Of Love and War: 1864

A Civil War Novel for the North

Charles Hammer

authorHOUSE®

AuthorHouse™
1663 Liberty Drive
Bloomington, IN 47403
www.authorhouse.com
Phone: 1-800-839-8640

First published by AuthorHouse 9/14/2010

ISBN: 978-1-4520-6775-9 (e)
ISBN: 978-1-4520-6776-6 (sc)

Library of Congress Control Number: 2010911980

Printed in the United States of America
Bloomington, Indiana

This book is printed on acid-free paper.

Photo courtesy of U. S. Army Military History Institute, Carlisle Barracks, Pa.

Cover design and photo illustration by Elise Ray,
eliseray.com

Commentary on *Of Love and War: 1864*

This action-packed novel presents a unique perspective on the Civil War. A white Confederate deserter joins a band of black irregular soldiers, including the woman he loves, who have escaped from slavery. Eager to free more slaves, they serve as auxiliaries to Sherman's army as it marches through Georgia. The book is a good read and will expand the horizons of its readers.

—James M. McPherson, Civil War historian, whose "Battle Cry of Freedom" won the Pulitzer prize.

Hammer works accurate historical detail seamlessly into dialogue and scenes to portray the overlooked role of black and white irregulars in winning the Civil War. They drive the last nails to box in the "noble," slave-holding rule of whites who started the fighting. Billy Leidig, a hapless Georgia conscript, deserts and discovers that the cause of these rich whites is not his. He fights for that of his sweetheart, Lenora June Moffat, an escaped slave girl. Helplessly in love, defying both white and black conventions, Lenora and Billy take up arms to free slaves on the fringes of Sherman's March. Hammer has written a great war novel here, brilliantly informed on munitions and the horrors of close combat, mixed with a love story that breaks the bonds of history. This is a Northern novel, with echoes of Michael Shaara's "The Killer Angels"; but it also evokes the deep-South narratives of William Faulkner, and even, in the author's sympathy for poor white Peckerwoods, the bleak, cracker comedies of Erskine Caldwell.

—John Mort, Vietnam combat veteran and author of the award-winning Vietnam novel, "Soldier in Paradise," "The Walnut King and Other Stories," "Tanks: Short Stories," and other works.

This is a gripping tale of inter-racial love told against the backdrop of the closing events of the U. S. Civil War in the Western Theater. It's fiction, to be sure, but also military history in a keenly instructive format with good insight into the U. S. Colored Troops and how they were led. Personalities are sharply delineated, moments movingly described.

—*Herman* Hattaway, co-author of "How the North Won," and "Why the South Lost," author of "General Stephen D. Lee."

This heartfelt novel of first love amid the trials of war takes the reader through battles during the Civil War, from ground level. The story is historically accurate and emotionally true. The young protagonists' experiences pull the reader into the story and compel him to keep turning pages. A satisfying story.

—Lenore Carroll, author of "Annie Chambers," "One Hundred Girls' Mother" and other historical novels.

As for the slaves...

How long their subjugation may be necessary is known and ordered by a wise and Merciful Providence...While we see the course of the final abolition of human slavery is onward, and we give it the aid of our prayers and all justifiable means in our power, we must leave the progress as well as the result in His hands who sees the end; who chooses to work by slow influences; and with whom two thousand years are but a single day.

—Gen. Robert E. Lee, from a letter to his wife, Dec. 27, 1856—

Whatever [General Lee's] feelings, they were entirely concealed from my own observation; but my own feelings, which had been quite jubilant on the receipt of his letter, were sad and depressed. I felt like anything rather than rejoicing at the downfall of a foe who had fought so long and so valiantly, and had suffered so much for a cause, though that cause was, I believe, one of the worst for which a people ever fought.

—Gen. Ulysses S. Grant at Appomattox, from his *Memoirs*—

1

A large proportion of the wealthy class of people have avoided the fevers of the camp and the dangers of the battlefield, and have remained at home in comparative ease and comfort with their families.

—from Georgia Gov. Joseph E. Brown's address to his state legislature, 1863.

BY LIMPING PITIFULLY BACK FROM Rebel lines as if wounded, Private Billy Leidig skulked untouched through two battles against General Sherman's army south of Atlanta. Then his Georgia militia platoon got roped in with a retreating column of real Confederate troops. Billy personally—little as he'd had of fighting—he thought it was plenty. So, sidling off the road, he angled into scrub oaks, steadying the Enfield musket on his shoulder with one hand as he fumbled with the fly of his breeches.

"Get in line!" yelled one of the real Confederates, a corporal of the 41st Mississippi. He waved Billy back with a bandaged hand. "We be taking a leak break here right quick."

"I ain't regular army," Billy told him. "I'm Georgia Guard. We just militia the governor called up."

The corporal's own Enfield swung around to catch Billy across his gut.

"Back!"

"The Confederacy ain't my boss!" Billy shot back. "*You* ain't my boss. Only boss I got is Governor Joe Brown. I thought we fightin for State Rights. Ain't that what the war's all about?"

"This here Confederacy is *DY-ing* of gaw-damn State Rights," the corporal said. "Get back in them ranks, you cracker sum-bitch!"

The musket whacking him solidly across his navel, Billy hustled back to meet the amused hooting of the Mississippi regulars and the

1

glum faces of his Georgia Guard buddies. Hell, most militia men didn't enlist to fight. They joined the Guard because Governor Brown vowed it would keep them safe from conscription by the South, a matter of State Rights, as old Joe declared. Governor Joe was hot to fight for Georgia but not for other sovereign states of the Confederacy.

"Well, if it ain't about State Rights, what's it about?" Billy demanded. The corporal didn't answer. "Governor Brown done recalled the Guard," Billy grumbled. "We ain't *s'posed* to be here." Again no answer. As part of General John Bell Hood's Army of Tennessee fleeing its bloody defeat outside Atlanta, they all sloshed westward through a chill autumn drizzle, an endless triple file of raggedy men. To the north, a tower of smoke rose above Atlanta.

"Yankees set the town afire?" Billy asked the corporal.

"They ain't even took over yet. That dumb Hood blew up our ordnance trains right by the depot to keep Yanks from gettin'em. Not one train. Four whole trains! He knocked down about half the town."

If the Confederacy is dying of gaw-damn State Rights and the general is dumb, Billy wondered, how come this corporal sticks so tight by him? General Hood's army was one of the South's last two with the other, Robert E. Lee's Army of Northern Virginia, getting chased back toward Richmond by that devil Grant. Nearly four years into this war, things didn't look promising. Billy said none of this aloud. Just this once he kept his big mouth shut and made up his mind.

That night he sneaked out between the Mississippi pickets, waded a flooding creek to get past, holding his Enfield and haversack high. He didn't head toward home but instead circled back south of Atlanta and then moved northeast, because he had to find somebody. Finding that somebody is why he'd let himself be dragged along with the Georgia Guard in the first place. Just as easy, he could have laid out in the woods for the rest of the war like so many others. But Billy wanted to find her.

Marching on different roads and trails, on winding paths, across countless fields and through trackless woods, he tried one plantation after another over a wide swath of central Georgia. Many times he ducked quick into brush, dodging General Joe Wheeler's Confederate cavalry patrols, thinking they might mistake him for a deserter. He drank creek water and ate yams and ear corn raw from the fields, occasionally begging something better from a kindly farm woman.

Still, he walked into the Hunnicutt plantation weeks later heavy on his feet but light in his head because he was so hungry. The Mansion loomed up against cedars rising beyond it—an ugly building, half of it like an old-timey temple with tall columns, the rest big add-ons that didn't match. His own shadow stretched out toward it, lying long across a low rail fence. The setting sun shone blinding bright on some things, leaving others in black shadow. Billy figured the slave cabins would be out back. Starting that way, he passed a vegetable patch too big to be just kitchen garden. It covered two or three acres, including one whole acre planted to pure-dee fall turnips.

He leaned his musket on the rail fence. Stepping over, he waded in and started yanking at the green tops. This was good loose Georgia dirt. Fat turnips came right up. He scrubbed off grit with his coat sleeve and bit into one, hot and tender, the spice of its purple hide burning in his nose as he wolfed the white meat down. He went along the row, yanking turnips, nipping off tops with his bayonet and stuffing every pocket with them, all the while chewing, swallowing, feeling turnip lumps crowd down past his Adam's apple.

He was so busy that until row's end he didn't notice two men standing on the far side of a second rail fence, a colored man and a white one with a black beard. Wearing a cap pulled low over his eyes, the colored one had a shotgun pointed so Billy could see little of it except the fat black double holes of the barrels.

"Howdy!" Billy said, grinning. "I come in here lookin for a nigger gal. Y'all got a gal here name of Lenora June Moffat?"

"You are stealin my turnips," the white man said.

Billy took one backward step.

"Wellsir," he said, "this gal back at Highland Forge—that's where I come from, Highland Forge, way over east of Millen—this Lenora June, she got sold to a slave trader about seven months ago, got sold somewhere out this way. I thought maybe..."

"Peel those turnips out of your pockets," the white man said. He looked to be not much over thirty and wore a black broadcloth coat, mighty rich looking.

"Well, heck now, I been yonder fightin them battles around Atlanta. We mighty near had the Yankees licked, but they kept slippin off to one side, then the other. They got around us. That damn Sherman, he'd flank the devil outa hell. I just got real hungry for turnips, that's all."

His breeches and coat, even his shirt pockets, were tight packed with them. Shrunken as the fabric had become, it *was* a sort of peeling job, hard to get them out, and he tore the right-hand pocket of his breeches. The two men stood ominously quiet.

"On that plantation a mile back, they told me there was a nigger gal on the Hunnicutt plantation who could rightly read all the news outa the Atlanta paper," Billy said. "Are you Mister Hunnicutt? Is Lenora June here?"

"She *was* here," the man said. "Throw those turnips down."

He kept dropping them, at last sighing, "That's all."

"Those in your shirt pockets, under the coat, throw them down." So Billy did.

"How did y'all happen to be out here?" Billy asked. "Y'all stay out here full time just guardin these turnips?"

"People like you been comin through here thick the last week," he said. Then he spoke heatedly, as if to the general world. "These Georgia Guard bastards! They won't fight, and they're worse than Yankees for stealin crops. What you doing out this way anyhow? General Hood took the army west."

"I come this DI-rection figurin to protect y'all from the Yankees. And I was tryin to find Lenora June. I got somethin to give her."

"Lenora June's a runaway. Slave patrols been looking two months for her. You're runnin off yourself. You've thrown down our sacred Cause. You're a goddamn deserter!"

In the Confederacy they hung deserters, Billy understood, or shot them, the transgression itself often followed seconds later by the punishment. He started backing down the row away from the men. This was exactly the time to keep his mouth shut, of course it was.

"I don't notice you doing much fightin for any sacred Cause," he told the white man. "Where was you back yonder at Jonesboro? I didn't see *you* nowhere, duckin Minie balls and them twelve-pound Napoleon roundshots."

"Keep your gun on him, Ezra," the white man said.

"How come you get to stay home and don't have to fight?"

The white man cleared his throat.

"We have eighty-seven Nigra servants on this plantation," he said, real dignified. "Somebody has to look after'em, keep the corn planted, plant these turnips you came on my place to steal."

It was a terrible time to talk out. Still, Billy saw that because of the fence the men stood behind, they couldn't quick run after him. By now he had backed nearly thirty yards away. This was getting to be a long shot for a scattergun.

"Sure, now, that's the twenty-nigger law, ain't it?" he jeered. "If you own twenty slaves, you don't get conscripted. You don't have to fight."

He turned and ran.

"Ezra, shoot the sonofabitch!"

"That's the rich-man's-war, poor-man's-fight law," Billy yelled gleefully.

He ran faster than ever he ran from the battle at Jonesboro. It surprised him, how many mighty bounds he took through the turnips, the white man yelling, "Shoot, dammit, shoot!" before Billy heard the whizzzzz of birdshot over his head, hoped it was birdshot anyhow because even at this range buckshot could kill him dead. Suddenly a flame of hot lead raked his scalp, blood from one ear spurting forward past his face, Billy only then hearing the second boom of the shotgun.

At field's end he jumped the fence, squatted and swung around. Now Ezra had his ramrod out, stroking methodically up and down as he reloaded the shotgun. Billy grabbed up his musket and leveled it across the top rail, aiming at them. White and colored, both hit the ground. At this range his weapon could be a sight more deadly than Ezra's—if it happened to be primed, which it wasn't. But Billy was running from one fight and didn't want to die now over a mess of turnips.

He crawled straight away behind the fence, blood drops from the ear splashing his left hand as he moved. He laid up in the wood's edge, clawing through his cartridge box for a percussion cap, plugging it onto the primer nipple of his musket in case they tried to follow. Struck by the hammer, that cap would ignite the cartridge powder in the barrel. Billy always kept the musket loaded, with just the cap missing to prevent accidental discharge.

But nobody followed him. The pain raged hotter for a minute or two—shit, that hurt! Slowly it eased off. The lead that hit his ear took a little piece and went right through, but his fingers found three wounds in his neck and scalp with round lumps of shot lodged under the skin. He couldn't see to cut them out.

After resting awhile, Billy felt his way into a thicket , then circled wide to get behind the house, exploring a more open woodland until along with pine scent he smelled hog sties, cook smoke with a meat taste, maybe cornbread mixed in, maybe yams roasting—the rich musk of slave cabins. They were scattered widely through these woods, rickety, poorly-chinked log pens roofed with broad planks laid on from eaves up to ridgetops. They were sorry lodgings compared to the decent slave cabins at Highland Forge. He was coming up quiet behind one when he saw two scared eyes shining in dusk light.

"Howdy, babe," Billy said.

A white smile leaped on the little boy's face, which he hid against a tree trunk that half concealed him. Billy laid his musket down and knelt on pine litter to bring his own face level.

"Do you know Lenora June Moffat?" he asked.

Shyness kept the child's forehead glued to the tree, but he was still grinning, sticking out his rosy tongue, making funny faces as if to himself.

"What's your name?" Billy asked.

"Lovage."

"Lovage, do you rightly know Lenora June?

"Yup."

"Where'd she go?"

He came from behind the tree, a kid maybe five years old, barefoot in this chill, his trousers so torn they hung in strips. He walked right up to Billy

"I got a button," he said. He stuck out a brown fist, opened it to show a shell-pink palm on which lay the brass round with its military crest.

"Can I have that button?" Billy's own grin widened, aggravating the pain in his lacerated ear. The boy's fist snapped shut and vanished behind his back.

"Well," Billy said, "I give you a penny if you take me to Lenora June's place."

"Uh huh!" the kid grunted.

Billy took a chance and picked the boy up, just swept Lovage up and rose, spinning under the trees till his panicky gasp turned into a giggle. Billy liked the sweat smell of him. Lovage reached a hand out toward the ripped ear.

"I see blood."

Billy's own hand flew up, fingers walking delicately backwards on his neck skin toward the throbbing lumps where shot had lodged. He took up his musket and, following the boy's pointing finger, strode through woods awhile and then into an open space before three of the cabins, dim in twilight, the major brightness a fire with a gridiron over it. A woman worked there, turning meat and something that might be yams. A cottontop colored man sat on the ground, winding cord tight around a broken shovel handle. Right away he jumped up. They stared at Billy, an armed graycoat appearing like some sinister ghost.

"Howdy!" Billy called out. "Ole Lovage here, he promised he'd show me Lenora June's cabin."

Lovage was still pointing. "It yonder."

The woman walked quickly toward him.

"You got my boy. Lenora June, she gone."

When she reached for Lovage, the boy clung to Billy's sore neck, mewling at him.

"I wants my penny!"

Gently Billy tugged the boy loose, stuffing him into his mother's arms while searching with the other hand in his own pocket. He planted a shiny copper beside the button in Lovage's palm. That smile blazed again. The woman, a golden sheen to her skin in dusk light, looked keenly at Billy's torn ear.

"You from Highland Forge, ain't you? Brought somethin to give Lenora June. That was you Ezra shot, a-stealin turnips."

Billy was amazed.

"How did you know that?"

7

She didn't answer the question, just said:

"Me, I'm Martha." She placed a square of hoecake in his hands. "Set yonder by the fire. Be supper here in a minute." As if stealing turnips in itself were qualification enough for hospitality. The old man had already sat again on folded burlap, leaning back on a log that faced the fire. He patted the sacking beside him.

"Set yourself."

So Billy did, sagging wearily, gratefully, back into the Negro night-time life he had come to love in his long childhood at Highland Forge. Biting into the crusty cornbread, he chewed and swallowed. He thought slavery wasn't all that bad compared to the deal they gave his own daddy and Billy himself. Colored folks had a good time together, not always trying to beat each other like white folks. They stole apples in season from the orchard, and peaches and cherries, yes, and turnips too from the kitchen garden. Now and again they would steal a sheep for a mutton barbecue off in the woods, with crazy dancing after.

That's where Billy learned dancing, Lenora June teaching him steps wilder than any Irish jig, walnut-dark Lenora, a house Negro who read books, bringing this white farm boy in under the wary stares of field workers, dancing with him to fiddle and banjo and tambourine, in firelight, moonlight, starlight, dancing through the best times Billy Leidig could now recall. He thought colored had a pretty good life, but it seemed like every damn one of'em wanted out of it. All over Georgia slaves were busting for what they called freedom, the same sorry, work-your-ass-off deal Billy already had. The old man put one index finger to Billy's chin, turning the back of his head to firelight.

"Oughta get them shot out," he said. "Otherwise won't heal."

Martha hustled away toward the nearest cabin.

"Just set still, Ezra, I fetch your razor."

Billy stared, offended, at old cottontop.

"Hell, you're Ezra, you the one shot me!"

Ezra looked back at Billy with foggy eyes, yellowish in the whites.

"I'm right sorry."

"All I done was steal turnips. Why didn't you just miss?"

"First shot I did. I didn't touch off the next till you about reach the fence. That's a ten-gauge, full choke. You lucky you alive."

Deepening his vexation, Billy then noticed what appeared to be a heap of purple and white cannonballs piled beside the cabin. He pointed at the stack and spoke accusingly.

"Them's the turnips I pulled, ain't they? They the ones got me shot!"

"Sure 'nuff! Master Hunnicuttt, he just let'em rot in the field, so I fetched'em home. Help yourself."

Martha returned with the razor and a leather strop, on which Ezra carefully honed the edge. Then he cut slits over the lumps and one by one pinched the birdshot balls out. Damn, it hurt!

"If you'd just pulled up a little on that scattergun, you coulda clean missed me."

"Cain't miss'em all," Ezra sighed, "not with master right handy."

"Anyhow, colored ain't *s'posed* to shoot white folks. Colored ain't s'posed to have guns."

"Master talkin about givin us guns," Ezra said. "Not like that shotgun. I mean guns like your soldier musket. Want us slaves fightin them bluecoats, give us freedom if we do."

Billy just shook his head.

"I thought we fightin to keep the slaves. That's what State Rights is for. I mean, HELL, won't be nobody left to do all this work but us Peckerwood whites!"

Hot as he felt about the political question, he was also starve-gut hungry. He shut up suddenly and gestured pleadingly toward the gridiron, glancing up at Martha.

"It's ready," she reassured.

Served up on a tin pie pan, the meat was gamy goat haunch roasted dry as jerky, tough to choke down. He ate all Martha gave him, along with three yams cooked in the coals and another square of hoecake. Billy washed the bites down with water from his canteen, heaving sighs between swallows. By home standards it was sorry fare, still way better than the hard biscuit he got with General Hood's army. Now other cookfires were flaring at cabins along the winding road through the woods. Other slaves bent to them. A quarter moon halfway up the sky shone through bare tree branches, lighting drifts of smoke.

Martha sat beside Ezra, leaning back against the log with Lovage's head on her lap. Already the boy was blinking sleepily. Of course she was Hunnicutt's rightful property, but he wondered who else Martha belonged to. Maybe Ezra, but he was too old. With slaves all the time getting sold south and sold west—husbands and wives and their children, sometimes together, sometimes apart—it was hard to say who belonged to who. Not that slave weddings were legal anyhow in the State of Georgia. Billy reached one foot out to boost a log farther into the fire.

"Back at Highland Forge," he said, "slave cabins all got fireplaces to cook on in winter. Don't have to cook outdoors. Two of them cabins got little iron stoves." Billy's own mother had both a fireplace and an iron stove.

"Big house, it's got a cook stove, real nice," Martha said proudly. "Iron stove in every fireplace." She reached out a brown hand and touched his haversack. "What-all did you bring Lenora June?"

He loosened the buckle and drew out a leather-bound book. Embossed in gold on the cover was a frowning mask of Tragedy. Billy's finger followed, letter by gilded letter, the printed title.

"It says, 'Romeo and Juliet by William Shakespeare.'"

"I hear about that story," Martha said. "It all about *love*."

Billy knew what it was about, but her use of the word made him shiver. He had to clear his throat before speaking again.

"See, I raised a mess of Shanghai hens. Sold just one of 'em to buy this. A plucked hen fetches top dollar now, even if it is them Confederate shinplasters."

She held the slim book in both hands, caressing the leather with her thumbs. Then she glanced sharply up at him.

"Ain't this a mighty long trip just to give her a book? What you come all this way for?"

Billy felt a heaviness like lead in his gut, even seemed to taste the metal on his tongue. He knew the reason, but he didn't want to say it. He just sat quiet. She smiled at him.

"I reckon anyhow you ain't no slave catcher. What for you want Lenora June?"

He didn't like to be laughed at, this white boy trailing off after a nigger slave who never even let him hold her hand unless they were dancing. Let others do more, by god! And wouldn't let Billy so much as hold her hand. Shouldn't be no mixing of black blood with white, she told him. Of course Billy believed it, though he had noticed—and even proved to Lenora June—that when you shed blood, black or white, it always comes out red.

"Did Lenora June ever talk about me? She ever talk about Billy Leidig?"

"Oh, she mention you. Talked about Billy at that Forge."

His heart beat slowly, powerfully in his chest, a dull ache spreading downward through his body. He thought he might be sick, but he had often felt so since the Forge sold Lenora June west.

"She gonna like that book," Martha said. "She can read it too, she could, I seen her read stuff. She read that Atlanta newspaper, grab up every one they threw out the big house. She read in the paper about General Sherman, talkin all time about Sherman comin."

"Well, he ain't comin this way. Sherman's follerin Hood yonder to the west." He stared eagerly into dying embers of the supper fire. "Lenora June, she learned readin in Pennsylvania, when she lived up yonder with them Quakers. Then the slave catchers caught up to her whole family, dragged'em right back to the Forge. We didn't have no school at Highland Forge. Lenora June taught me readin. Right onto five years, every day we was readin together." He lifted the book from Martha's hand and brandished it before him. "I could read this right now if I wanted to."

Martha looked doubtful.

"That Romeo book, I heard it's hard."

"Okay, reckon I'll just prove it to you. Here now." He paged through to a maple leaf he had stuck in as bookmark. "In the story it's comin on dawn, and that Juliet, she's wonderin how Romeo ever climbed them high orchard walls to see her. She knows her folks won't like it, Romeo'll get killed if he hangs around in yonder. So she asks him how the heck he climbed them walls. Then Romeo pops back and says...." his finger searching for the place. "He says, 'with love's light wings did I o'er perch these walls, for stony limits cannot hold love out. And what love can *do*, THAT dares love attempt.'"

"Well ain't it the truth!" Martha said. "And you read good."

How well he could read had brought him problems with Lenora. She thought he should also talk like he read—give up his Peckerwood speech, as she had given up the Quaker "thee" and "thou" because the words no longer served the original purpose. But Billy liked his homey way of talking. Happy now, he leaned back against the log.

"Lenora June, she didn't just teach me. She was teachin all them slaves to read, the grown-ups and the kids, just flat out teachin against Georgia law. She wouldn't stop teachin, either. That's how come the Forge Master sold her west to Hunnicutt."

Billy felt Martha's hand as she took hold of his wrist. She squeezed the wrist, staring into his eyes.

"If you lookin for Lenora June, go find Sherman in Atlanta. That's where she be. Master Hunnicutt thinks she scat north like them other runaways. I know she run west lookin for Sherman."

"Hell, I already *been* to Atlanta," Billy said. "I already *been* to Sherman. I seen his Napoleon cannons shootin' grapeshot and cannister. I seen all of Sherman I wanna see."

Her face in the firelight was stubborn as stone, like smooth and frowning stone.

"If you lookin for Lenora June, go find Sherman."

Billy slept that night in Lenora June's cabin. It had no glass in the windows, just openings in the log walls with burlap covers. Billy pinned back the fabric to let in starlight. On the dirt floor there was a pallet filled with springy tips of hemlock, their resin scenting the room. He had never before slept in a room where she had slept, not to say in her very bed. It retained no smell of her, she with her Quaker cleanliness, who seldom smelled like anything at all. He had noticed her absence of odor and once announced to her that, despite common conviction, it seemed niggers actually had no stink particular to them. They just had less chance to wash than white folks. That started her grinning.

"You don't wash much yourself, Billy," she told him. "Maybe you haven't noticed, but you've got your *own* particular stink. Oh, Billy, you're a funny boy!"

He didn't like being laughed at, even by Lenora June.

Nigger nigger nigger—most colored folks didn't seem to mind the word, often used it themselves. After her sojourn in the North, Lenora

June did mind, and Billy stopped using it in her presence. Here, where she had slept, he sensed that presence. Tired as he was, much as he savored feeling for what just might be the lanky shape of her body still pressed into the pallet, he lay a long time awake watching stars move across the window squares, trying to keep his mind off it but now and again returning to that foreboding thought:

Oh, shit, *Sherman!*

2

Behind us lay Atlanta, smoldering and in ruins, the black smoke rising...
and right before us the Fourteenth Corps marching steadily and rapidly,
with a cheery look and swinging pace...Some band, by accident, struck
up the anthem of John Brown's soul goes marching on. The men caught
up the strain and never before or since have I heard the chorus of "Glory,
glory hallelujah!" done with more spirit or in better harmony of time and
place.

—Gen. William Tecumseh Sherman, from his Memoirs.

MARCHING WESTWARD IN SEARCH OF Lenora June, Billy figured that by
the time he reached Atlanta, Sherman wouldn't even be there.
He'd be chasing Hood, marching off westward into Alabama. Still,
Billy kept a sharp lookout—not an easy thing in this country. It had
woodlots aplenty, great runs of old forest, farms with fields that once
grew cotton but now raised mostly food, dry corn standing unharvested
in many places, even a few yams dug but not yet gathered. Often as
he walked he gnawed corn kernels from the cob—better than nothing
if you're hungry enough.

The second day out Billy spied a big snapping turtle crossing the
road from one slough to another. It seemed to know what was coming,
waddling faster when Billy approached. He primed his musket and
shot its head off, then quickly reloaded, first biting the paper bottom
of the cartridge to expose black powder, tasting peppery saltpeter.
Pressing the cartridge, topped with the rounded cone of its Minie ball,
into the muzzle, he tamped it twice with his ramrod. Billy butchered
the snapper on the spot, wedging his bayonet into seams of the shell
to pry it apart. He wrapped the meat joints in an old towel from his
haversack.

He had risen to move on when he noticed a glint of movement from the steaming heap of innards on the road. It was the snapper's heart, a beating purple center amid globs of yellow fat. It squeezed inward like a clenching fist, relaxed, squeezed again and yet again with a rhythmic, wave-like motion. He watched awhile, expecting the beat to stop. It didn't stop. He pondered whether he should put the purple thing out of its misery, then shrugged and left it beating there in the road.

That night in his creek bank camp he heaped poplar twigs together and started a fire with a single friction match from the corked bottle in his haversack. He roasted turtle on hickory sticks propped over the flames, cooked yams in the coals. The smoky meat tasted as he knew it would, like chicken, as so many good things do. It was a power better than goat jerky.

After the meal, he walked off into the woods to piss. Then he took off his clothes and stood shivering on a rock at the water's edge, halfway washing himself with a wetted cloth and a sliver of lye soap. Ever since Lenora June mentioned Billy's own particular stink, he'd felt sore about it and washed when he got a chance. Tenderly he splashed his neck and scalp where the birdshot wounds were scabbing over. He shivered back into his uniform, then built up the fire and sat close, watching creek ripples blink flashes of fire back at him.

Lenora June, born the same year as Billy, had roamed the woods with him around Highland Forge. She taught him how to tie a bacon slice to a weighted line and carefully lift from the creek crawdads not even hooked, just stupid enough to grab the bait and hold on till you shook them into a bucket. Her mama made savory gumbo out of crawdad tails. Lenora June talked a lot about black blood and white blood until one day Billy snapped open his pocket knife and pulled her open palm onto his knee.

"Naw!" she grunted and snatched it away.

But he talked her into it. First he nicked his own palm, squeezing out a shining bead of blood. Her open palm as it lay in his hand was the color of cinnamon. She took the knife from him and pricked herself deep, blood welling around the point, pooling in the cupped hand. Billy dipped a finger in and tasted the salt of her. As she tasted his blood, he looked into her eyes. They were a light bright brown, like

Indian summer maple leaves he'd seen pressed to the rocky bottom under clear water of the spring branch. He saw himself in those eyes, reflections of his own eyes, of sky behind him.

"See," he said, "ain't all the blood red?"

"Oh, Billy, everybody knows that!"

Of course she knew that, at least. Still, as a little kid Lenora June had been dumb as a crawdad, dumb as Billy himself—couldn't read a thing, not even the hymnal. Then one day she and her family were gone, vanished from the world, and without trace. The hounds never caught so much as a scent, as if a whole family of slaves had flown off in the air, Lenora June and her mother, Reba, and her father, John Marion Moffat. It was way too clean and complete to be anything like an ordinary escape into the woods. Once Billy overheard the Forge Master in angry accusation:

"Gaw-damn abolitionist sonsabitches, comin down here, stealin our servants!"

Billy's dad didn't even have his own land. He was just a farmer for the boss, raising food for the iron workers. Anybody could do that. But Lenora June's dad, he was a master forge man, he could take them red-hot blooms of pig iron and beat slag out of them, turn them into wrought iron, which could be shaped into hinges, gate latches, harness buckles, wagon tires, plowshares, musket barrels, cannon parts. He even knew how to reheat wrought iron over charcoal to that mysterious zone between red-hot and melting which changes iron to steel.

Once Billy stood with Lenora between the two fires, between the finery forge and the chaffery forge, and watched John Marion do it, watched him make this very bayonet. Billy held it up to firelight, the blade stained now with snapper blood, wearing back a little from much use, many sharpenings. That's why the Forge Master was so mad, because not many could do what the escaped slave did. The Forge really needed John Marion.

They were gone six years before slave catchers found him working with Quakers at a little forge in Abington, north of Philadelphia. Billy was glad, he was glad for the Fugitive Slave Law. It was the reason the Quakers couldn't help the Moffats stay up there. The law brought the whole family back, including Lenora June. She was all changed, she was fourteen years old with little pointy bosoms that pushed out under her slave cloth smock. By then she was big for a woman, and he was small for a man. They looked level into each other's eyes.

He was glad he could teach her at least one thing. Colored not being allowed to mess with guns, Billy secretly taught her how to shoot with his own little squirrel musket—not even a percussion piece, not even rifled, just a damn old flintlock smoothbore. He taught her to shoot, but she taught him everything. She could read good and do figures, she knew about Tahiti and William Shakespeare, knew about the whaling fleet at Nantucket, knew about Paris and Rome and Athens, the pyramids of Egypt and the Fugitive Slave Law. This was the law that took away all the money John Marion saved from his work up North and gave it to the Forge Master. Lenora June hated that law, but Billy was happy it brought her back. And just in time, too, because pretty soon the war started.

Now, more than five years later, he sat watching the creek move in firelight, wondering why he was heading west toward that war instead of east toward home, a little scared, in fact, by this—his foolish conduct. At Jonesboro he got close enough just once to see war, that same Mississippi regiment clawing through an abatis of thorny cut brush toward bluecoats entrenched behind a breastwork of logs.

For the first time he heard the POW-POW-POW-POW-POW-POW-POW POW of the Union's Spencer repeating carbine, eight shots almost without pause, just one bluecoat firing and four Confederates falling. It was like the Union men were pulling off a stunt, showing what their new weapon could do. Then their battery of Napoleons like giant shotguns blasted cannister at the 41st Mississippi, a hornets' swarm of musket balls ripping through the Confederates, spraying blood into bright sunlight, shreds of flesh and gray cloth and leather from their uniforms leaping out behind the men. That's when Billy started limping, at first backwards, then turning to hobble out of the battle like a spavined mule.

So he sat here tonight by a no-name creek, and around him this great war was going on, hundreds of thousands of men trying to kill each other—General Hood by now in Alabama, Lee up in Virginia, both struggling to sweep back that Union tide. He thought about the snapper heart, beating back there in the road. It might still be drumming away. That's just how Billy felt. He didn't want to turn loose of everything, didn't want to turn lose of **anything**, no more than the snapper did.

Yet he walked on west the next day, walked on toward trouble. In the morning lots of wagons passed, all going east away from Atlanta, none toward it. A sign he passed said "Decatur 9 Miles," which meant he was only a few more than that from Atlanta. As he climbed a hill, a graycoat cavalry troop suddenly swarmed over the crest coming his way at a canter—too late for him to hide. He stood there breathing fast, figuring to be arrested as a deserter or outright shot.

The troopers came with a jingling of sabers, canteens and musket carbines, the single-shot, short-barreled weapons Confederate cavalry used. Stuff hung from their saddles, whole hams, chickens and farmyard geese headless but unplucked, towsacks of what looked like ear corn and turnips. Their horses wheezed, winded, with flanks mud spattered from fording creeks. The leader went by and a couple dozen more, Billy standing in the middle as they passed on both sides. They didn't even look at him.

"Who are y'all?" he yelled. Nobody answered until he yelled again. The last rider pulled up and turned in the saddle.

"We're out foraging for General Wheeler," the man said, "gettin on to meet the regiment." The rider was an older man, sitting heavy in the saddle, his blue eyes casting an amused glance down on Billy. "Son, if you are deserting, you headin the wrong DI-rection."

He turned again and spurred the horse onward. After that, the road ahead of Billy was empty. He saw no more wagons, no more graycoats. Even the farmhouses seemed deserted, no smoke from their chimneys. He stopped at one, drew a bucket from the well and drank. A shutter on one window inched open, and he saw a face there. Nothing happened. He refilled his canteen, hung the bucket on its post and went on.

There were lots of birds, bluejays squawking from tree to tree, a cardinal singing rich and sweet, lost amid the shining leaves of a live oak. It didn't look dangerous out here. Near noon he sat behind a tree at road's edge and ate a sweet potato cooked the night before. Not that he meant to be careless, but the next thing he sensed was a sound, the quick pad of feet on dry clay. Jerking out of his nap, Billy jumped up with his musket and spun to face a colored man in the road.

They stood there panting, staring wide eyed at each other. The man's face and hands were a mess of deep scratches, his clothes ragged, ripped as if by thorns. His feet were bare and scratched worse than his face. One ankle oozed red from bloody teeth marks. Grabbing a long breath, the man said:

"Howdy! Master Harwell up the road here ahead, he raised him a big heap of oats. My own master, he send me yonder to fetch home a sack."

"Oats?" said Billy, slow to come fully awake.

"Yah! Master, he didn't give me no pass. He figured it's such a little way, I ain't gonna need no pass. I'm s'posed to just get that sack of oats and run right home."

"You been runnin through brush," Billy said. "You bad cut up. Looks like you're dog-bit on your ankle."

He was older than Billy, yet still young and powerfully built. Warily, he looked Billy's gray uniform up and down. He clasped his mauled hands before him as if in prayer and dropped his eyes, staring into the hands.

"You ain't no slave catcher," he said. "I hope you ain't no slave catcher. Oh, damn! I was just about free here and now you got me ."

"Damn right back," Billy said, "'cause I ain't no slave catcher."

"You can go ahead shoot me. I sooner be dead as go back now."

"Hell, I ain't gonna shoot you. Get on down the road."

"I go ahead, then you shoot me in the back."

"Like hell I will. This musket ain't even primed. Come on, I"ll walk right with you."

The man seemed just as fearful of that prospect but limped along anyway, favoring the dog-mauled ankle. Billy offered him a drink from his canteen. He flinched back from it, like the water was poison. They walked slow enough, but the man was so scared he kept right on panting. They hadn't gone a mile together when he edged toward a path angling off into the woods.

"See, I'm scared of them cavalry soldier. They most nigh got me back yonder. You not minding, master, I'll just get on off this road."

But Billy saw cavalry wasn't this man's real worry. He was staring at this grayback soldier before him, his brown eyes bright with fear. The man thought he was being tricked. Never before had anyone in the world been so afraid of Billy Leidig. The slave was the one scared, but it was Billy's own gut that the fear infected, leaving him with something like the curdling sickness that comes before a vomit.

"Wait!" Billy cried. The man stopped, stood trembling before him. "That old devil Lincoln, he already done it, but after you called me master, I see you need the same thing again." Like the preacher in the Baptist church at the Forge, Billy raised one hand high, the man's eyes following the open palm as though expecting it to strike him down. "Mister slave, sir, I emancipate you! I hereby emancipate you! You are a free man!" Hollering like the preacher now. "*GO*, and sin no more!"

As from a madman, the negro fled along the path, falling down, getting up to hobble onward. He was still running when he went out of sight through bare-limbed brush. So, as did the Quakers, Billy had helped steal the lawful property of some plantation owner like Hunnicutt. He walked on, uneasy that—having committed a crime under Georgia law—he felt so good about it.

After awhile he noticed that the birds sang no more. He heard his own brogans tread the dirt, now and again the hush of a breeze through roadside grass. The sky was still rich blue, clotted here and there with puffy clouds. Then, from behind him and to the south, he heard something like a chord of music. Somebody was singing. Another half-mile and he heard a spatter of gunfire, again from behind but this time to the north.

He ran back to the hilltop he had just crossed, climbed a burr oak there, from which he still could see not much more than big woods with scattered fields. Then, southeastward where a distant road ran alongside a pasture, he saw blue-clad soldiers marching. For the moment they had fallen into step and were singing, words coming erratically on a south wind.

"....soul is marchin on....glory, glory hallelujah..." A long pause, and with swinging blue-clad arms they started the song again.

"John Brown's body lies a-mouldering in the grave..."

His eyes searched the woods farther east along where that road must lie, finding another break in trees. Many more bluecoats. The road there was crowded with them, marching men and wagons and a battery of cannon hauled by four-horse teams. To the north he could see nothing unusual—no road anyhow—but he heard again that spatter of gunfire, first a musket or a Confederate musket carbine, a single BOOM, a minute later another, BOOM, maybe Joe Wheeler's cavalry. Then, POW-POW-POW-POW—that bluecoat Spencer repeater. Load it on Sunday and fire it all week. A half-mile to the west, rising over a hill on his own road, he now saw another column of soldiers, flags flapping ahead as they marched straight toward him.

"Damn!" he breathed, heart pounding in his chest.

Billy hugged the tree trunk as he shinnied down, hugged and let go, grabbing branches, breaking them, skidding, half-falling out of the big oak. He yanked up his musket and ran, heading north away from the road because there seemed fewer of them that direction. Fewer, but noisier. POW-POW-POW-BOOM! It scared him, but he had to run that way, right toward the gunfire, or be overrun by Yankees on the road. He went down a wooded valley beside a little stream, huffing along a good mile before he encountered a dead man, a graycoat thrown all askew into the brush, and then a live bluecoat, yelling.

"Help me! Water! Oh help me! Mother!"

The man drank greedily from Billy's canteen, groaning as he choked the water down. The runaway slave wouldn't take it from a grayback soldier, but this man did. He was hit in the thigh, hit square, bone broken so the leg lay at the wrong angle. He wouldn't walk on that leg again.

"It's just your leg," Billy said. "You ain't gonna die."

"It hurts! Don't leave me!"

"Keep yellin for help," he told the man. "Plenty Union men coming."

He ran through open woodland, downhill to what looked like a millpond all ruined, the dam broken, the pond only part full. The old mill had been torn down for rebuilding. A locomotive boiler had been mounted on stone cradles to trade steam power for the water mill. They must have part finished it before war stopped the work, its fresh lumber already gray from weathering. He had just figured that out when bark on a hickory beside his head exploded, POW. He hit the ground, crawled behind the tree, tried to get his musket up. POW-POW-POW. Slugs searched dirt along his right side, kicking up spurts of dust. Shit! It was another Spencer repeater. Billy crawdad-crawled to his left, more behind the tree, and tried to get his musket ready. Of course, it wasn't primed. His right hand scrabbled in the cartridge box, groping for a percussion cap.

"Surrender, you gaw-damn Reb!" sounded a huge voice. "I'll kill your ass!"

It came again, POW-POW-POW, as the gunman levered cartridges in. Slugs whacked through the tree, cutting little branches that fell onto Billy. A half-second pause and then one more, POW. Seven shots in the magazine and one in the chamber, eight altogether. Billy had counted them. He knew the Spencer was empty.

He found the cap and plugged it onto the primer nipple. Trembling violently, breathing deep to calm himself, he jumped up. Out beside the mill foundation was a handsome bay horse with a rider, a bluecoat cavalryman pawing into a long box at his belt for what must be his next cartridge magazine, the horse kind of bouncing, jigging delicately sideways. No wonder he missed, shooting from a horse. After reloading with the magazine, he would have seven more chances. Billy sucked in a breath to yell.

"You quit that! I got you in my sights."

He raised the musket, aiming just left of the man's head.

The bluecoat leaned down and dropped his carbine to the ground, swung his right arm across the saddle and yanked back, sucking a long saber from its scabbard. The rider came in a rush, hacked at Billy as he scampered around the tree, fell down, got up and ran toward the mill. He got his musket raised again as the bluecoat swung the horse and started back, saber swinging.

"Surrender, you little turd. I'll cleave your skull!"

"Nawsir," Billy said, "you're the one ought to give up. I got my musket right on you, and it primed to shoot."

But Billy couldn't get the musket aimed before the enemy was after him, hacking at lumber joists of the unfinished mill floor as Billy ducked and crawled under them to get away, dragging his weapon behind. He scrambled out the other side and fled again as the cavalryman reined in the prancing mount, deftly circling the building's stone foundation to get at him. Winded from running, Billy hauled up in a tall tangle of sunflower, goldenrod, elderberry, now bloomed out and gone, all tied together with bindweed. He turned to face his pursuer. He decided now that capturing the man was impractical.

"So stop! Just stop it. Let's just quit right now and call it even!"

"Like hell quit! Surrender or DIE, Secesh!"

Billy knew he personally never seceded from the Union, even if the Sovereign State of Georgia did. Hell no. He wasn't any Secesh. Still, this Yank was fixing to kill him for being one. Billy had his musket up before he realized it had never been cocked. The rider raced down on him, the bay's sides heaving, mouth foaming. Billy's thumb clicked the hammer back just as the muzzle swung around to the cavalryman's head. The weapon shot half the man's face away, not quite the full job it had done on the snapping turtle. The rider pitched right into Billy, splashing him with blood. He pushed the man away, fought off the limp weight. The horse whirled, stirrups flinging outward, and shot off into the woods. The body drew another breath or two, sucking air through the liquid mess of its face. Then the noise stopped.

Billy stood there gasping, wiping at the blood on his uniform, halfway bawling. He wished he had never left home, even for Lenora June. He wished he could take it all back.

"Oh shit, oh shit, oh shit..." He lay down amid tall weeds beside the dead man. "He tried to kill me," Billy murmured. "He woulda too. He woulda."

Looking at the sky, he saw the sun was still shining, the clouds still sharp against the blue, but it couldn't be the same day. He closed his eyes and stared up into the rosy world behind his eyelids. He wanted to stay there, it was so cozy and quiet. Then he felt hoofbeats in the earth under him, heard a sudden splashing. Warily, he sat up from the weeds and crawled to the wrecked mill, inching up to peek between two boards.

A Union cavalryman sat astride his horse, which noisily sucked water from what was left of the millpond. Another rode in to water his mount. The soldiers sat companionably, stirrup to stirrup, one sharing tobacco in his pouch as they both filled pipes and lighted up.

"Where'd Evans go?" one said.

"I dunno. He came this way."

As they puffed contentedly, a blue cloud grew up around them in November sunlight. It smelled good to Billy, smelled like home. Their horses wheeled in opposite directions and waded dripping from the water. The men rode away eastward. Billy had just started to rise when someone yelled from the south end of the clearing. A soldier walked out of the trees, another bluecoat holding his musket at the muzzle, carelessly dragging its butt through the dust.

"Hey, here's water!" Nearing the bank, he yelled. "Well, look at that, wouldn't you know, them cavalry sonsabitches muddied it up."

"Pray they didn't piss in it," said another, emerging from the trees. A bunch more came out, following the first toward the head of the pond where the water looked clearer. They knelt along the bank and began filling canteens.

So this wasn't just wide-roving cavalry. Sherman's army was supposed to be off west chasing after Hood. But already here east of Atlanta Billy was in amongst Union infantry, sure enough Sherman's army. He could hear men calling now to the north. They were all around him. From where he huddled, he could see through weeds to the man he'd killed. When the bluecoats left the pond, Billy crawled back to the corpse. The dead man wore gold-embroidered second lieutenant's straps on his shoulders.

"I didn't mean to," Billy told him, "I didn't."

The blue uniform was hardly touched by blood. Billy himself had caught most of that. The big struggle was getting the lieutenant's coat off without raising his arms high enough to be seen by some passing soldier. He had to roll the body onto its front, and back again. He wasn't so horrified now, just more and more numb. The boots were easy. He had to remove them before he could tug off the breeches. Billy didn't like boots, but his own brogans were badly worn. He took neither shirt nor small clothes. At Jonesboro he had seen dead men left naked on the ground, peeled-potato white. He didn't want to leave this one like that.

Lying on his back, he stripped off his own uniform, using the coat lining to wipe clotting blood from his face and hands, from the patent-leather bill of the Union forage cap. The lieutenant had called Billy a little turd, but he was small himself. The blue uniform with its short jacket, its single row of brass buttons, fit pretty well, as did the boots. Billy rose from the weeds, brushing sunflower hulls from his hair. He thought again how much it looked like the same day, the same sky, sunlight shattering like diamonds on the pond when wind brushed the water. But he felt older, as if years had passed.

A faint shuffling from behind caused him to turn. Six bluecoat infantrymen emerged from a leafless sumac thicket there, muskets held at waist level, bayonets fixed. They came straight toward him at a trot. He felt so dull this didn't much surprise him, didn't even make his breath come quick. Of course he couldn't fool them, not with the dead Union officer lying at his feet beside Billy's own gray uniform. He started buttoning the open jacket anyway, for some reason wanting to make a halfway decent-looking prisoner or corpse, whichever way it turned out. The strangest thing, he noticed, was that under the bills of their forage caps, the faces of the soldiers rushing down on him were black—no, two of them brown, one very light brown.

They came thundering up to him, wary from the first instant, angling their bayonets toward his throat. A soldier wearing corporal's stripes, studied the ground where Billy's uniform lay.

"He's a Reb!"

"Gaw-damn Secesh!" said another.

Billy saw the musket butt coming too late to duck. Then he was looking up at blue sky, in which many bright lights blinked wildly on and off. He realized he was seeing stars. It was the first time he'd seen this kind of stars. He felt the prick of bayonets at his throat. Above him now was a regular ring of black faces, brown faces, all shadowed by forage caps.

"Re-MEM-ber Fort Pillow!" somebody yelled, and Billy sensed the eagerness of the bayonets.

"Let's just stop now," another voice said. "Let's pull away now." Like someone talking down a high-strung brace of carriage horses. "Just step on back now."

"Do what the sergeant say," the corporal ordered.

Grudgingly, the bayonets drew back. A dark hand reached down to him. He took it—this small hand—and was hauled to his feet. The hand didn't let go. It belonged to a sergeant, broad gold stripes on the uniform sleeve. Under the bill of the sergeant's forage cap, out of the dark walnut face, shone those same clear eyes he'd seen so often, eyes of light bright brown. Once more he saw himself in them, himself reflected and the woods behind him, and sky. Among all those scowling faces, this one alone beamed a wide-mouthed smile, struggling, it seemed, to suppress its pleasure. The left eyebrow lifted, giving the face a bold, commanding air, as she gazed into him. Her eyes were telling him something, maybe no more than, *be quiet, let me talk.*

"He's Georgia Guard," Lenora June said in a strange husky voice, "but I know him. We can use him."

3

When I got there I saw some soldiers. They wanted I should enlist and so I did...All the money I send you I want you should spend it for the family... If you want to save anything to remember me by, keep that spotted calf and if I ever return I want you to let me have her again.

—Letter of Nov. 24, 1862, by Sarah Rosetta Wakeman of the 153ʳᵈ Regiment, New York Volunteers, one of about 400 women who in disguise fought for the Union and the Confederacy.

DALTON, GEORGIA, NORTHWEST OF ATLANTA was Union territory, already conquered—so Lenora June had been told. She had to enlist in the army there, they said, because General Sherman in Atlanta refused to sign up colored fighters. Walking into the little town, she found it hard to believe Dalton was Union controlled. A saddlery proprietor came out on his shop porch to jeer as she passed.

"Looky who's comin in, some shit-ass contraband. Get yonder to the Post! They're lookin for niggers to enlist. They gaw-damn well gonna *need* you!"

Contraband—it was a word Lenora June hated. She was no contraband of war, mere property seized by one of the belligerents. She had freed herself from slavery. Far from being seized, she would offer herself, body and mind, to the Union side. A nicely-dressed woman stepped into the street ahead of Lenora, hands lifting the hem of her skirt. She said nothing, just hawked up a wad of phlegm and then didn't, after all, spit. She stood, purse lipped and threatening, causing Lenora to veer away. Other whites stopped on the street to stare cold eyed.

Wearing much-patched breeches, a child's shift to flatten her breasts, a man's homespun shirt and a tattered frock coat, she walked in among the tents of the Post through a ferment of effort. Black troops shoveled furiously on the south side, throwing gouts of dirt against a low log wall that was becoming an entrenchment. On the east side, a crew of men leaned into a cannon, rolling it up to the line. A colored soldier came past pushing a wheelbarrow loaded with wooden boxes labeled, "Cartridges, Rifle Musket, .58 Caliber."

"What's going on?" she asked, lowering her voice to its gruffest register.

"Hood's comin! He's comin quick."

"I thought Sherman was chasing General Hood out west of here."

"Sherman done quit chasin him. Now Hood's chasin us."

She found army headquarters in a two-story building, what might once have been a boarding house, set amid a clutch of military tents. A white captain in a ground floor room, glancing quickly at her, commented:

"You're a skinny one." He slapped the enlistment paper down on the desk before him. "At least you got a little height on you. Go ahead, make your mark."

He rose from his chair and disappeared through a door into the next room. The paper said she was enlisting in the 44th U. S. Colored Infantry Regiment. She dipped the steel pen and signed her father's name in a careful hand, "John Marion Moffat." The man returned with a cup of coffee. He glanced idly at the paper, then studied it closely.

"Can you read?"

"Sure."

"How much can you read?"

"I've read Shakespeare, of course, and Dickens and Browning..... both Brownings. I like her better, the sonnets."

"What's nine times nine?"

"Eighty-one."

"You ever shoot a musket?"

"A squirrel musket, just an old flintlock smoothbore."

"Percussion's easier by far—nothin to it. And you can hit somethin with a rifled musket. That rifling inside the barrel spins the slug, makes it shoot straight." He turned and shouted behind him through the open door. "Colonel Johnson, we got another sergeant!" The captain looked eagerly up at her. "Sergeant Moffat, take this paper, go quick to the quartermaster tent and get yourself equipped."

Four hours later she stood with her infantry squad, the dozen men she commanded, in the south entrenchment watching General John Bell Hood's Army of Tennessee slowly approach the post, then lap around it, 30,000 graybacks, they were told—what was left after Sherman whipped them at Atlanta. Hood had circled behind Sherman's army and was trying to cut his rail connection to the North by destroying, among other things, this little post at Dawson. The day was cloudy and cold, gray light from the sky gleaming dully on the bronze of Confederate cannon.

She'd been told Corporal Ben Densmore couldn't read but was expert already with loading a Springfield rifled musket, which was different a little from Billy Leidig's squirrel gun. Densmore helped her with loading, in particular with the primer, a percussion cap which she didn't understand. He knew this recruit had only just enlisted, but knew also that his noncom could read. He was respectful, never addressing her except as "Sergeant Moffat." She was surprised, and naturally pleased, that so far no one had detected that she was female.

She stood in the trench behind the head log, running her hands through the stiff leather box at her belt, puzzling it out. The box was stuffed with paper cartridges, the primer caps in a little pocket at one side. Glancing up, she saw Hood's men were rolling the cannon out from their lines, arraying them in batteries of four. Love your enemies—so her Quaker teacher had taught in Pennsylvania. Bless them that curse you, and pray for them which despitefully use you. What she cursed just now was the intrusion of these crippling thoughts.

"They're damn near in musket range," the corporal said. "We oughta be shootin grapeshot and ball to keep'em back. Looky yonder!" A little knot of Union officers rode out through an embrasure toward the Confederate mass, accompanied by a single Negro sergeant. A white flag fluttered from a staff in the sergeant's stirrup socket. "Oh, shit," Densmore said, "hope we ain't gonna give up!"

As the Union contingent was swallowed into the Confederate line, Corporal Densmore shouted:

"Re-MEM-ber Fort Pillow!" The cry echoed then on all sides. "Fort pillow! Fort Pillow!"

"What's Fort Pillow?" Sergeant Moffat asked.

"It's up in Tennessee, where they shot down nigger soldiers after they surrender. Shot down most all of'em, burnt their bodies. Killed some Tennessee white soldiers, too, cause them boys were from a Secesh state and fightin for the Union. Traitors, they called'em. I seen it myself, what happen." He put a hand up to his forehead, massaging it as if to ease a headache. "That Bedford Forrest, that cavalry man, he done it. He been a slave trader. He said niggers cain't stand up to Secesh whites like him."

The musket iron chilled Lenora June's hands as she stood there, trying to steady down her trembling. We must tremble at the Word of God—so the Quakers had explained the shaking that had given the Society of Friends its common name. Hood's army was not the Word of God—quite the opposite, she thought. Still she trembled. Slowly the sky cleared in the west. Shafts of sunlight broke through there, as if portending some heavenly hope. After awhile the Union horsemen rode back from the Confederate line, came in through the embrasure.

Densmore was forty years old at least, his cropped hair nearly all gray. He knew a world of things Lenora would never know. Good at rough carpentry, he was the one with wit to install the head log of this entrenchment, so they could shoot under it with some protection. The white captain had told her Densmore's thick fingers could load and fire a musket three times a minute. Now he looked at her with an expression of deep puzzlement.

"Sergeant Moffat," he asked, " how come them Secesh hate us so? They been fightin Yanks three years already, three years bloody fightin. Us coloreds just got in it. How come they hate us so bad?"

Lenora June studied her new, high-topped federal shoes, planted on raw clay of the trench bottom. Without looking up at him, she said:

"Because we're the reason for it. They know we are the cause of this war."

Reaching this point in her story of how she became a U. S. Army sergeant, telling it to Billy by firelight, Lenora June saw the lines in his face sag, as if he'd been slapped. From times long before, she knew this expression. She had hurt his feelings.

"I don't hate coloreds," he said. "Best people I know are colored."

A year ago, she thought, he would have said the best people were niggers.

"Corporal Densmore was talking about Secesh," she told him. "Are you Secesh?"

"Reckon I'm from Georgia. I wore that grayback uniform."

"Now you're wearing blue."

"Sure, just tryin to keep from gettin captured by the Union." He smiled and lifted his hand to rub the smile away. "That didn't work good."

"No, I caught you."

They sat before a fire sheltered behind a barn, doing a shift as lookouts. A little reflected heat shone back on them from the log wall. The other squad members lay asleep inside. Billy's hand fished into the inner breast pocket of his Union officer's coat and came out with something, which he handed her. It was a little Daguerreotype, cleverly fitted into a frame with a heavy steel back. The portrait, coppery in firelight, was of a sober-faced young woman who looked straight ahead, deep into Lenora's eyes.

"I bet she gave him that," Billy said, "told him wear it over his heart, like it was gonna turn the musket slug. Wisht I'd shot him there, instead of the face. I had to shoot'im. He was chasin me with a saber. He mighty near got me."

He took the portrait from her, tucked it back into his coat and buttoned the lapels against the chill. That young woman's lover, the Union lieutenant, lay now where they had buried him, his grave marked only by plank of timber taken from the ruined mill. The squad dug the shallow hole because Billy wanted him buried. Billy's wind-burned face, beginning to show feathery whiskers, still sagged in every line. She had always liked the faint dusting of freckles on his nose, under his eyes. Lenora June pulled a warm hand from her overcoat pocket and laid it on his cold one, surprised at the sudden thump of her own heart. She struggled to control it. Everything she'd learned, North and South, had taught her this must not happen.

"Remember how I took your hand to pull you up?" she said.

"Uh huh."

"Well, that—and this right now—this is about the only hand-holding we're gonna do. You understand?"

He shook his head and looked at the fire.

"Back at the Forge, at them dances, you let others do more."

"Sure I did. Isaac Stoneman kissed me—kissed me back after I kissed him. Once. But he's of my race. Billy, you and me, we *can't*."

She didn't want to hurt his feelings again, was relieved when he turned his blue eyes up to her and smiled ruefully. He laid his other hand, just very cold, just icy, on top of hers. She fought back the surge of pleasure it gave her. Then, grinning at the ground, he pulled both hands away and hid them behind his body, as if renouncing temptation. Billy rose, walked off to one side and looked past the barn into the valley below, gesturing for her to join him.

In the valley to the south, on the next ridge, and the ridge beyond, on and on to a dim horizon, ten thousand campfires flared, maybe a million, winking through the midnight woods. Smoke hung in the hollows, brightened by a moon that night after night had been growing, now almost filling its full circle.

"How come us to camp way over here," he asked, "and the Union army yonder?"

"Sherman doesn't want us. He wants no Negro fighters. Colored soldiers fight in units everywhere else in the Union army. Not with Sherman. If we go over there, he'll turn us into teamsters or laborers."

Together they walked back to sit on their ground cloth before the fire.

"Tell the rest," he said. "What happened at Dalton?"

What happened was a surrender, which their white captain quickly tried to explain as triumphant Confederates were rushing in to take them prisoner. The 44th U. S. Colored Infantry was outnumbered thirty to one, he said. During the truce parley, General Hood had asked another Confederate officer if he thought they could "take those damn niggers out of the fort."

"Hood himself, the commanding general, he's the one spoke that," Lenora June told Billy. "The other officer told Hood his troops just itched to storm the fort and kill every damn one of us. Ben Densmore said it back in Dalton. It's true, they really *hate* us."

Colonel Johnson surrendered them all, Lenora June said, and—though some soldiers of the 44th were shot down—it didn't quite become another Fort Pillow.

"They marched us off toward Alabama, said they were turning us back into slaves. I'd been free twice in my life, the last time only two months. Damned if they were gonna make me a slave again! The first night they were so worn out, and they thought so little of us, they didn't mount much guard. Ben and one of the privates staged a scuffle. That Texas picket came running over. I took him from behind—whopped him with a stick of firewood. My squad and a lot more got out that night."

She sat frowning into the fire, feeling her breath come quicker at the memory. Do good to them which hate you—the words crowded forward in her mind. But *damned* if they would make her a slave again! Lenora June kicked a foot out, knocking logs together, sending a storm of sparks up toward a starry sky.

Even as a child at Highland Forge she'd sensed the difference between slave and free, above all freedom's prize of reading. At the age of six she became personal servant to the Forge Master's daughter, Parthenia. They wouldn't let her join the tutoring sessions so much dreaded by Parthenia and her older brother. But Lenora was amazed at the result when Parthenia proudly read to her from books—how many words could be decoded from every page, how many far-off worlds took shape, how many scenes flowed before the eye of the mind.

That genius was denied Lenora until they escaped to the forge near Philadelphia. In Abington she learned to read in a Quaker school, the Bible, of course, which proved wonderful when you could page through to parts seldom studied: wise Ecclesiastes, the beautiful Song of Solomon, the four Gospels, especially the verses reporting what seemed almost the sinful kindness of Jesus, sheltering even the woman taken in adultery. She compared that to the heartless commands of Ezekiel, of Deuteronomy. The Bible, she decided, is a book at war with itself.

She read everything else she could find, Beadle's dime novels, *East and West*, and *The Gold Fiend*. Much of this her Quaker teacher frowned on, but he didn't stop her, even told her where to borrow yet more books. She read William Harvey on how blood coursed through her own veins, from heart to lungs to brain to limbs and back again. She read Dr. Louis Agassiz on how continents had been laid up like wedding cakes in layers through eternities of time, how the land had been shaped in great Ice Ages. During a rail trip she saw for herself the evidence in granite boulders carried by glaciers and dropped among limestone hills where they didn't belong.

What a brilliant man, she thought, this Dr. Agassiz, until later she read his statement that Negroes were not born of Adam and Eve but were instead a different species, not human. She admired him for discovering those ages of ice and, as her teacher advised, tried to pity him—not hate him—for the other.

Still, the persuasive power of his racial fable was proven one day when a canvas-topped wagon rolled into the Abington Forge, only one teamster on the bench but three men with shotguns hidden inside. They took her father, then her mother and Lenora captive. They riveted manacles on John Marion's wrists and ankles, also on her own wrists and her mother's. Dragged them all the way back to Georgia in that wagon under the Fugitive Slave law. Nevertheless, Lenora kept on reading—read every newspaper, studied every book that Parthenia's tutor passed along to her. She kept reading. She taught reading to other slaves, right up to the day she was sold to the speculator in slave property, who took her west. Violently, she kicked the fire again, sending up another tower of sparks.

"They have laws in Georgia too!" she announced to a surprised Billy. "There's a law here against teaching Negroes to read." She glared at Billy, caught unawares by her sudden heat. "Their churches send missionaries to heathen across the waters. Here, they won't let us learn to read the Bible."

"Reckon I knew that, Lenora June. Of course I did."

"I tried to teach those people, and the Forge Master sold me west."

"I was right there all the time, Lenora. I cried when it happened. That's why I come out here a-follerin you."

"Master Hardesty is *ignorant*, Billy. I talked to him. He doesn't know anything about the world. He can read, but he never reads anything except invoices and bills of lading and the cruel parts of the

Bible. He runs a forge, but he doesn't know how to make steel like my pa can. He put us in manacles. Just like he owns the Forge mules and the Forge mill, he *owns* my ma and pa."

Billy looked wide eyed into her, his freckled face, his scraggly beard, flickering in light from the fire.

"Lenora June, I never much thought about it back in them days. I didn't see much difference between us, even you being a slave. That didn't seem so bad. But me killin that Union lieutenant," he said, "that's about all I'm gonna do for Secesh. Killin that man, I reckon that's plenty for the South."

Lenora let out a held breath, feeling her anger begin to die. She yawned, wondering whether she should be waking someone for the next guard shift. Billy, too, seemed to lose his edgy alertness. On his down-turned face, that challenging smile of his peeped out.

"How come you to join the army anyhow, you being a Quaker? Way you talked back at the Forge, Quakers ain't s'posed to fight."

His question cut into her, made her turn quickly to him.

"Jesus whipped the money changers out of the temple," she said.

"Oh!" he barked. "That's what you call war—whoopin money changers?"

"If Jesus could do violence, if he sinned like that, I can too. I'd go to hell for it, if Quakers believed in hell. The ones who taught me don't." That struck her as funny. She glanced up at Billy and felt the grin widen on her face. "Anyhow, bad as I am, Billy, I'm a better Quaker than you are a Secesh."

"I ain't no Secesh—reckon I never was. But I'm Georgia born. I ain't no Union man, even if I am wearin this blue coat. What kinda sense you got, anyhow, going with Sherman, and him not wantin colored?"

Actually, she had done worse than merely go with Sherman. Before that they had escaped from their captors in Hood's army and hiked back to Dalton, got themselves equipped again with weapons and ammunition. Then she led her squad out—five of them anyway, the ones willing to take the chance. They deserted and traveled cross country to hang at the northern fringe of Sherman's columns on the eastward march toward the sea.

"Billy, Sherman doesn't like colored. He'd just as soon we all stayed slaves. But he's marching sixty thousand Union soldiers right through the heart of slave country. He's gonna free more slaves in one campaign than all the other generals put together. That's why I'm going with Sherman."

Billy added a knot of wood to the fire and sat quiet for a moment, staring gloomily into it.

"I come out this way lookin for you. I didn't come out here to go with Sherman."

Now that he'd found her, she didn't want him to leave. Still, she said:

"You don't have to. I'm going."

4

In all social systems there must be a class to do the menial duties, to perform the drudgery of life...It constitutes the very mud-sill of society... Such a class you must have, or you would not have the other class which leads progress, civilization and refinement... Fortunately for the South, she found a race adapted to that purpose here to hand...We use them for our purpose, and call them 'slaves'.
—South Carolina Sen. James Henry Hammond to the U. S. Senate,
March 4, 1858.

THEY NEEDED A WHITE OFFICER. Turned out that's what Lenora June had meant when she said, "We can use him." Army regulations required colored troops to serve under white officers. It would look better if her squad had one. No Union man himself, Billy was perversely pleased to find himself promoted from lowly private with the Georgia Guard to second lieutenant in the U. S. Army. He lacked the horse officers usually rode, but he didn't mind walking.

He damn well did mind that a grinning Sergeant Lenora June had told the squad his full name was Wilhelm Ludwig Leidig. The middle name honored a prince of Bavaria, where Billy's pa was born. But the whole damn squad didn't need to know it. Anyhow, Sergeant John Marion Moffat awarded him the dead lieutenant's Spencer carbine, with five loaded magazines and a box of fifty copper-jacketed rimfire cartridges. With her rumpled blue jacket buttoned to her throat, she stood before him, her full lips pulled down at the sides, her chest swelling as if she were holding back a guffaw. Then she handed him the weapon.

"You could always pop a squirrel, Billy Leidig," she told him. "You might make the best use of this."

What was so damn funny? He *was* a good shot, though he had no idea how, deranged as he'd been, he had shot the Union lieutenant in the face. Fingering the carbine's loading lever, he pondered whether he could shoot anyone else, blue or gray. Staying away from major roads, they marched eastward mostly on foot paths and game trails following ridge lines through a poor farm country. At an open place, where they couldn't be ambushed, Lenora called out an order, and the squad broke into song. Billy recognized the melody, *John Brown's Body*, but had never heard these words.

We are done with hoeing cotton, we are done with hoeing corn,
We are colored Yankee soldiers now, as sure as you are born.
When Master hears us shoutin, he will think tis Gabriel's horn
As we go marching on. Glory, glory hallelujah....

At the first piss break Lenora June told him, as she had told the others long before, that rank has its privileges. She walked off into a thicket to do her business alone. No one questioned this. The others thought she was a man, yet they showed a respect in her presence befitting a woman—no, actually more befitting a lady. They also spared the Quaker sergeant their worst outbreaks of profanity. Hell, she'd led them out of Confederate captivity into Sherman's emancipating army—reason enough for respect.

Billy noted that even corporal's rank rated privileges, since—imitating his sergeant—Ben Densmore also crashed off through the brush in another direction to meet his need. That left Billy on the trail with four privates, Ike Spears and Aaron and Hubert Smallwood—all escaped slaves—and Leon Duffy, the squad's one freedman, come down from Detroit to join up and emancipate. So, rank having its privileges, Lieutenant Leidig was obliged to strike out on yet another angle to piss in genteel solitude.

When they were little, he and Lenora June had felt no such need for privacy. Often they pissed together, Lenora's skirt thrown up on her back, her smooth butt protruding as she squatted. Many years had passed since he'd seen that walnut-brown butt. Still, he cherished hope of seeing it again. After buttoning his breeches, he walked back to rejoin Lenora, who said:

"What are you grinning about?"

"Oh, nothing."

As they marched ahead on a foot path, they saw boiling pillars of smoke to the south marking foundries, gristmills, cotton gins, railroad trestles, occasional plantation houses torched by Sherman's troops. Lenora told him Sherman's men sometimes did burn houses, but her squad so far had not. Nevertheless, they had robbed food from a well-stocked plantation the day before. He noted with pleasure how their haversacks bulged with hoecakes, jars of canned preserves, two sides of bacon and a ham. Passing through Georgia in a colossal raid, this army had no supply line stretching back to the North, Lenora told him. Forage liberally off the country—that was Sherman's order. So they foraged. At that first plantation the Negroes had already run off—no slaves to emancipate there.

But on Billy's first day of marching with the squad, they found some. The house was half log and half lumber, nothing like a Mansion, just a family's farmhouse. But behind it stood a clapboard cabin, leaning crazily, with rot in its sills. Two colored boys and a white one played mumbletypeg in the dirt with a pocket knife. When the squad deployed at quick step around the house, the boys jumped up and fled into the half-open back door.

"Don't scare the people any more than we have to," Lenora June said. "Cock your muskets and watch the back door. Corporal Densmore, you and Billy come with me."

Billy held the Spencer slanted across his chest, finger on the trigger, studying the black shape of the open door, from which a charge of buckshot might blast out—just good white folks plugging their fellow Georgian, Billy Leidig, even if he wasn't Union like the rest of the squad. But, hell, he himself had emancipated that slave he met on the road. Emancipating, he had to admit, seemed like a good idea. Instead of buckshot from the door, a skinny colored man came forth, shoulders tucked back, hands resting easy in the hip pockets of his overalls.

"Howdy!" he greeted them. "How y'all doing? Reckon y'all lookin for dinner? About all we got's a half-bushel of parched corn. Grayback cavalry took everythin else, took them plow horses too. They said Yankees get it anyhow, so they took about everythin we had. But y'all sure welcome to a bowl of corn mush." He looked warily around at the circle of faces. "I heard the Union got nigger soldiers. Y'all the first I seen."

"Thank you, we don't need dinner," Lenora June told him. Did you know President Lincoln emancipated the slaves, those anyhow in the rebel states? He set you free."

"Yah, I heard. That right nice."

"We came here to set you free. You can leave right now, go anywhere you want."

With a brown hand he stroked his chin downward.

"See, the lady is sick, she sick yonder inside the house." He drew one calloused hand from a back pocket and waved at the door behind him. "Hus-bin shot dead in that fight up on Kennesaw mountain. He's daddy to the baby she got."

Billy was still worried about that open door.

"Somebody tell you to say that?" he asked. "Who's inside? They got a musket?"

"They's an ole scattergun yonder, hangin over the mantel."

Billy shouldered past him, sheltered a moment against the house wall, then hinged around the doorjamb with the carbine raised and rushed inside, surprised at his sudden courage. Ben came right behind him. For a moment Billy stood, heart pounding, seeing nothing except a high window on the far side, hearing the scuffle of feet on the floor. Lenora June darkened the door for an instant and then stopped beside him. Slowly the room lightened around them.

A tall colored woman stood behind the wooden kitchen table, all three children—black and white together—hanging about her legs. Her lips dragged down in a ferocious frown, not angry—just bad scared. Here Billy was doing it again, scaring this woman as he had scared the shoeless runaway slave. But in a pleasant, quavery voice she said:

"Howdy. Set y'all down. I get the stove fired up and fix corn mush. Wisht we had more to give."

"Reckon we didn't come to eat," Billy told her. "No, maam, we come to set y'all free. You don't have to stay no more. Y'all can go."

The woman glanced back and forth between Billy and Lenora.

"Well, that's real nice. We go right soon. But Miz Rawdon, she sick." The woman pointed toward the window.

Under it, as Billy now made out in the dimness, was a bed constructed of some dark wood. Billy and Lenora moved closer. A white woman, flushed faced and panting with shallow breaths, lay on the good feather mattress. Between her and the wall was a newborn baby, asleep on its back but with hands raised, fingers moving, its face crossed and recrossed by a grin that came and went. The woman's eyes were open but didn't seem to see. Lenora lay a hand on the pink cheek and pulled it away.

"Touch her," she told Billy.

He touched her cheek and jerked back, surprised at the heat. The Negro woman had come up beside them.

"She got that youngin out just fine, then two day later come down sick."

"How is she down below?" Lenora June said. She had asked for an answer Billy didn't want to hear.

"Miz Rawdon tore up some," the woman answered. "Real red, kinda swole up today."

The Negro man had drifted back into the room, along with the rest of the squad, Ike Spears, Leon Duffy and Aaron and Hubert Smallwood. Duffy moved close to face the black woman.

"Y'all free now," he told her. "Take what y'all want and get."

"Sure, thank-ee," she said. She looked at the floor and then up into Lenora's eyes. "Miz Rawdon, she got milk for the youngin, but she ain't good. What you reckon is wrong?"

"It could be childbed fever," Lenora said.

"Ain't that bad?"

"It's bad. Just keep her clean as you can down there. Keep her warm. Make her drink water, help her eat. Most important is the water. She has to drink."

Duffy pushed close to Lenora June. He was a good-looking fellow, Billy decided, of light complexion with a pointy, almost Norwegian nose.

"We ain't here to be takin care of white folks," Leon said.

"Private Duffy, get outa here!" yelled Sergeant Lenora June.

Duffy spun in place and marched toward the door.

"I thought we gonna free the slaves. Come to find out, it's just more takin care of white folks."

Duffy groused about it. Still, he obeyed. Billy couldn't help but notice he regarded the sergeant—not the lieutenant—as his boss. They left the family a side of bacon, half the sweet potatoes, half the preserves, then traveled on down a woodland trail so little used it wasn't even rutted. Billy walked beside Lenora June, glancing amiably across at her frowning face.

"That story you told about the day before you found me," he said. "You hit this plantation where the slaves already run off. Now today we come on a farm where the slaves *won't* run off. And here I thought we gonna free the slaves."

"Oh, Billy, just be quiet!" she huffed.

They marched onward north of Sherman's streaming army, close enough to flee back if attacked by Wheeler's cavalry, far enough out so they could call on plantations with slaves the army wouldn't reach. On the third day they followed a trail through forest much worked in the past for timber. The old stumps had resprouted into dense thickets of vertical trunks. Ben Densmore, in the lead, dropped back to walk beside Lenora June.

"That way you learned readin must be hard. I study on readin Bible. Cain't make nothin out of them scriptures."

Walking behind them, Billy saw Lenora's face turn brightly up to Ben's.

"You could learn. Billy did. Didn't you learn it, Billy?"

"Sure!" he answered. "Sergeant Moffat taught me, back when she was a slave. Taught a bunch more folks at the Forge. It took awhile."

The subject interested Leon Duffy. He caught up to walk beside Billy, listening as Ben spoke up again.

"Reckon you could learn me readin?"

"We could start," Lenora told him. "Evenings we could both teach you."

"Might be I'm too old. Be obliged, though, if you tries."

In his haversack Billy still carried the leather-bound *Romeo and Juliet.* His using it as an excuse for chasing after Lenora June had made him shy about giving it to her. But it might be useful if she taught reading. Beside him, Private Duffy tucked down his chin, swelled his chest and spoke in a booming voice.

"Sergeant Moffat, he gonna teach readin to the id-jut nigger. Sergeant Moffat the big per-FESS-or, all time talkin like one."

Lenora June stopped abruptly and swung around on him. Throwing her arms out like a scarecrow, she danced a jig, her brogans kicking up dust. The whole squad listened in wonder as she boomed out:

"Here be ole LEE-on Duffy, dat big freedman fum DE-troit! Y'all get schoolin up yonder, LEE-on? Learnt y'all t'talk good wif that big mouf a'yourn?"

They stood in stunned silence, Lenora beaming her white grin at them, its corners squeezing her cheeks upward, her eyes nearly shut. They laughed. When it died out in a volley of coughs, Leon said:

"Well damn me to hell! I reckon Sergeant Moffat so bad I got to teach ole Densmore myself!"

Ever the teacher, Sergeant Moffatt couldn't leave it at that. As they walked on, she reminded Billy once again that, reading aloud, he could speak the English of books.

"With good language, you can say what you mean in few words," she told him. "Billy, you don't have to talk Peckerwood all the time. Just like me, you could talk either way."

Chewing over this lesson, he walked in sulky silence.

"I like the way my folks talk," he said at last.

Her mocking grin brought warm blood to his ears.

"Yah," she said, "dot's de vay ve talk in Bavaria, eh? Mit Deutsche spraken. Verdamnte youngin! All dot stuff."

"All right! NOT the way my pa talks. The way MA talks, the way them other folks around the Forge talk. That's what I like."

Then he picked up the pace and walked on ahead of her. It was almost noon when they came out into a logged-over clearing cluttered with stumps. as they reached the middle, a Union officer spurred his horse from where the trail emerged on the far side. Two more Union horsemen followed him. The last Union officer Billy had seen was the lieutenant who'd tried to kill him with a saber. Now he felt a powerful urge to flee. Lenora's presence steadied him. He stood fast as the Union men approached. The officer was heavy set, triple chinned, sitting a mount too small for him. He pulled the animal up before them.

"Who are you people?" he yelled, looking straight at Billy, here at last recognized as ranking officer.

"Forty-forth U. S. Colored Infantry," Billy answered, regretting his words even as he spoke them.

"You musta fought one helluva battle," the officer said, "seeing how there's only seven left from a whole regiment."

Maybe the truth would work better.

"Reckon we just out here trying to free the slaves," he said.

The officer—Billy could see now he was a major—smirked at them across the thirty yards that separated the two groups.

"Lieutenant, that is not General Sherman's intent. We are trying to win this war. I happen to know the Forty-fourth got sent back to Memphis. You deserted your outfit."

First Billy deserted from the Confederacy, now he'd deserted from the Union. Shit, he couldn't keep it straight!

"Goddamn niggers," said one of the two sergeants who sat their horses beside the officer. "They never gonna make soldiers. That lieutenant talks like a damn Secesh."

"I'm Major Ballard, with the 179th Illinois," the officer boomed. "You people fall in behind us. I'm taking you back to my command."

Desperate for a way out, Billy saw to the north a green cedar tangle like all the surrounding forest—big trees cut off maybe for house logs, re-sprouted now into a thicket. He turned to Lenora, whose eyes were wide with alarm. She yearned to free slaves—not become laborer for an army that didn't want her.

"Sergeant Moffat," Billy whispered, "let's just walk real quiet into them woods."

"I said FALL IN, gaw-dammit!" the major yelled.

"Let's go," Lenora hissed to the squad, inclining her head toward the thicket. They moved together toward the trees.

"Did you hear me?" the major yelled. "That's an order! You niggers gonna be teamsters for my battalion. General Sherman wants no nigger troops on this expedition. I warn you, now. Stop or we'll shoot!"

Before he even thought about it, Billy felt himself swinging around, Lenora turning with him. He heard the snapping of buckles, the click of musket hammers, as other squad members turned behind him. The major had leveled his revolver at them, the other two horsemen their carbines, which looked to Billy like breech-loading single-shot weapons.

"Don't raise your muskets, don't threaten them that way," Lenora said. "Let's just stand quiet here a minute."

Abruptly, the Union horsemen found themselves facing double their numbers of armed and primed infantry soldiers. Billy displayed his weapon in profile so they could see it was a Spencer repeater—far better than their single-shot carbines. First the pistol went back into its holster. The carbines came down. Lenora turned then and led them into the cedars. The squad sank into resiny dimness, squeezing between close-placed trunks. Billy's coat sleeve caught on a branch and stopped him. Lenora plucked it free, pushed him forward. Looking back, he saw that Major Ballard had advanced his mount to thicket's edge, which barred entry by any horseman. The officer shaded his eyes, straining to see into deep-woods gloom.

"That's an order! You come back here! That's a direct order! You niggers, don't listen to that white officer. He's an outlaw. You hear me, lieutenant? You gonna be court martialled for desertion. You will hang before I'm done with you!"

Billy wondered what they might court martial him for if they found out he was a Rebel private, killer of the Union officer whose uniform he wore. An hour later and a mile distant, Lenora June walked beside him, shaking her head, her teeth clenched, her chin thrust defiantly forward.

"Those are our liberators!" she seethed.

"Like hell!"

Billy had to wonder why those three were even fighting the damn war. Hell, he was a Georgian, he was a *Southron*—what Confederates had taken to calling themselves instead of Americans—and still he hoped for Lenora June's sake that the Union would come to more than this.

5

...like demons they rushed in. To my smokehouse, my dairy, pantry, kitchen and cellar like famished wolves they come, breaking locks and whatever is in their way. The thousand pounds of meat in my smokehouse is gone in a twinkling, my flour, my meat, my lard, butter, eggs pickles of various kinds both in vinegar and brine, wine, jars and jugs are all gone. My eighteen fat turkeys, my hens, chickens, fowls, my young pigs are shot down in my yard and hunted as if they were rebels themselves.

—Dolly Sumner Lunt, Covington, Georgia, comments in her diary on the arrival of Sherman's troops.

LENORA JUNE HAD TO CONCEDE the woman showed grit, shouting defiance from the porch of her plantation house as the squad approached.

"Y'all not welcome here! Get off this property!"

The Mansion was of brick, its pitched roof sheltering deep gallery porches on two sides. Four big dormer windows frowned down from the shingle roof two stories above. Between the curtains Lenora could see into the richly-furnished parlor, its pianoforte set prominently near a window. Behind the house, shaded from the sun by huge green live oaks, stood a brick smokehouse, many barns and sheds, a carriage house, a whole street of slave cabins. There was no trace of horses or mules and, aside from the middle-aged mistress, the place was mysteriously vacant of humans.

"Where are your slaves?" Lenora June asked.

The woman didn't look at her. She stared pleadingly into Billy's eyes.

"Oh, sir, as a white officer and gentleman you must protect me from this Nigra outrage."

"Answer this here sergeant," he told her. "What you done with the slaves?"

"From your voice alone, sir, I discern that you are Georgia born," Mrs. Lowery said. "You *must* help save our magnificent civilization from this heathen assault."

She was making true tears, dabbing at her eyes with a handkerchief. She wore a lace-collared black velvet blouse over a long blue gown, ruffled at the hem.

"The slaves!" Billy demanded. "What happened to them?"

"Thanks to the cursed Union, all our servants have run off. I am a lone woman, without help."

The house, the yard, the nearby kitchen garden seemed well kept. Lenora June found it hard to believe this silk-skinned aristocrat could cook her own meals, empty her own chamber pot, not to say till gardens or tend livestock. She was too fine-fleshed for work.

"If Mister Lowery were only here," the woman said, "he would not put up with this Nigra trespass. I appeal to you, sir. In my husband's absence, and as a white southern gentleman, won't you stand in his stead?" A hard hand grasped Lenora's elbow, shaking.

"Burn it!" hissed Leon Duffy. "Burn the damn thing, like white troops been doing. How come we don't get to burn nothin?"

She pulled free and, without answering Duffy, addressed Corporal Densmore.

"Ben, take the Smallwood brothers and search the house. Don't take anything out of there except food. Get under the house and search the crawl space. Let's find the slaves."

"You will not!" the woman screamed. "You niggers will not come in my house! Oh, lieutenant, you *must* stop them!"

When Densmore's men went up the steps, she blocked their path. They picked her up as they might a wriggling river catfish, carried her down and set her in the dirt, weeping and screaming.

"Y'all will never defeat us! We will NEVER give up the Cause. We will fight y'all for-EVER!"

At this sight Lenora fought back the surge of pleasure that choked her throat—not a decent Quaker response. With Billy beside her, she moved behind the house, found a big detached kitchen there with twin chimneys. Billy took a crow bar from a tool shed and broke the padlock. The building's shelves were loaded with rounds of cheese, canned preserves of all kinds, sauerkraut and pickles. There were barrels of flour, corn meal, rice, sorghum molasses. He broke another padlock on the smokehouse and pulled back the plank door. They walked into a darkness pungent with hickory smoke, surrounded by a hoard of hams, bacon sides, jerked beef. Lenora had just turned back to the door when a child darted in, seized a ham and staggered out with it.

"Hey, now, you wait. You stop!"

The little black boy wobbled onward, trying to run with the ham, glancing back over his shoulder. Lenora ran ahead and again yelled, "Stop!" He stood panting before her, hugging the ham to his dirty shirtfront.

"Where you taking that?"

"Down yonder by the creek."

"Where's your mama?"

"Mama dead. Aunty Sooze, she take care me."

"Where's Aunty Sooze?"

The boy sighed out his vexation.

"I'm *tellin* y'all, down yonder by the creek. They hongry down yonder."

He wouldn't let Billy carry the ham. He struggled onward with it, leading them first along a well-used path beside a corn field, then across pastures a half-mile to a wide creek bottom.

"How come they down here?" Billy asked. "How come they don't go to the house?"

"Cause Master chain'em down here. Master, he say Sherman comin, Sherman whoop niggers, Sherman kill niggers. Master hide'em by the creek. He didn't cotch me. I run in them woods."

The boy led them down a steep earthen bank toward the creek, teetering on the path, then skidding in with a splash. He rose, dripping, from the shallow water, the ham still clutched to his chest.

"Binky?" somebody called from the other side. "Who comin?"

"Me comin," the boy yelled. "I got a ham!"

Voices went up. "Praise the Lawd! That's a good boy!"

They crossed the creek at a rocky ford and climbed the far bank, moving up among widely-spaced trees, giant sycamores trunks ascending to a canopy of bare white branches. Around the base of one tree were men and women and children, fifty or sixty of them. They huddled in ragged coats and shawls and blankets, sitting in leaf litter. There was much coughing and throat-clearing as Lenora approached. An older woman rose from the ground. The boy staggered over to her and handed her the meat.

"I got it, I got it, Aunty Sooze." Binky prodded into ham fat with one thumb and sucked it. The woman gazed warily at Lenora and Billy, cradling the ham against her belly.

"Y'all Sherman's army?" she said.

"We're Union," Lenora answered.

The woman's ankle was clamped into a fetter, bound by a long chain to an iron ring encircling the sycamore trunk. Lenora moved past her, moved out among the people as others crawled to their feet. Except for the tiniest children, they were all fettered that way, bound by chains radiating from the iron ring. Chained up like foxhounds. The smell of rotting feces thickened the air. She turned back to Aunty Sooze.

"How long you been here?"

"Five days, pretty near. About five days, seem like. Master Lowery, he say Sherman get us. He hide us here. He got the stock penned up down the creek about a quarter, them hosses and mules. Hounds penned up yonder too, them *slave* hounds. Done hid everthin so Sherman won't get it."

"Where's the master?"

"He gone. Master and Bossman, they got pistols, they chain us up. Then they go, reckon they run from Sherman."

Fetters, chains—Lenora recalled how well they had worked in holding her mother and father on the wagon ride back from Pennsylvania. She saw the people had dug holes at two places in the sandy soil for latrines, now swarming with flies as the November day warmed. They had been lying chained here five days, unable to move, yet they looked exhausted, drawn and thin. A sour smell rose from their clothing.

"Did the master leave food?"

"Naw, bossman say they comin back. Nobody come. Binky, they didn't cotch him. He pick ear corn out the field for us. We got gourd dippers, reach down to the creek for water."

"Mrs. Lowery is up at the house. Didn't she bring any food?"

Aunty Sooze shrugged.

"Naw. She lady from Charleston. She don't do nothin."

Billy, who had moved out to the edge of the slave circle, dropped to one knee and picked up a chain.

"What-all is this?" he asked.

It was a puzzle. Lenora saw one end was hitched to the iron ring. The other just disappeared into the earth beyond Billy. Her breath came quicker then.

"Did somebody die?" she asked.

"Uh-huh, Cornelee die. Cornelee old, she sick when Bossman put us down here. Third night, she pass on." The woman looked away, up into the trees. "I'm shamed, we just scratch a hole, no preacher to say somethin. Couldn't get that chain off."

Lenora felt the blood beating in her face. Billy moved close and, looking at his shoes, spoke in low tones, for Lenora alone to hear.

"Wasn't too good back home at the Forge, I mean, the way y'all colored was treated. But I never seen nothin like this."

Would *this*, then, be enough to make him a Union man at last? She was angry at him as well as the slavers who'd done *this*. Anger had blinded her to everything else. Now she realized Binky, shivering in his wet clothes, was yanking urgently at the woman's skirt.

"Aunty Sooze, let's eat!"

When Billy drew his bayonet from its sheath, the woman took one step away. He passed it toward her, handle first.

"Reckon y'all hungry," he said. "Cut that up, give all of'em a bite. Plenty more yonder at the house when we get them chains off."

Aunty Sooze took the knife and stood blinking at them.

"Abe Lincoln done 'mancipated the slaves, so we heard. Y'all come to set us free?"

Never in her life had Lenora wanted more to say a word.

"Yes!"

"Praise God!" the woman shouted. "We free!"

"Hallelujah, praise God!" went up the chorus around her.

Lenora June turned and walked away from them to hide tears that sprang up in her eyes. She took deep breaths, panting almost, struggling against the feeling that weakened her knees. Then she turned and shouted back at them.

"Free, if you can stay free! You may yet have to fight for it."

Indeed, it turned out that even the first step was hard. Bossman had the only key for the fetters. Billy ran back to the tool shed for what he needed. He returned with Corporal Densmore and the rest of the squad. Moving from person to person, he would carefully place the bolt of a leg fetter on the steel face of a sledge hammer. Using the sledge as anvil, he would set a cold chisel on the bolt and strike it sharply with a mason's sledge. One by one the fetters fell away.

Lenora June liked watching him in this deft use of tools. He worked with a little half-smile on his face, biting his tongue between his teeth. On one thick bolt he had to strike hard and bloodied the man's ankle. Still, when the fetter came off, the man rose, walked into the creek, lifted water in his cupped hands and splashed his face.

"Hallelujah, jubilee!"

Lenora June stood at the place where the one chain sank into dug-over earth.

"Cornelee," she said, "don't forget Cornelee."

Billy glanced up at her, surprised.

"Not the fetter on her ankle?"

"No, just break the chain."

He trailed the chain across his sledge and set the chisel on it. With a sharp hammer blow, he shattered one link, the two ends flying apart. Billy stared gloomily at the end disappearing in the earth. t least Cornelee wouldn't spend eternity chained.

"Let's keep the hammer and chisel," Lenora told him.

Standing among the milling people, she let out a long-held breath. Aunty Sooze had cut the ham, passing out pieces. The people chewed as they moved about, shaking their legs, loosening their joints. They brushed leaves and dirt from their clothes, patted and hugged each other, the children trying their feet again in little chases across the creek bottom. To make herself heard, Lenora June yelled.

"Some of you might want to stay. This army is just passing through. Stay behind and you'll be slaves again when we're gone. But follow the army if you want. Take what you like from the kitchen and smokehouse." This time—thanks to how these slavers had treated Cornelee—it would be more than kitchen and smokehouse. "Take anything you want from the house. Plenty of wagons and buggies up there. Take'em. You built this place with your labor. Take anything you need."

Without food from the pantries, these people would starve on the road. Anyhow, she had always thought property belongs not to those who own it, but to those who make it. She had doubts about the very concept, having herself been only that—property—just two months ago.

The people also would need the plantation livestock. She took Billy and Hubert with her to find them. The horses and mules—twenty four of varying quality—were penned in a log corral down the creek. Four Redbone hounds, the slave hounds, were chained to a tree there, chained as the people had been. They bayed and groveled and wagged as the squad approached. Lenora June had grown up with such amiable hounds at Highland Forge. She also had seen them in use.

"Shoot'em," she ordered.

"NO, Sergeant Moffat," Billy groaned. "It ain't their fault, what them slave owners made'em do. They just good ole hound dogs."

Like good old Peckerwoods, Lenora thought, who know not what they do in abetting slavery. Raising her musket, she shot the first one herself, calling forth a pitiful yelp before the animal sagged and died. Billy shrugged and dispatched two more himself with the Spencer before Hubert's musket killed the fourth. She stood for a moment, taking slow breaths. For though we walk in the flesh, we do not war after the flesh. That Quaker conviction came back to her as she watched blood pool in the dirt. For the weapons of our warfare are not carnal, but mighty through God to the pulling down of strong holds. Anyhow. She sighed inwardly. Anyhow, those hounds would never again be used to capture escaping slaves. That she had been forced to kill these dogs, even for such a reason—she ground her teeth against the slavers who caused it.

By the time they had led the livestock back to the Mansion, people were stripping the abundance of kitchen and smokehouse. Several men led horses and mules to the barn, began harnessing them to pull wagons. The women had started cookfires outside their cabins. Since

Corporal Densmore had searched it looking for slaves, no one else had dared enter the house, where Mrs. Lowery stood now on the gallery porch with a double-barreled shotgun. She glared down at Billy and Lenora, her face smudged, the dress disheveled. Without hesitation Billy climbed the steps toward her.

"Billy, don't!" Lenora yelled.

The woman aimed the shotgun at his face, her fingers scrabbling at one hammer to drag it back.

"I will kill you! I will."

Lenora threw up her own musket to shoot the woman, realizing only then she hadn't reloaded after the dogs. Billy's face had turned toward her with an amused look as he climbed. She heard a sharp click as the shotgun hammer fell. The gun didn't fire. Billy took hold of it. He twisted it from the woman and pulled her back down the steps, she pounding him about the head with her hands.

"You will not defeat us!" she moaned. "We will die in the last ditch!"

Lenora ran to him, grabbed both his shoulders and shook him.

"You damn fool! I don't want you dead!"

"Hell, that scattergun wasn't primed. I seen that clear. You not loaded and she not primed." He grinned at her and lowered his voice. "Y'all women cain't seem to get full ready to shoot."

Lenora stood before him, trying to breathe. She'd seen a whole regiment surrendered at Dalton and then this little scuffle, but never a real battle. Still, she found war hard. Here it was mid-afternoon, and she worn out with the day.

She ordered the woman to stay out of the house and called the former slaves in to take what they wanted. Soon they were trooping out with their prizes, a stereoptican viewer with its twin scenes of fancy places far across the sea, ladies' hats and shoes and gowns and gloves, Venetian glass vases, tailcoats, cufflinks and broadcloth trousers from the master's wardrobe, a silver candelabrum, porcelain platters and bowls, four muskets and another shotgun from a hidden closet cache. Lenora resolved to arm the freed people at every opportunity. A woman came out holding two fat gold pocket watches, one to each ear, smiling at their ticking. Private Duffy emerged wearing a wide-brimmed woman's hat with an ostrich plume.

With Billy beside her Lenora climbed to an upstairs guest room. She stripped a linen sheet from the bed, folded it over into a smaller square, then another yet smaller to make an easy-to-carry package.

"How come you want that?"

"I'll soon need it," she said, and nothing more despite Billy's puzzled look..

Descending the walnut staircase, she saw a tall-chimnied oil lamp, fueled, as she saw, no longer by scarce whale oil but by milky, half-melted lard. She lifted it and smashed the glass base on the marble tabletop. Lard splashed the carpet. She drizzled the rest across a horsehair couch. From a pocket she drew out her corked bottle of friction matches, scratching one on the tabletop.

"Hey, don't!" Billy yelled as she lowered the flame toward the carpet. "Lenora June, don't! You ain't s'posed to burn houses. That woman out yonder, she ain't the one chained up them slaves!"

Lenora dropped the match and, before Billy could stamp it, flame ran across the carpet to the couch. He jerked a pillow up from a chair to beat at the fire. Near the window she found another lamp, broke it, soaked the fringe of the damask drapes and lighted them with a second match. By now Billy himself was afire, the cuffs of his trousers anyway. The pillow worked at least to save his pants. As flames rose around them, he stood staring amazed at her.

"Oh, Lenora," he sighed, "Lenora June..."

"That woman could've fed them!" she screamed at him. "She could've let poor Cornelee off that chain before she died!"

By they time they got down the outside steps, smoke was boiling out of first floor windows. Mrs. Lowery stood looking at it, hands pressed to her cheeks. Minutes earlier her cry had been, "die in the last ditch." Now it was forlorn lamentation.

"No, no, no, no...."

Heat popped the glass of a side window. Reaching rich air, the smoke pouring out flashed into flame. It licked upward on the brick. From the street of slave cabins, Private Duffy came rushing up to them. He took off his fancy hat, slapped his leg with it, grinned wildly.

"Hot damn! Burn that sum-bitch!" He danced a crazy jig.

The freed people milled around the white woman. Now she didn't seem to mind the Nigras. She watched the house, softly moaning.

"Mama's letters are in there...."

For November it was a warm day and sunny, the shingles very dry. When fire reached them, it rushed up the roof to make a towering steeple of flame. It licked out through the front windows, eating at the gallery porches. Heat parched their faces.

Lenora stood beside the white woman, struggling to keep Cornelee in mind, Cornelee chained to a sycamore tree, buried coffinless in the dirt. Yet once she had seen Mrs. Lowery's tears, she felt some baffling urge to hug her. She didn't hug the woman. It was Lenora herself who was hugged—by Billy, who had moved close and seen Lenora's own tears. He came up beside her, with one arm hugged her to him. She wiped her eyes and sharply pushed him away. hissing:

"Billy, NO!"

Then she glanced across his shoulder and saw Leon Duffy watching them, his mouth open, his eyes wide with astonishment. Billy's eyes were also wide but not with astonishment, the lines of his face sagging with the wounded look she'd seen so many times before. His mother had reared him too tenderly. Once again, Lenora realized, she had hurt Billy's feelings.

6

Any free person who shall teach any slave to read or write upon conviction shall if a white man or woman, be fined not less than 100 dollars, nor more than 200 dollars, or imprisoned; and if a free person of colour, shall be fined, imprisoned or whipped, not exceeding 39 lashes, nor less than 20. And for a similar offense, a slave shall receive 39 lashes on his or her bare back.

—(34 Revised. Statutes of North Carolina 74: 209.)

THE SQUAD TOOK TWO PLANTATION mules for their own use, husky animals with the delicate hooves of race horses. Working together, the Smallwood brothers turned a stock saddle and a lady's side saddle from the barn into pack frames, which they loaded with food, a pot and skillet from the kitchen, a pair of lard-oil lanterns chosen by Lenora June for outdoor use.

She had meant to begin a reading class that night but found it impractical. Private Duffy had unearthed a jug of whisky at the plantation. It passed back and forth along the line of marchers, and by evening the soldiers wanted only sleep. Next day, despite the intermittent drizzle that wet their rubber ponchos, the squad covered ground well, often singing from what seemed endless variations on the melody of "John Brown's Body."

They said, "Now colored brethren, you shall be forever free,
From the first of January, Eighteen hundred sixty-three."
We heard it in the river going rushing to the sea,
As it went sounding on. Glory, glory hallelujah...

That one, Billy recognized, was about the notorious proclamation—which, of course, Lenora June had celebrated with a wild jig when the word reached Highland Forge that winter of sixty-three. On and on they sang.

They will have to pay us wages, the wages of their sin,
They will have to bow their foreheads to their colored kith
and kin,
They will have to give us house-room, or the roof shall tumble in!
As we go marching on. Glory, glory hallelujah...

At sunset that day they made camp where a creek emerged from hills into bottom land fields of corn and sweet potatoes. It was here, after they cooked supper, that Sergeant Moffat began teaching Ben. With the last glow draining westward from the sky, the creek gargling over the stones of its bed, she lighted the two lamps and cleared a space of dirt between them.

Long before at Highland Forge she had learned never to teach the entire alphabet at the same time. Tonight she started with a few letters, BEN, scratching them into dirt with a willow stick. These letters he already knew. She added D, named the letter, then bowed the willow twig to show him and said, "bend."

"Mmmm," Ben murmured.

With one hand she erased the last two letters to add AN, naming them as well.

"Bean," she said. She added another letter, S. "Beans, with an S, means a lot of beans, what we had for supper tonight."

With his own stick Ben stabbed the S.

"That snaky thing, it change one bean into lots?"

"S makes a word plural, more than one. Most of the time, S is all you need."

"Cracky, if that ain't sharp!"

She went on to BEAR, BEARD, BEAST, BEAT. Watching her move through the words, Billy realized she was a better teacher now than when he knew her at the Forge. She was dressed like a man, her hand-me-down blue jacket already worn to white threads at the elbows, yet showed a woman's softness in her features—cheeks darker than the kernel of a red oak acorn but with the same silky shine.

At the Lowery plantation she had pushed him away so violently that he still felt heart-stabbed. Of course she had to do it. He couldn't be caught hugging her. Already Leon seemed curious about Billy's friendship with Sergeant Moffat. Still he felt the hurt of it, actually savoring little shivers the recollection sent down through his body. He stood behind her as she taught, the squad. After a half-hour, some began yawning, staring upward to a sky winking with stars. Bored, Leon spoke out.

"What good all this doing," he demanded, "learn this stuff and still ain't got no book to read?"

"I've got a Bible," Sergeant Moffatt announced.

A moan rose from the group.

"Not that ole BI-ble," someone said.

"Don't be givin' us none of that ole E-PHE-sians," groaned Ike. "Servants, obey your masters."

"I know something good in the Bible," Lenora said.

"Don't want none of that ole Saint Luke stuff," Hubert sighed. "Don't do what the master say, then you get beat with many stripes. White preacher back home, hell, he sermon on that every Sunday."

"Give me minute here." She dug the Bible from her haversack and sat marking passages with a burnt twig end from the fire. "We'll do a dramatic reading. I do one part, Billy the other."

"Me?" Billy said. This scared him. "What kinda readin?"

"Dramatic reading. I learned it with the Quakers. I showed you this chapter before. You've read it—just not with people listening."

She had marked verses for herself and short passages that were his. They knelt facing each other before the open patch of dirt, one lantern on each side. She would read, she told him, then turn the book on the ground and mark his place with her finger.

"I ain't that good readin, Sergeant Moffat."

"Just do it."

Her smile glowed on him, eyes bright in her dark face as he'd seen them so many times. Now the yawners gathered tight around, eager to see Billy make a fool of himself—so he figured. Lenora looked somberly down at the book and spoke low voiced.

"I am black, but comely, oh ye daughters of Jerusalem, as the tents of Kedar, as the curtains of Solomon. Look not upon me, because I am black, because the sun has looked upon me." She took a breath and moved her finger on the page. "I am the rose of Sharon, and the lily of the valleys. As the apple tree among the trees of the wood, so is my beloved among the sons. He brought me to the banqueting house, and his banner over me was love. His left hand is under my head, and his right hand doth embrace me."

"Whoa-ho!" shouted Leon. "Whoa-ho-ho-ho!"

Ben Densmore slammed down his big open hand, banging Leon's bare head.

"You shut that now. We gonna listen." Leon cowered, sidling away from Ben around the circle.

Billy knelt looking across at her face. She was black, at least in this light, and she *was* comely. The lanterns shone on her high forehead, the slope of her nose, her wide moist lower lip. She turned the Bible on the ground and placed her finger on a verse. He saw the first three words and choked up. Urgently, her fingernail tapped the page.

"Read!" she commanded. He coughed once and tried it.

"Thy two breasts are like two young roes that are twins, which feed among the lilies. Until the day break and the shadows flee away, I will get me to the mountain of...." He looked up at her. "What-all is this?"

"I will get me to the mountain of myrrh and the hill of frankincense," she read.

He glanced at the next words, then looked up at her to say them.

"Thou art all fair, my love. There is no spot in thee." A smile grew on his face, because she herself was after all, a spot of darkness lighted by the lanterns' flicker. He looked down again. "Thou hast ravished my heart, my sister, my spouse, thou hast ravished my heart with one of thine eyes, with one chain of thy neck. How fair is thy love, my sister, my spouse! How much better is thy love than wine, and the smell of thine ointments than all spices. Thy lips, O my spouse, drop as the honeycomb. Honey and milk are under thy tongue."

"Ooooooooooooo," somebody moaned. This time it wasn't Duffy. Ben let it go.

Lenora June turned the Bible to herself but didn't read. She gazed straight into Billy's eyes and recited.

"My beloved is white and ruddy, the chiefest among ten thousand. His head is as the most fine gold, his locks are bushy and black as a raven. His cheeks are as a bed of spices, as sweet flowers, his lips like lilies, dropping sweet smelling myrrh. This is my beloved and this is my friend, O daughters of Jerusalem."

White and ruddy, he could believe that. But chiefest among ten thousand? Hell, he couldn't hold his own among these seven. Still he felt fire in his face, his breath coming so quick he could hardly read when she turned the book and showed him his next verse.

"How beautiful are thy feet with shoes, O prince's daughter. The joints of thy thighs are like jewels, the work of the hands of a cunning workman. Thy navel is like a round goblet, which wanteth not liquor. Thy belly is like an heap of wheat set about with lilies. Thy two breasts are like two young roes that are twins."

When they were children, Billy had seen her titties, touched her nipples, as she touched his. Then, male and female, they were shaped much the same, his a freckly white centered as if by a copper penny, hers a silken brown with a darker, larger center. Now, swaddled in a sack-like blue uniform, she had no more breast than anyone else in the circle. Her fingernail slid down the page. Impatiently, it tapped at another verse.

"This thy stature is like to a palm tree," he breathed, "and thy breasts to clusters of grapes. I said I will go up to the palm tree, I will take hold of the boughs thereof." He'd never heard such words spoken in public. Here he was, speaking the words himself, panting them out for everyone to hear. "Now also thy breasts shall be as clusters of the vine, and the smell of thy nose like apples."

"Whooooooo-eeeeeeee!" someone said. Lenora turned the book back to herself but didn't look at it. Again she looked at Billy.

"I am my beloved's, and his desire is toward me," she said. "Come, my beloved, let us go forth into the field. Let us lodge in the villages. Let us get up early to the vineyards. Let us see if the vine flourish, whether the tender grape appear, and the pomegranates bud forth. There will I give thee my loves."

When she fell silent, they heard the rush of creek water again over the stones. In his chest, along his throat, Billy felt the pounding of his heart. Then Duffy threw his arms wide, clapped the plumed hat on his head and danced in mincing little steps back down the trail.

"Come, y'all beloved, let us go forth into the field," he warbled. "I'm a-goin back to that plantation, catch me one of them little gals. Get me some tender GRAPES!"

As Duffy disappeared into darkness, Corporal Densmore moved closer to stand, looking down at Lenora.

"That the best Bible I ever heard. If you learn me, then can I read it?"

"You can."

"Sure, but after you quit teachin, I forget. I just get dumb again."

"The mind once enlightened cannot again become dark," she said.

"Huh?"

"That's what Tom Paine wrote. After you get smart, you don't get dumb again—if you keep on reading."

"Who-all Tom Paine?"

Billy knew Tom Paine, had read him in a book Lenora borrowed. He was about to answer Ben's question when she sighed out:

"Oh, he's a hero from the past."

"Sure, then I quick learn readin," Ben said. "Quick as a hiccup." Grinning, he looked around to see if anyone else was. "Y'all hear that? Quick as a hiccup." They had heard this before, too many times. No one else grinned. He gave it up.

Returning from his sashay down the trail, Private Duffy came back into the lamplit circle and stood for a moment, staring keenly at Billy and Lenora, who still knelt on the ground facing each other.

"*Some*thin goin on here," muttered Leon Duffy.

7

Our new government...its corner-stone rests upon the great truth, that the negro is not equal to the white man; that slavery—subordination to the superior race—is his natural and normal condition...He, by nature, or by the curse against Canaan, is fitted for that condition which he occupies in our system.

—Alexander H. Stephens, vice president of the Confederacy, in his speech of March 21, 1861.

HAVING HURT BILLY'S FEELINGS, LENORA June had mended them—or so she hoped—by staging that warm dramatic reading. Two days later the good cheer boiled away in the flames of a burning house, this time, regrettably, no mansion.

Where their one road forked into two, she had sent men ahead to scout the best route. Billy took the left fork. Leon advanced on the right while the rest waited at the divide. Hubert Smallwood lighted his pipe and puffed contentedly beside his sergeant. He passed it from man to man, each sucking at the tobacco, making it crackle, until the pipe reached their sergeant. She drew the tiniest nasty smoke taste into her mouth. Then they heard a BOOM and its rolling echo. Shotgun, she was sure. She listened for the answering bark of Leon's musket. It didn't come—a bad sign. She coughed out the smoke and thrust the pipe back into Hubert's hand.

"Let's go!"

They went at quick trot until they could trot no more. Then, out of breath, they walked. The house, just two big lumber rooms with a shed kitchen behind, was afire. Flames eating their way up one wall licked at the shingled eaves. Circling the building, they found Leon in the barnyard behind, one foot on the back of white man who lay belly down in dirt. Leon's musket muzzle pressed tight against the man's ear.

"Get him offa me!" the victim squealed, rolling a wild eye up toward Lenora June.

A tiny spot of blood on Leon's chin grew into a droplet and fell away. Lenora June had just reached a hand up to search for a wound when a woman appeared in the door of the log barn behind. Barefoot, she wore only a ragged muslin shift and cradled a baby in her arms. For a moment she stood quietly in the door. Then she stepped out toward the Union soldiers. She had almost reached the squad when four children trailed across the barnyard following her. She turned, flapping a hand at them.

"Get! Get back yonder! Y'all get back to the barn!"

They didn't get back. Shrieking and wailing, they circled her, tugging at her skirt, three little girls and a boy about ten. Lenora heard the rapid thump of boots as someone came quickly around the house. Billy ran to her, sucking for air as he caught up to the squad. He looked hopefully into the woman's face and shouted to make himself heard above the clamor of the children.

"Need water to fight fire! Where's your well?"

She shook her head so violently the baby rocked in her arms and set up its own mewling.

"Ain't got none. We haul from Brushy creek about a quarter down the path."

Which made fire fighting hopeless after all. The shingles were blazing now, thrusting a column of smoke into a blue noontime sky. Lenora raised a hand to shield her face from the heat. Billy stood for a moment staring into the blackness of the open back door. Then he ran through it, emerging seconds later with a wadded armload of fabric, quilts and blankets and bed sheets. He dumped it on the ground and glanced up at a gawking Lenora June.

"Come on!" he roared.

Again he vanished inside, to be followed in train by other squad members—all except Leon, who kept his foot on the back of the groaning man. They got out the clothing, a single oil lamp, even a few chairs and a small table. Lenora staggered out, coughing from the smoke, and dumped an armload of kitchen goods. The woman handed the baby to her son. She began tugging her possessions farther from the heat. Billy made one last foray and emerged dragging a feather-filled bedtick. His uniform jacket smoldered at the collar, adding to the reek of his singed hair. With quick fingers Lenora pinched sparks out of the charred wool. He coughed a few times, bending low, and stood up to catch his breath. Then he waved a hand at the woman, who had retrieved her baby and now held it close.

"What's going on?" he demanded. Under scorched eyebrows he looked accusingly out at Lenora June. "These folks just Peckerwoods. Ain't hurtin nobody. How come y'all to burn the house?"

Lenora had no idea. She opened her hands and shrugged. Leon stepped away from the prostrate man, who sat up feeling at his head as if to be sure it was still there. Leon himself looked a little baffled by these circumstances.

"Hell, I was out yonder just passin by on the road, that's all. This white sum-bitch yells, 'gaw-damn dirty black nigger contraband.' Sure, I'm dirty and I'm a nigger, but I ain't no contraband of war. I ain't NO-body's piece of property. I'm a freedman, a free DE-troit nigger! Free before this war even start. Bastard called me contraband. I went right at him, gonna fight him is all, and he pops up with that damn twelve gauge. Hit me too."

He lay a hand at the side of his face where a single pellet had raked it.

"Sum-bitch skipped back in the house. I run in behind to cotch him before he could reload. Knocked him down. I was mad, I kicked over the iron stove in yonder. Hell yes, I set the house afire! Let it burn!"

It burned. The growing heat drove them all back toward the barn. The children clustered around their mother, still wailing, making snot and blowing their noses on the fabric of her shift. The white man now stood close beside his woman, as if she might offer some protection. For all the weeping of their children, both man and wife were dry eyed. The woman stood stolidly beside her husband. Her wide nipples had leaked milk through her shift, leaving dark circles on the fabric. Lenora June noticed that Billy had put on his sullen little-boy look, as if once again she'd hurt his feelings. He waved a hand at the bruised husband.

"He ain't fightin for the South," Billy said. "These folks are just a buncha Peckerwoods. What they gonna do now, with no house and winter comin on?"

"They can live in the gaw-damn barn!" Leon shouted back. "Plenty niggers live worse! That Secesh shouldn't ought shot me!"

"You shouldn't a-gone at him!" Billy yelled back.

"He shouldn't ought call me contraband!"

Lenora June could see where this was going. She didn't know how to stop it. Billy stood looking level into her eyes, breathing as hard now from the argument as from his exertions.

"Y'all just burn any ole house," he said. "Ain't just rich folks houses. Ain't just these slave owners. Y'all burn poor folks' houses. Reckon I seen about enough of this house-burnin shit!"

He spun around in place and stepped off, going wide around the fire. She didn't want him to go. She didn't think he would. She watched for him to turn at the road and come back. Once outside the front gate, he turned eastward and if anything picked up his pace.

"Look at him go," Leon said. "Looky how he strut. Cocky sumbitch! You gonna let him walk right off with that quick-shootin Spencer gun?"

"He's the one who took it. From the Union lieutenant."

"Sure, but we gonna need quick shootin before we're done."

Lenora June didn't respond. She watched Billy. She hoped he would turn and come back. He just walked on, abruptly going out of sight behind a low-branched juniper.

8

I am weary of war, of powder and ball,
I am weary and sick of the glory and all,
too much blood has already flowed like a river,
too many fond hearts have been parted forever...
footsore and weary over path steep and rough,
we have fought, we have bled, we have suffered enough.
   ---Diary entry, April 25, 1864, by Confederate Pvt. T. B. Kelly---

WAITING IMPATIENTLY FOR SLEEP TO come, Lenora June kept recalling that house fire, how ardently the flames chewed at the shingles. By the time the squad arrived, nothing could have been done to stop it. Still, the remembered eagerness of those flames, like chaos, like riot let loose on the world, tightened the inner muscles of her gut.

With no good stream handy, they had camped that night beside an abandoned farmhouse, this one at least equipped with a dug well. The well pulley, its bucket and chain, rose between her and a waning moon in the eastern sky. Hubert perched on the brick rim standing watch with a musket across his knee. Lenora lay rolled in her one thick blanket, a rubberized ground cloth wrapped tight around that. Leon, sleeping a few feet distant, sighed and shifted in his blankets, Lenora feeling a tinge of irritation with him. Why, after that day's trouble—which was so much his fault—did Leon sleep so well when she couldn't sleep at all?

The moon hung against the stars for what seemed hours and didn't move. She blinked and opened her eyes and found the moon, after all, had shifted beyond the pulley crosspiece. A friction match popped against the bricks as Hubert lighted his pipe. The pipe gurgled when he sucked fire into the tobacco. The match flare hung a long time in her eyes, laid over her vision of the burning house.

Then she saw fire in the huge water-powered bellows at Highland Forge, its pleated leather sides already burning furiously. The chaffery forge retort, where raw blooms of pig metal were heated for pounding into wrought iron, was white hot now, too hot to look at. She looked away and saw John Marion Moffat running. Her father carried two buckets from which water splashed with every step, wetting his pantlegs. He was running toward her parents' cabin, where the chimney was already on fire. So hot! Lenora raised an arm to shield her face from it. Her mother, Reba, scratched up dirt with her hands to throw on the fire. Her mother's hands were bloody, they were all bloody. Lenora couldn't help her. She wanted to. She struggled to help her mother, struggled just to move her paralyzed arms and legs.

Someone was holding her. She felt the grip on her wrists and heard a voice.

"Sergeant Moffat! You just fine." It was Leon, looking down into her face as he freed her wrists. "Be easy now."

"I saw Highland Forge burning," she told him. "Where I grew up. I saw my folks' cabin burning."

She lay on her side. In the darkness Leon knelt over her. Someone stood behind him, a shadowy soldier with forage cap cocked forward on his head.

"That's Ben. His shift on picket duty," Leon said.

Beyond Ben the moon stood high in the sky, already past the zenith, so bright she could see dirt on her fingertips, real dirt she'd scratched up to help her mother in the dream. She breathed, struggling to ground herself again in what was real.

"I'm all right," she told him. "Thanks. Go back to sleep."

She lay back too, looking at the moon. She hadn't yet recovered from the agitation of the dream. Ever since meeting Billy on this march, she'd dreaded riding with him back into Highland Forge. Seven months she'd been gone since she was sold west by the Forge Master. Billy had left home two months ago with the Georgia Guard. She had worried that when they rode in together as federal bluebacks, their parents would see it as more than coincidence. With him gone, that worry now seemed laughable. What had happened was so much worse.

Billy and Lenora had both grown up as only children, no brothers or sisters to play with. Fearing the too-common deaths of infants, couples wanted many children and hoped some would live to adulthood. Their own parents were unlucky, so they thought, to be given only one each, one child all the more cherished for it. And one lone child is likely to fall in with another.

They played as children in the village where the forge workers lived, freely crossing the little creek that separated the many slave cabins from the Forge Mansion and the other three dwellings of whites. They fished in the millpond. They skipped rocks across its glossy surface, freckled with dogwood petals in springtime, yellow poplar leaves in fall. They ran the April woods, finding poke greens and lamb's quarter, picking mushrooms, some of them deadly toadstools, as Lenora's mother warned. They picked blackberries in July, often came home smeared purple around their mouths, chigger bit with ticks lodged in their skin creases, ticks ballooned with child blood.

Once in a woodland thicket she showed Billy what was hidden under her raggedy skirt. He dropped his stripy overalls to show her his puckered pink nubbin. Only a nubbin he had, but she found the contrast between them distressing—what he had that she didn't. Why had she been so dreadfully shortchanged?

Considering that they were slaves, after all, her own family had a better life than that offered slaves on the richest of plantations. The Forge Master dare not try to whip skilled forge workers into pounding quality iron. They had to be urged toward it, rewarded at least a little for good work. But a better life still was a free one. She was eight years old when, at dusk on what would be the longest night of winter, her parents led her through woods to where a wagon waited. She rode away with those scared abolitionists, those sweet slave stealers—not Quakers but instead Baptists, native Georgians, who hauled them on the first leg of their journey to Pennsylvania. In the wagon she bawled out loud over leaving Billy.

The whole six years in Abington, where the wide world opened to her, she never forgot him. There was only one good thing about being dragged in chains back to the Forge: Billy. When the slave catcher's wagon carried her in, she saw him pitch-forking clover from the stack, over the fence to the dairy cows. He threw down his fork and ran behind yelling her name. No, *two* good things: Billy and dancing, which was something the Quakers in Abington couldn't abide.

They were both fourteen years old, he doing farm work, she back in service as personal maid to a spiteful Parthenia. The Forge Master's daughter never forgave her servant for escaping such a fortunate condition of slavery.

"It's the privileged and pampered ones," Parthenia fumed, "them who are given everything, they are the ones who run off from their benefactors!"

Lenora found Parthenia's enmity easy to forget at those slave dances in the Quapaw creek bottoms. The first time she went alone. A week later she led Billy through the dark woods into that firelit clearing where the fiddle sang and dirt throbbed with pounding feet. Abruptly, the fiddle squawked and fell silent. The dancers stopped. Everybody looked at them—all those eyes.

"What you bring him for?" demanded Isaac Stoneman, an apprentice to her father at the chaffery forge. "Ain't no Peckerwoods allowed down here."

"Who says?"

"I says!"

He stepped close to Billy and with a heavy iron-pounder's hand boxed his left ear. The head flopped sideways with the blow and recoiled. Billy's lips were level, his eyes frightened. Isaac did it again. Billy didn't back up, just came erect and stood, staring up into Isaac's face.

"Fight, you sum-bitch!"

If he fought, he would lose—that she was sure of. Even if he won against Isaac, in the circle around them milled a half dozen grinning young men, ready to take him on in turns. This dance was *theirs*, one of the few things truly their own. The crowd murmured its anticipation. Billy's hands clenched themselves into fists but hung stubbornly at his sides. Again, Isaac slapped that side of his head.

"Fight! How come you don't fight?"

Billy raised a hand to finger the lobe of that buffeted ear, which throbbed dull red in the firelight. He said:

"Man strike you on one cheek, you s'posed to offer also the other. It says that."

What he'd said was right, of course, but more than that, smart. It was his only chance. She felt a flood of feeling rise in her body as she watched the two, a bellicose man with big fists raised against this slump-shouldered boy, still open eyed, ready for more.

"Righty-right, sir!" Isaac pronounced. "Glad to O-blidge!"

His left hand shot out and whacked Billy's head on the other side, staggering him.

Lenora, the Quaker pacifist, didn't know she'd moved until her fists thudded into Isaac's chest. It was like hitting a blanket hung on a wooden wall. He didn't budge. She hit him again, leaning into it. This time he sucked in a breath and stepped back. He stood there, mouth hanging open, looking at her.

"Isaac, I'll bring who I want!" she yelled. "Leave him alone!"

All she could hear was her own panting. A huge silence had gripped the crowd. She heard the trill of crickets, of treefrogs in the woods around. Isaac's face had lost its scowl. It was twisted now into a mask of sorrow, as if Isaac himself were the victim here. He didn't hit her back. The people looked worriedly across the circle at one another. On the far side the fiddler, old Charley Broomfield, sat down again on his wooden stool and began stomping one foot in the dirt. The people found it easier to look at him than at one another. He stomped and stomped, finding the beat, and from his instrument unwound a silvery thread of music, *Turkey in the Straw*. Then he sang.

It's gettin mighty late when the Guinea hen squall,
And you better dance now if you gonna dance at all.
If you don't watch out, you'll sing another tune,
For the sun rise and cotch you, if you don't go soon.

To Lenora's relief, they took Charley's advice. Two began to dance together, a kind of shuffling polka, then another alone, who was joined by a fourth.

"Bow to your ladies!" Charley commanded.

So it would be the Virginia Reel. Already quick-stepping to the fiddle's rhythm, the people formed two lines, men on one side, women on the other.

"Bow to your ladies," Charley called again. The men did as he ordered, skipped forward to the next call. "Right hand to ladies."

Still leaden in their hearts, burdened with the fight mood, they danced stiffly. By the light of the huge log fire, they moved through do-si-dos and sashays, the dancers weaving a pattern, every hand clasping every other only to come apart and reach eagerly for one more, every man swinging every woman. All eyes wide, they began to grin at one another, helpless to resist this bleeding away of rancor, this inhalation of good cheer. The grudge Lenora nursed against Isaac began to fray. She swung on his hand and smiled up at him. He smiled meekly back. That night the dance lasted long, though not till the guinea hen squalled.

Very late, when Charley slipped his fiddle back into its canvas carry-sack, Isaac marched over to where Lenora stood with her partner. He balled up a fist and socked Billy lightly on the shoulder. This time Billy returned the blow, hard enough to jar Isaac.

"Oh ho!" Isaac grunted. "He *do* hit! How you reckon that squares with the Bible stuff?"

And that was it. Billy was in. Lenora grabbed Isaac and kissed him on the cheek. Delighted, he kissed her back on one cheek—the source ever since of Billy's upset that she'd done more with others than with him.

During that long-ago summer they danced every Saturday night. Sometimes it went on till dawn. As if drugged with laudanum, they sleep-walked through their Sundays, which anyhow were the biblical days of rest. In that first summer back at the Forge, Lenora had some free time. Georgia gallants were courting Parthenia. She was gone a lot to parties and on visits with friends in Millen or Augusta. During those lucky hours Lenora taught reading to the slaves—those who could finish their work early. The teaching made her more useful and the dancing happier, if not freer, than she'd ever been.

One October night that first year big sycamore leaves were spinning down in the Quapaw bottoms, flaring into flame on the bonfire. To bolster his fiddle, Charley had found a woman at the next plantation who played hammered dulcimer. They started with a waltz. Charley made it a broom dance to loosen them up. With a wicked smile shining in his face, he handed Billy the broom. Lenora was proud to see Billy so game. He waltzed as grandly with the broom as all the other men with women partners.

"Time to CHANGE!" Charley yelled.

Billy flung the broom down and ran for her. She shucked off her first partner and ran for him. They banged together, laughing. This time everybody found partners except the burly Isaac, who was left standing over the broom. Sour faced, he anyhow plucked it up and began to mince about with it. Billy's hand slid around the curve of her waist, and they waltzed with the others across the packed earth of the clearing, feet crunching in the leaves, couple following couple as they circled past the musicians. He whirled her so wildly that she lay back into the outward pull, looked up at the firelit white trunks of the sycamores, at leaves still spiraling down.

Then a powerful hand gripped her upper arm. It jerked her to a halt. Sucking in a panicked breath, she saw her father. A frowning John Marion tugged her away from Billy, whom—she now realized— had been seized by his own father. The music stopped. The dancers all stared as Billy and Lenora were led out of the circle, John Marion still clutching her arm, his right hand pressing her waist to guide and propel her.

Their mothers, each carrying a lard-oil lantern, waited on the path. They said nothing, just joined the procession as Billy and Lenora were marched onward. She heard the music start again behind them and fade as the distance grew. They were led through the open door of a little milking barn, right to the back, where oats were stored in tow sacks. In yellow lantern light, Billy looked scared.

"Y'all sit!" her father barked. They plopped down on the sacks, staring at four parents lined up before them with military precision.

"Ve be easy, John," said Billy's Bavarian father. "Ve talk vid'em. Straight dem out, yah?"

August Leidig was an affable man, often funny. Lenora liked him yet now watched him fearfully. Her mother lay a caressing hand on John Marion's neck, but he was not appeased. A long breath hissed out of him.

"Sure!" he said, and pointed a finger at Lenora. "But what you been doing, it's agin the law. Agin Georgia law. You got to stop!"

In Abington her father and mother had learned to read but refused to carry it further. Like Billy, they stuck by the language they'd learned as children.

"Pa, we just dance together," she told him. "That's not against the law."

"Vot it leads to," August said, "dot's agin de law. Must be no mixin de blood."

"Daddy, we ain't mixin no blood," Billy told him. "We just dancin."

"Uh-huh, uh-huh, I SEEN that dancin," John Marion said. "Way you do, it's closest thing I seen to mixin blood."

"Neither shalt thou make marriages with them," said Billy's mother, Essie. "Thy daughter shalt not give unto his son, nor his daughter shalt thou take unto thy son."

"Aw, mama," Billy groaned, "that ole Deuteronomy, he's talkin about them Amorites and Canaanites and them Jebusites. He ain't talkin about colored."

Listening to this, looking into the grim faces of their parents, Lenora felt the cast-iron block of gloom in her gut begin to heat at the edges, like pig metal in her father's chaffery forge.

"The Forge Master mixed blood with Rachel," she answered. "Master Hardesty went to her and went to her, till Rachel had Theophilus. He went back just yesterday to make another baby." Lenora felt her tongue grow acid in her mouth. "If the Forge Master does it, is that against Georgia *law*?"

A Guernsey cow in a stall at one side raised her moist black nose above the slats and mooed uneasily. This was not her usual late night in the milking barn. The yeasty smell of her manure was so familiar that Lenora found it comforting—the only such feeling she would ever recall about this barn. Essie, herself Georgia born, leaned close and looked into Lenora's eyes.

"Honey, poor ole Mister Hardesty is just like King David. Rachel is his Bathsheba. And he don't confess that chile to the world, except he keeps givin' Theophilus presents. Treats him better'n the others. That's as far as it goes with the Forge Master. But I know you two. You get started, it will be more than just going in unto. You be tryin to get married. That prosecutor in Millen be right over here."

Lenora was amazed to see the tears that now streaked Billy's cheeks, shining in the lamplight.

"Mama, lotsa laws ain't right!" he groaned. "Daddy says it too, that tariff law. Tax laws hurt the poor man and help the rich. Bad laws. All the time pa says that." The lines around August's eyes, his mouth, sagged as if he too were about to weep.

"Yah, youngin, but dis law right. This law keep de blood pure."

Billy's weeping face twisted itself into something like a grin.

"Sure, papa, my blood's pure! Pure-dee Peckerwood, that's what I am!"

"Cain't be no mixin bloods," John Marion said.

"Papa," Lenora cried, "your blood is mixed, *your own blood.* There's nothing wrong with you. Everybody knows you're the best man at this forge."

John Marion's hand flew to his brow, as if she'd struck him. Lenora's mother, Reba, turned and sat beside her on the oat sack.

"Lenora June, don't be throwin that up to your daddy."

She felt the tears on her own cheeks now, looking around at these parents, so glum-faced in the lamplight.

"We ain't mixin no blood!" Billy sighed, his fingers wiping at snot that ran from his nose. "We just dancin! We DANCIN, that's all we doing!"

The distress of that remembered moment lifted Lenora's head from her pallet, made her jerk upright beside the dying fire. Leon still lay on his blanket, his open eyes turned up to the sky.

So in the argument with their parents, they had circled back to where they started, and there it remained. She and Billy danced anyway, secretly, so they thought, till the news got back. They took their punishments—never very serious, their parents being too fond, victims of these only children. They danced again, once more trying to keep it secret, and yet again, five fine years right up to the day the speculator in slave properties seized her for transport west and eventual sale to the Hunnicutt plantation.

If she had not been sold west, she would not have run away from Billy. Tonight she wouldn't be on this trek across Georgia. She'd be with him—not that it would make life any more possible. Since that argument with their parents, the world's view of their affection had not changed. It was just as well that Billy yesterday had walked away mad. She turned to Leon, who by now was as wakeful as herself. She said:

"They make cannon parts at Highland Forge, and iron for wagon tires. That's all Rebel iron. Sherman will attack it. I want to go there, get there before the army."

"Sure!" he answered. "That's yonder side of Millen, ain't it? Long ways yet."

"We must go to the Forge," she said.

9

I saw more dead bodies of the right kind, covering broad acres, than it was ever my pleasure to see before or since. Those who have never battled often think such expressions as this are brutal. If they are correct, all courageous soldiers are brutes; for they enlist to battle, if so ordered, and as fighting is a dangerous thing, the more dead the less risk.
—Confederate Private William A. Fletcher on the aftermath of the battle of Fredericksburg in his *Rebel Private: Front and Rear.*

FOLLOWING A MEADOW PATH ALONG the edge of woods, Lenora heard the rumble of wheels far back in the trees but somehow heavy and ominous. A hundred yards ahead, their path crossed a road. From their right on that road, something was coming. It was hidden in the woodland while they stood exposed at meadow's edge. Beside her, Ben turned his face up to the sky, listening.

"Ain't no wagon," he told her. "Might be one them twelve-pounder guns with a caisson."

She led the squad at a run, intending to cross the road quickly before the cannon reached this point. The triangle of woods between their meadow and the road shrank as they dashed forward. They had almost reached its apex when—from a dense tangle of bloomed-out goldenrod directly ahead of them—a figure stood up. He held a carbine slanted across his chest.

Lenora jerked to a stop, clawing at the hammer on her musket, trying to get it cocked. She couldn't breathe. Ben slid to a stop beside her, also struggling to get his weapon up. The figure ahead raised one open hand above his head and brought it quickly down. He did it again. The man wore a scorched and dirty blue uniform. She saw his weapon was a Spencer repeater.

"That's Billy!" she hissed, starting to breathe again. Once more he gestured downward with that open hand. She turned to the rest of the squad and, low voiced, called: "Get down!"   They hit the ground and crawled toward cover, toward the wood's edge. Then, very near, a voice came to her through the trees.

"...ain't never gonna get that gun close enough."

"We can! Major got a notion how to play it."

Thirty yards ahead two Confederate horsemen came out of the woods where the road emerged into the meadow. If they glanced to their left, they would see her. Lenora crawled desperately on toward the woods. She didn't want to look at the graybacks, didn't want to know whether her squad had been discovered. At last she made herself look, sighing when she saw the two horsemen ride on.

She should have known an artillery commander would send mounted vedettes ahead to warn of ambush. She whispered orders that squad members should hide in the narrow band of woods between road and meadow. Then she remembered: Billy! After three long days, he was back, and just in time to warn them of the approaching vedettes. She caught herself smiling against her own will. Moments later Confederate cavalrymen crowded the road as they passed the squad. If they veered off the track, their horses would step on Lenora's bluecoats.

Through bare-branched trees, she saw the bronze shine of the cannon, heard its iron wheels grind over gravel. A four-horse team hauled the Napoleon, its caisson following, along the ridgetop road and across the meadow. She turned her face down into green moss smelling richly of the earth and waited it out. When the last Confederate had passed out of sight, she jumped to her feet. Already Billy was standing at the edge of the trees, looking steadily at her. She waved for him to come and led the squad across the road through yet more woods to a spot where they could see what was happening.

The Secesh were unlimbering the cannon on a cliff overlooking a bottomland farm to the south. Where were the horsemen? Most of the cavalry troopers had transformed themselves into infantry, swarming down now to throw up a cliff-top battle line. Already hastily-erected breastworks there crawled with grayback soldiers. Not all graybacks, of course. By now a good half the Confederate army was wearing butternut uniforms, that brown dye being cheaper now in the South, cheaper even than gray. Billy came forward on hands and knees. He lay down beside her and said nothing, just looked into her eyes. In a hushed voice, she said:

"What are you doing here?"

He smiled down at the dirt.

"Just sidling out the way of them graybacks. Didn't wanna get caught wearin' this Yankee uniform."

"And you couldn't help but warn us about those vedettes?"

"Reckon not," he said, "y'all being right in the way of where I wanted to go."

"Thank you," she said.

His only response was a nod toward the swarming cliff top

"Looks like a battalion of Wheeler's cavalry. Easy enough for us to back away from'em. We can go north a little, go clean around'em."

His eyes were smoky blue, flecked with yellow in the iris. That blue would fade, she suspected, as he grew older. His father's blue eyes were much paler.

"No," she said, "not yet. Maybe they'll move out of *our* way. Let's see what happens."   To her right, southward and parallel with the ridge, was that bottomland valley of farms, cloud shadows gliding across cotton fields there, the ragged bolls still unpicked. It was one of the few fields of cotton she'd seen, there being little market for it now that the Union naval blockade had blocked exports. Peering backwards, she saw other squad members in various poses, some already falling asleep, Leon Duffy on his back, knees up and crossed as he bit through the papery peel and munched a cooked sweet potato.

Billy found a chunk of hoecake in his haversack, broke it, passed her the half. His hands were begrimed with wood ash, sticky still from what looked like peach jam. She was dirty enough herself, they were all dirty. Deep in her gut Lenora June felt the beginnings of pain, a cramping there, like a slow heartbeat. Was she afraid, or was she only hungry? She munched the hoecake and nodded to the Confederates on the cliff.

"If it comes to that, can you fight those people?"

He swallowed his first bite with difficulty, then said:

"Reckon so, if they try to kill me. That Union lieutenant, he came damn close. Trick is to fix it so that don't happen. Don't go through 'em, go around 'em."

"They're fighting for slavery, Billy."

"Hell, I know it!" He said it so loud Lenora hissed a warning at him, and his voice fell. He nodded toward the graybacks. "But lots of them people yonder, they don't know it's slavery they're fightin for. They just Peckerwoods like me. I told you, I done all I'm gonna do for Secesh, but damn if I'm lookin to kill them boys."

Hearing this, she wondered what would happen. As the sun crawled up the eastern sky, they lay side by side on their bellies, munching hoecake, watching the Confederates, who settled down to a stealthy immobility. Her right hand pressed the earth beside his left. His was split-nailed, seared brown and freckled by sun, wrinkled and cracked like an old man's.

It was almost noon when Union infantry appeared in the valley below, dribbling eastward through the fields, throwing fence rails down to open passage for wagons that would follow. It was at least a battalion, three or four hundred men. They trudged along with bulging haversacks, most of them trailing muskets over their shoulders, blue ants crawling widely scattered over the valley bottom.

"Those Secesh on the cliff," Lenora whispered, "are they gonna attack the Union troops?"

His eyes shone with pleasure at her question. She knew he liked being asked. And, after all, unlike herself he'd at least seen some battles—even if he hadn't fought much in them.

"They cain't attack from yonder," Billy said. "Them bluecoats is a good three musket shots out. Shootin cannister, even that Napoleon wouldn't reach good."

Now, from brushy trees at the base of the cliff, a squadron of cavalrymen, both butternut and gray, rode out, their mounts romping and wheeling, to form a thin line ahead of the Union troops. They dismounted and, leveling their musket carbines across their saddles, began firing. The husky BOOM of their weapons echoed up and down the valley. Union foot soldiers fired back, pimpling the valley floor with little bursts of powder smoke. Nobody fell. The range was too great.

That scattering of blue ants quickly scrambled together into a braided line laid across the fields, regimental flags flapping from guidons held here and there along it. With a grumbling roar from a battalion of Yankee throats, the infantry line swept toward the cavalry. It bent backwards where fences slowed the troops, forward where clear pasture made the going quicker. A few leaders would pause to fire, swiftly reloading and running to catch up. As the range closed, the Confederates stopped firing and leaped onto their mounts. One grayback had barely swung his horse around when he fell backwards from the saddle, stirrups flying. The others spurred toward the brushy grove from which they'd come.

"Aw-oh!" Billy said. "Them Yanks gonna catch hell."

"Why? How?"

"Just watch."

The Secesh cavalry quickly drew out of range, the Union infantry rushing after them. When the horsemen vanished back into the brushy grove at the cliff bottom, Lenora June understood.

"It's a trap!"she groaned

"Uh-huh! I seen it once, by Jonesboro, only Yanks done it that time. That's when I started backin away."

She saw a ripple of movement on the clifftop as Confederates in their breastworks leaned to their weapons. The Union troops—very close now—rushed onward in a mass, to be met with a spurt of gunfire from horsemen in the brushy grove and then a crashing barrage from the cliff top. A dozen bluecoats went down, writhing and kicking on the ground. Lenora June saw Union faces beneath their caps flick up in surprise to the cliff. The cannon fired with a mighty, WHUMP, its charge of cannister plowing a path through the blue ranks. Bright blood splashed the ground there.

"No, no, no..."

Those who fled straight away were shot down by marksmen on the cliff. The others scattered to what scant cover they could find behind rocks and small trees. Some tried to fire back at the cliff top, now boiling with powder smoke as the avalanche of Confederate fire fell on them.

"We've got to help them," Lenora said.

"No!" Billy shot back. "Y'all cain't do nothin, just get yourself killed. Wouldn't help them bluebacks none."

She heard the words but found them hard to understand.

"We're gonna help them, Billy. We have to."

"Hell, no! I seen battles like this. We can go right around while it's happenin. Anyhow, I ain't got nothin against them Peckerwoods." Now he pointed to the Union troops cowering on the valley floor. "Them bluecoats don't like colored neither. They won't let y'all soldier. They want to turn y'all into a bunch of teamsters."

"Billy, like us or not, they don't fight for slavery. They *free* slaves. Ye shall know them by their fruits."

He stared into her, hot and desperate.

"Well, I ain't gonna do it," he said, "ain't gonna kill them Peckerwoods, not unless they try to kill me."

His words tormented her. So, on the Confederate side, he had fled from the battles around Atlanta. He didn't want to fight on either side. She turned away from him and rose to her feet.

"You don't have to go with us."

"Wait. Wait now," Billy said. "I thought you was a Quaker. It's bad enough, burnin houses, but Quakers don't kill people."

"I'm a lapsed Quaker."

She turned away from him, walking in the open. Powder smoke lay so thick over the cliff that the Confederates couldn't see her anyway.

"You just pickin and choosing your scripture, Lenora June. You ain't listening to what it says. It SAYS if a man smite thee on one cheek, you got to give him a chance at the other."

She didn't answer. She walked back to the other squad members and raised her voice above the din of gunfire.

"We're gonna assault those Secesh on the cliff, take'em in the flank. Maybe we can do some good. Are you with me?"

"Yes!"

"We do it!"

"Re-MEM-ber Fort Pillow!"

His face bleak, Billy stood away from the others as they formed up, swinging haversacks up to their shoulders, priming their muskets, checking cartridge boxes. Then he stepped close to Lenora June.

"Tell'em drop the haversacks," he said. "They cain't fight right carryin that load. Tell'em tote their canteens and ever damn cartridge they can haul."

Private Duffy eyed Billy skeptically. He had overheard their argument.

"*They* cain't fight right. *They* cain't. If that damn Secesh, ole Looooo-tenant Ludwig, ain't goin with us, lemme have the Spencer."

Lenora June didn't respond to Duffy. She told them to drop their haversacks, carry only water and cartridges. Billy kept pacing forward on the path to stare at the clifftop, back to the squad as they readied themselves. She looked again at the seething smoke, trying to steady herself. She recalled waking up that morning, waking to watch stars wink out one by one as dawn blued the sky. That seemed impossibly long ago.

"Let's move," she said.

Billy stepped in front of her, palms raised to her, his eyes pleading.

"Wait, wait now, let's don't get y'all killed for nothin. I been figurin. That's cavalry yonder. They got horses picketed, maybe just the other side the ridge. Gonna be a few horse holders back there guardin'em. Go for their horses, and them cavalry soldiers'll quit shootin bluecoats. They'll run after their horses. They don't want to get caught afoot and Sherman's whole army comin."

He was panting as if he himself had been running.

"Where?" she said. "Where over the ridge?"

"Right yonder, I figure," he said, pointing. "If I was them, that's where I'd picket the mounts."

She looked at Corporal Densmore, who shrugged.

"Sound good. Might serve better'n us six wading into that whole mess of graybacks."

They took a narrow path across the meadow in plain sight of the smoke cloud and were not seen. Billy hustled through weeds alongside her like a feist dog chasing a butcher's cart, still not exactly with them, now and again half turning to shag sideways, glancing anxiously at her as he passed earnest advice.

"Get over the ridge yonder, then y'all get off the path and deploy."

"Billy, we know how to deploy."

The horses were where he had pointed, in a steep little ravine that led down from the ridgetop. The squad came through dusky woods six abreast but spaced well apart, with the seventh, Billy, trailing ten feet behind Lenora June as they came out on the cleared valley floor. He was not exactly with her. Still, she felt the comfort of his presence there. Disturbed by the gunfire across the ridge, the animals snorted and stamped, tugging at leads tied to the tree stumps that remained after logging.

Lenora had seen corrals at livery stables but never horseflesh in such abundance—bay horses, spotted horses, buckskins, burly Belgians and Clydesdales galled by plow harness, horses white as Pegasus but mud spattered. Most looked worn down by cavalry duty. They were skinny, losing hair in spots, but all were saddled and ready, reeking sourly of their own dried sweat.

Sitting on a boulder amid them was a horse guard, slumped over the shotgun on his lap with a greasy felt hat tilted down over his face. Already Lenora, like the others, had cocked her musket. Now she squeezed the stock and trigger guard to keep her hands from shaking.

"Wake up, soldier," she said.

The head rose, one hand came up to lift the hat, and his mouth began shaping itself to a lazy smile until his eyes came fully open. His glance raced back and forth along the line of dark faces, noting the muzzles of weapons raised against him. He laid the shotgun on the ground and stood up.

"Y'all got me," he said. His breath came in little gasps. He caught one gulp of air and spoke again. "RECKON Y'ALL COME FOR THE HOSSES. THEY'S A RIGHT SMART OF'EM HERE, AIN'T THEY."

"Shut your damn mouth!" Ben hissed at the man.

Lenora's eyes flashed along the wood edge around them, jerking to a stop at the sight of a man forty yards distant. He'd thrown up his musket, bracing it against a tree trunk, and was leveling it now so the muzzle settled precisely down on her. Just that quick image of the man aiming—that's all she saw before his head erupted with a red splash, the huge POW! of the Spencer resounding behind her. The horses bucked and danced and jerked at their leads.

"Gonna be more of'em!" Billy yelled.

"Re-Mem-ber Fort Pillow!" Ben roared.

The squad's muskets swung around the line of woods. Smoke spurted well back in the dimness as a weapon fired there. They shot into the Confederate gun smoke, four musket blasts and two from the Spencer, breathing the sulphurous bite of their own powder.

"Oh! Oh, hell!" somebody groaned from the woods. "I'm a dead man."

In the silence that followed they heard running feet, still more horse guards who'd given it up, crashing through brush in the ravine as they ran toward the main force on the other side. Their captive horse guard stood rock still, beseeching Lenora with his eyes.

"Drop your cartridge belt," she told him, and he instantly complied. "Now get on across that ridge."

"Don't shoot me."

"Go!"

He ran crazily up the ravine, dodging through the stumps, glancing fearfully back.

"Ben, take Aaron and see about the man we shot."

But Aaron Smallwood had opened his coat to tug shirttails and long Johns up from his trousers, exposing a swath of dusky skin pierced by entry and exit wounds. His index finger stroked woolen threads from his underwear, which the slug had rammed into the frontward hole. The rearward hole oozed a trickle of blood. He studied it with an amused intensity.

"Damn if I ain't took a slug my own self," Aaron breathed.

Lenora told Ben and Leon to check the downed Confederate. Then she knelt beside Aaron to study the wound.

"It went in and out along your side," she told him. "Probably didn't hit your gut. Can you ride a horse?"

He took a breath and thought about it.

"Reckon so. Only just now comin on good to hurt."

Corporal Densmore and Leon returned to say the grayback was far from dead, had in fact left his musket alongside a splash of blood on the ground and fled. At Lenora's order, Ben Densmore quickly chose the best of the horses, more than thirty—all Ben figured they could ride and lead away from the ravine. They quickly stripped bridles from the rest and set them free, flapping their arms and hooting as the animals bolted away through the trees.

We EEEE-mancipating!" crowed Leon Duffy.

That din of Confederate gunfire from across the ridge abruptly slowed to a desultory crackle, then died out. The horse guards had carried the news that their mounts were endangered. Now Lenora's squad members were choosing their own animals, heaving themselves into the saddle, gathering reins of other horses. Hubert offered his brother help in mounting, but Aaron shooed him away. On his own, he clutched the saddle cantle and crawled up. Billy stood over the Confederate soldier he'd killed. Lenora moved close as he stared solemnly down at the dead man.

"You wore that same uniform," she said.

Billy's eyes were raw red at the lids. He coughed and drew out a rag to blow his nose, then looked down at the blood-splash he had made of the young face.

"First I killed that Yankee lieutenant. Now this one, just a dumb Georgia Peckerwood, that's all he was. I dunno what the hell I'm doing."

"He was aiming his musket right at me," she said.

"I seen him."

The lines in his face were sagging again, as if once more his feelings had been hurt. She coughed, leaned forward to blow her nose on the ground, then stood once more, looking at Billy. She reached out to his coat sleeve, her hand clasping his stringy bicep through the fabric.

"Come on. Those Secesh are gonna be down here."

With everyone mounted, Ben Densmore stood high in his stirrups, his eyes roving to meet faces of the others, as if in challenge.

"That Bedford Forrest, he say colored cain't stand up to them Secesh. Reckon he was right about me. At Fort Pillow, I run, I run clean out. Then I turn around and watch them Forrest cavalry kill nigger prisoners. Shot'em like hogs. I been shamed, shamed. This day I didn't run. This day I stand up to'em."

They rode through the forest, back toward the ridgetop where they had left their haversacks and the pack mules, each rider leading four or five horses. Climbing out of the ravine, they heard far behind the curses of Wheeler's cavalrymen, raging at the loss of their mounts.

"Hey, Ludwig!" somebody shouted. "Looooo-tenant Ludwig!" Of course it was Leon Duffy.

"My name is *Billy*, dammit!"

"Looooo-tenant Billy!" Leon shouted. "You done good this time. That were smart!"

"Thankee," Billy said, smiling at his saddle horn.

With the danger behind them, Lenora June once more felt that painful cramping in her gut. So it wasn't hunger, and it wasn't fear. It was *that* again. When the squad emerged on the narrow path at the top, they saw Union infantry pouring across the ridge toward them.

"We oughta run," Billy said, "get the hell outa here."

Lenora June said no. Those blue-clad troops were on the ridge now, not entrapped under fire below the clifftop, because of what her squad had done. She thought how calmly she had given the orders that made the battalion's escape possible, a little bubble of delight rising through her. She felt proud. As the line of infantry moved close, a pair of officers rode out.

"Well, I be god damned!" one officer said, turning to the long-bearded fellow beside him. "Colonel Langley, it's that nigger squad I told you about."

Lenora groaned. This was Major Ballard, who had wanted nigger teamsters for his battalion.

"I knew we shoulda run," Billy said.

Major Ballard beckoned one of his men forward and pointed to Billy.

"Sergeant Perry, arrest that lieutenant. Drag him off that horse." The officer sat erect on his mount, eyes roaming the dark faces. "The rest a'you niggers, you are not walkin away this time. You going to my labor company. Climb outa them saddles. Where'd you get all them horses, anyways? God damn mess of horse-stealin niggers!"

Before Lenora could open her mouth, the sergeant and two other soldiers dragged the struggling Billy from his saddle.

"Billy, stop it!" she yelled. "Stand quiet now. Rest of the squad, stay on your mounts."

He quit struggling but one by one stripped away the hands that had seized his arms and shoulders. Lenora June looked at the bearded officer.

"Colonel Langley, where *did* we get these horses? Just look at them. Who do you suppose we stole them *from?*"

Abruptly, the colonel spurred forward on his bay, reining the animal, making it dance sideways along the line of Lenora's squad, his skeptic's eye studying the seven soldiers with their throng of restless, stamping horses, all saddled and bridled. Loud enough for all to hear, he said:

"Look at those Jenifer saddles. Most of this is Confederate tack, all these carbine boots." He glanced at Billy, standing between his soldier guards. "What did you do with the rest of their horses?"

"Run'em off," Billy answered. "Couple hunnerd of'em anyhow in that holler other side the ridge. We high-tailed out of there right before them Secesh came howlin down to see after'em."

"These you brought along, these are the best of their mounts then?"

"I reckon." He nodded to Ben. "Corporal Densmore picked'em, best we could fetch away."

Lenora June felt faintly irritated that instead of herself, the colonel had addressed Billy, as the only supposedly commissioned officer present.

"The regiment can use these animals," he said. At last he looked at Lenora again. "We thank you, sergeant."

"You are most welcome, colonel."

He reined his horse around to face the other officer.

"Major, let these people keep the mounts they're riding. If they need ammunition replenished, coffee, corn meal, molasses, my quartermaster will issue it. I suspect they haven't had a payday since the campaign started. Pay them a month's wages."

Leon Duffy bounced impatiently in his stirrups and raised one hand.

"How much pay we get—thirteen dollar like whites, or that lousy ten for colored?"

"Soldier, I see your problem." The colonel smiled. "But now colored troops also receive thirteen dollars a month. We got that corrected."

"They are not on the regimental rolls," the major objected, standing tall in his stirrups..

"Pay'em anyway. Now do what I say!"

The major sank back onto his saddle.

"Yessir."

"Could your surgeon treat a bullet wound?" Lenora June said.

"No!" yelled Private Smallwood. "I'm stickin tight to y'all. Don't want no doctorin. It's just smartin now, stings a little, that's all."

The major urged his horse forward and stopped close to the colonel, speaking low voiced, as if embarrassed.

"General Sherman wants no nigger troops in this army."

Above the beard, Langley's face reddened.

"Major Ballard, we have all sorts traveling with this army— bummers of every kind, bandit bluebacks, turncoat Confederates, all of them foraging liberally off the country. What you call these 'nigger troops' saved our bacon today."

"If you say so, sir."

"Major, that's what happened!"

The colonel wheeled his horse and rode along the line of the squad, stopping at Lenora June, who was, after all, the sergeant. The gold-trimmed breast of his uniform was stained, his beard still strewn with twigs picked up as he took cover below the cliff. He was so short in the saddle that their eyes met level as they sat their mounts. His eyes roved the squad.

"You all you need to understand the danger. President Jefferson Davis has ordered that Negro soldiers taken under arms, and their white officers, be turned over to the various states under their slave insurrection laws. That could mean execution. We hear now that most Confederates no longer even take Negro soldiers prisoner. They shoot them on the spot. They've gone into field hospitals and shot Negro wounded."

"Colonel Langley, we will not be taken," Lenora June answered.

He smiled, his face now brimming with amusement.

"When Major Ballard told me several days ago about his nigger squad, he said you intended to free the slaves. Is that correct?"

"Yessir," she answered.

"Well, I must say you're a peculiar squad, with your white lieutenant who talks like a Negro, and your Negro sergeant who talks like a professor. But that's all right. Just get on about your duties."

10

$50 REWARD——Ran away from the subscriber, his negro man Pauladore...I understand [U. S. Senator] Gen. R. Y. HAYNE has purchased his wife and children from [U. S. Congressman] H. L. PINCKNEY, Esq., and has them now on his plantation at Goose-creek, where, no doubt, the fellow is frequently lurking. T. Davis.

—advertisement in the Richmond, Virginia., Enquirer, Feb. 20, 1838..

STILL THEY WERE NOT CAVALRY and, except for Billy, they were still armed with cumbersome muskets instead of carbines. As mounted infantry, though, they could range farther and take more chances, swiftly cover ground if the need arose. Billy felt good as they rode eastward from the ridge-top battle ground. That evening they camped early because Lenora June felt sick in her belly. They stopped at a creek flowing down a south-facing slope, the sun yet high in the western sky, warm for the season.

"We stink like hogs," Sergeant Moffat told them. "Everybody's gonna go in that creek and wash up."

An unbelieving Leon Duffy shook his head.

"You tellin' me to get in that cold water?"

"I damn sure am." She tossed him a bar of soap. "Wash yourselves and rinse out your uniforms. If you wring'em real dry and put them on, after awhile they'll be warm enough."

Grudgingly, they followed orders. They stripped off and waded warily into the creek, Aaron bending to fill his canteen, then swinging the open neck of it to spatter his brother with water. Hubert danced away and didn't splash back, apparently mindful of his brother's wound. They were all hip deep now, the stream erupting water spouts in a general melee. The cold shriveled their peckers into dark little thumbs at their crotches. Billy's face smoldered with embarrassment, he thinking of Lenora's near presence. At a pause, Leon stood tall from the water and shouted:

"Sergeant Moffat, how come you ain't in here?"

"Rank has its privileges," she said.

Yes it did. Although Corporal Densmore had splashed in with the rest, Lieutenant Billy Leidig also enjoyed those privileges, standing dry and warm and filthy dirty on the bank beside her. She called Aaron out of the water. With his brown nubbin of a pecker dangling before her very eyes, she gently tugged at the woolen strands protruding from the entry wound. Aaron said, "ouch....oooooooo," as the threads pulled out along with a horn button from his long Johns. Then she washed the wounds with soap and water. The puckered little mouths of flesh no longer bled as she finished the treatment and sent him back to the creek. Then Billy knelt beside her.

"How's your belly now?" he asked her. "Feelin better?"

"No. I've had this pain before. I'll get past it."

"Down the creek here about a quarter, I seen a millpond. Water yonder be a mite warmer. Reckon I'll walk down there to warsh."

"Sounds good. Go ahead."

Carrying his carbine, he walked downstream through a glen of tulip poplars, occasional big leaves spinning down around him, blazing yellow in the last of the sunlight. What had been a sawmill was now just a standing chimney and a few charred posts. The circular saw blade jutted from the ashes, already showing rust. But the mill dam was sound and the pond ran full. The setting sun lay full on gravel of its eastern shore. Billy felt that warmth through the seat of his breeches as he sat to pull off the boots. Naked, he soused his drawers, his wool socks and the uniform in pond water, rinsing repeatedly. Then he wrung the clothes dry as he could squeeze. With a sliver of soap clutched in one hand, he waded into the pond and was waist deep before the shock forced gasping breaths between his clenched teeth.

"Whoooeeeee!"

He dove headfirst to wet his hair and swam three quick overhand strokes. Then he rose, spouting, growling between his teeth, and quickly soaped himself. He ducked once more and rose again, discovering how warm the air was compared to this water. He was eager to jump full up and out into that warmth when he saw Lenora, smiling down on him from the shore.

"Come out," she said.

"No! You got to turn your back."

"I've seen you before."

"Not since we was kids. I ain't the same now."

"You're not that different from the others."

"I *am* different. To you I'm different, leastways hope I am." He was whining now. "Aw, come on, Lenora June!"

She folded her arms across her chest and turned away from him to look at the burned mill. He danced, shivering, up onto the gravel bank, which hurt his feet. The drawers clung to his skin as he dragged them up his hairy legs. The uniform was heavy but easier to pull on. Fully dressed, with his socks but not his boots on, he felt the blood-blush in his skin warming the cloth. Lenora sat on a log beside her open haversack, head down now, holding her belly with both hands, rocking slowly back and forth over it.

"You gonna puke?" he asked her.

"No. I just don't feel good."

Billy sat down beside her, he clean and she still dirty—a situation which didn't bother him, though the opposite, he was sure, would trouble her. He figured at least that one Quaker part of her, the cleanly part, still hung on. The sun lay just above trees on the far side, shining in a V-shaped water wake left by something. What? A damn muskrat! At Highland Forge they hated muskrats, which dug dens in the millpond dam there and once breached it.

"How do you feel bad?"

"I've got cramps."

Then it came to him. She'd told him about this long ago back at the Forge, what women put up with to carry down the generations.

"This here's your monthlies?"

"Uh huh."

"You got somethin to handle it?"

"That bedsheet from the Lowery place."

The muskrat had reached the far shore, was busy now nipping off reeds, making them tremble and fall in the breezeless evening. Then it waddled back to the water and swam, green stems trailing amid the ripples.

"Them water rats make right good eatin," he said.

"Billy, don't talk about eating."

Arms folded, she rocked slowly back and forth over her belly. He heard her breathing, her occasional long sighs, as the first stars burned through the dimming sky.

"Sorry you feelin bad."

Her face turned to him, its smile widening her full lips, the upper one dark pink, its bird's-wing curve rising at the ends. Her hand groped for his and drew it toward her.

"Put your hand here."

She pressed it tight to the rough wool of her breeches—held it there for a moment. Then she scuffled the fabric, loosing buttons, drawing her shirt up, pulling his hand into her open drawers. She cupped it over the shallow mound of her belly, over her womb, where their baby would lie if he ever got a chance to make it. He looked into the bright shine of her eyes as into sweet lake water and saw himself there again, felt her belly move with her breathing, felt that breath on his face.

"You're clean," she said, "and I'm all dirty."

"Don't bother me none, Lenora June." His own breath was coming so quick now his words barely croaked their way out. "I like this. Your skin's right hot."

"Your hand is cool."

Inside his trousers he could feel his pecker contend against the clingy drawers, crawling down the pantleg to stiffen in an erection, which made him ashamed of himself. Jesus said you should not lust, not even in your heart. Lenora June needed comfort, that's all, and here he was, lusting in a mite more than his heart.

From a distance it would appear they were just two soldiers sitting side by side on a log—so Billy hoped, if anybody happened to be watching. If anybody were watching, he couldn't even hold her hand, but now his own hand warmed itself on her belly, exploring her roundness, his thumb caressing her little in-turned navel. She pressed the hand to her, sighing.

"That eases me."

For awhile he held very still, hoping she would forget he was there and let him abide. Then she pried up three fingers and gently pulled his hand away.

"You go back to camp. Tell'em I'll be along. I have to wash myself."

Slowly he rose, looking around at the pond, at the now star-thronged sky above the ring of trees, locating himself once more in the world. He found his boots and pulled them on over the wet socks. He picked up the carbine and, enwrapped still with the warm feel of her belly, turned to go up the trail.

"Billy?" He wondered why she made a question of his name. He turned back to see her face, now shadowed by something more than evening. "You left us. Why did you come back?"

He didn't intend to, not as he walked away mad about that poor family's burning house. But he thought he knew why he'd trailed them these three days through thicket and meadow. He shrugged.

"Reckon I was wantin to see you."

She shook her head ruefully and looked at the ground.

"Oh, Billy," she sighed, "why do you want it? Why do I lead you on? It's just a misery, what people go through who try that. I saw it even in the North, even with the Quakers. I knew one couple like that. People shunned them. It's a hard life."

She turned away from him toward the pond. He turned, too, and started back toward the squad, his heart heavy in his chest as a fistful of Minie balls.

That night, the leaden weight in his chest lifted a little. Chilled in their damp uniforms, the squad members slept "spooned" first on their left sides, later on the right—seven in a row, back to front to back to front. Spooning was a trick Ben had learned at Fort Pillow early in his enlistment. Billy had picked it up in the Georgia Guard. With two waterproofs and two blankets spread under them, they could layer the other five waterproofs and blankets on top and sleep crowded but warm.

Drifting off squeezed tight behind Lenora June, Billy recalled the spooning he'd done with those Georgia Guard boys, what a rank odor puffed out from under all those blankets. Tonight he breathed in damp wool scent and no smell at all from seven clean bodies—all equal in that respect. He took it as evidence of his notion that pure-dee dirt—and not plain skin of any color—was the root of stink.

11

Deer sister Libby,

I hev conkludid that the dam fulishnes uv tryin to lick Shurmin Had better be stoped. We have bin getting nothin but hell & lots of it ever sinse we saw the dam yankys & I am tirde uv it.

—letter from "Jim" to "Libby" quoted by Edmund N. Hatcher in "The Last Four Weeks of the War."

THEY BEGAN RIDING FARTHER OUT from Sherman's columns. Each evening they stopped early enough for practice in military drill—not the parade ground sort, but the combat drill that moves soldiers quickly in formation across the battlefield. Billy taught them all one little trick of marksmanship: hold the rifle on target and squeeze the trigger so slowly that the discharge surprises you. That way, he said, you can't jerk the trigger and pull the muzzle off aim. Every night Lenora June taught reading.

On that long outward foray they visited three plantations in just two days. As they approached the third, a shotgun blazed at them from attic windows of the Mansion. The squad's return fire didn't make it stop. Leon vanished into the barn and minutes later emerged pushing a handcart piled high with straw. Lenora June saw the flicker of fire on one side. In the mist of rain that was falling, the straw was slow to light.

"NO, Leon!" she yelled

He didn't seem to hear. Shoving the cart ahead, Leon dashed toward the house. Lenora ran after him. The attic shooter got off one blast at them—a miss—before they reached safety close under the house wall. Leon had just snugged the flaming cart up to the clapboards when Lenora June yanked it away. She glared at him through smoke that boiled out of the straw.

"I said *NO!*"

The policy of Sherman's army was to burn only houses from which soldiers were fired on. That had happened here yet she didn't want another house-burning, didn't want to drive Billy away. They would need him. Leon's eyes avoided hers, searching the ground. He shook his head.

"Second time this week them sum-bitches shoot at me!"

Of course, she had no real authority to punish him, except by withholding the thing he wanted most.

"You disobey again, I'll make you leave this squad. You will ride off on your own."

Instantly, his eyes flicked up from the ground. He offered a lingering, sober stare.

"You the boss. Yah."

The Mansion did not burn. Still, the mere threat of fire flushed them out, a sobbing little boy and his grandmother, a middle-aged woman who approached menacingly but then threw down the shotgun. Still in her nightclothes, mad as a singed hen, she confronted the sergeant.

"May God in his justice scald you Nigra Lincolnites with the fire of his wrath!"

The husband had left her and the boy inside while he hid in woods behind. That's the way it often happened, as Lenora had learned, the couple deciding Sherman's minions were less likely to kill the wife than the husband. Now, with the flaming cart pushed aside and things looking more peaceful, he also appeared. He walked slowly up to them, dropped his musket and stood with his woman.

It had become Lenora June's practice always to search immediately for the necessary equipage of slave ownership. This time she found it in a locked room of the barn: a dozen pairs of manacles, chains, several cats—not of nine tails, as it happened. These had only three whipping strands each of braided horse hide nailed to oaken batons. She also found a strange helmet-like device of wrought-iron bars, open where the face would fit but closed off across with a straight iron rod.

Having carried the whole mess back to the house, she held up one of the wrought-iron devices for the white man to see.

"What's this?" she asked.

The man's face was clean shaven, but a sparse growth of silky whiskers sprouted from his throat. With thumb and forefinger, he stroked them thoughtfully as he spoke.

"I call that the gag. Blacksmith in Macon forged it for me."

The blond grandson stared with interest at the iron thing. The rain had slicked down his hair, was dripping from his nose. Lenora June addressed herself to the boy.

"How does your grandad use that?"

"See, our Pompey, he's all time back-talkin. Grandpa locks it on his head. The straight piece, that goes between his teeth."

"How long does Pompey wear it?"

"Grandpa took it off him right 'fore y'all come. Had it on a week. Pompey, he bad to back talk."

"It works right good," the man said, "and a servant can get on about on pickin cotton, tending the stock Keeps him quiet, is all."

Even with their slave equipage laid out before her, even with her rain-damp gown clinging about her, the plantation mistress still smoldered, her face reddening from the chin upward.

"Yankees are not wanted here!" the woman shouted.

Slaves were beginning to come forth. The gunshots had brought them out. Children appeared, at first peeping from behind the row of slave cabins, then running out to flash smiles at the colored bluecoats.

"Are y'all DEAF?" the woman yelled. "We people of the South do not want you!" The woman's eyes blazed with anger. "Our servants are GOD given! Both thy bondmen, and thy bondmaids shall be of the heathen that are round about you. Of them shall ye buy bondmen and bondmaids." She raised her fist to the sky. "And ye shall TAKE them as an inheritance for your children after you, to inherit them for a possession. They shall be your bondmen for-EVER!"

Lenora, who also knew Leviticus, felt her own face warming. She selected one cat from the heap, displaying it for the woman to see.

"And if any mischief follow," Lenora said, "then thou shalt give life for life, eye for eye, tooth for tooth, hand for hand, foot for foot, burning for burning, wound for wound, stripe for stripe." She swung the cat hissing through the air. "STRIPE FOR STRIPE!" she yelled.

The woman flinched but didn't take a backward step.

"That's Genesis! You know that's out of context! As it was prophesied, Satan will quote scripture!"

Lenora just bundled the cats together with the gags and chains and gave them to Aaron to hide in the woods. Then she stood amid the colored people and gave her little speech, telling them they were free for the moment but would not be after Sherman's army passed. They could stay or go. Less informed than others, never having heard of Lincoln's proclamation, they stood more in awe than jubilation. Then a young woman came up, by-passing the white lieutenant to look anxiously up into the black sergeant's eyes.

"Y'all a-headin east on this road? Gonna free them slaves on Blankenship farm?"

"If it's on this road, we will."

Her somber face, shining wet with rain, opened in a smile.

"Reckon y'all gonna free Walton? He my man. He yonder at Blankenship."

"If he's your man, why's he over there?"

"Cause Master Sherrow won't lemme marry Walton. He say Walton too small. Month gone by, he sell Walton away to Blankenship."

Master Sherrow was small himself, pinched and withered in his face.

"Why won't you let her marry Walton?"

Sherrow looked at the ground, then shrewdly up at the sergeant, once more stroking the silky growth on his Adam's apple.

"It's what she said, Walton's too small. Small female like her, she's no problem, but you want big males for the heavy work. Man has to plan for the future." His eyes lingered appraisingly on Lenora's lanky figure. "You big enough," he said. "Husky male like you, that's the kinda mate Mary Etta needs."

A tense and eager Leon Duffy crowded forward to confront the white man.

"I'm just small myself," he told the master, "but reckon I could whoop your little ass. I lay down my musket, we go at it!"

The man's wife took three steps forward and dropped to her knees before the white lieutenant, clutching his muddy trouser cuffs.

"Oh, sir, you are their leader. As a white Christian gentleman, you must stop this torment. Do not let them torture us so!"

Billy and Lenora June exchanged baffled glances. She offered him a shrug, then addressed the slaves in a loud voice.

"You don't have to leave this place. It might be safer to stay here in slavery. But if you leave, take any food you need, anything else you want from the house. Take the wagons and carriages with the stock to haul them. Take every musket and shotgun you can find on this place. You are free people, if you can stay free."

That afternoon they also freed eleven slaves at the Blankenship farm. It turned out that Walton was truly small, smaller than Mary Etta. But when she ran to him, slapped herself tight to him, he squeezed her in his arms—a stocky little squirt—and danced around swinging her worn brogans two feet above the puddles forming on the ground.

Later, as they rode eastward, the squad passed many little parties of colored folk. A few had been freed only that morning from the Sherrow place, men and women, some with many children. Mary Etta, trudging side by side with her Walton, waved at them as they passed.

Their rutted back road curved on a hillside and swung down through tall timber, emerging abruptly on a major road that crossed a wide valley. Here they encountered marching Union infantry, the 179th Illinois again. Because Colonel Langley had accepted them, they felt free to march alongside, despite one blueback's sing-song objection.

"Tis hard to know, ain't it now, why white men walk and nay-gers ride."

His companion socked him on the shoulder, making the man stagger sideways.

"It's 'cause you immer-gant Irish ain't worth two cents, Cassidy, and them black folks on the hosses, they'd sell for a thousand dollars apiece at Savannah on the Coast—till we get there, anyhow."

Cassidy didn't hit back, just tugged at the bill of his forage cap and grinned.

"Mind you now, I don't oppose'em," he said. And he broke into song.

Some tell us 'tis a burnin shame
to make the nay-gers fight
and that the threat of being killed
belongs but to the white.
But as for me, upon my soul
So liberal are we here,
I'll let Sambo be killed instead a me-self
On every day in the year!

We *are* being killed, Lenora thought, and glad for the chance. Now the trickle of freed slaves from the back road had joined a river of them on this valley road. She felt the smile grow on her face. Without intending it, Sherman's army was emancipating slaves in thousands. They trudged through liquid mud like the soldiers or rode in anything with wheels—platform wagons, leather-topped buggies, two-seater surreys sagging on their springs from the weight of people and goods piled aboard, conveyances drawn by horses and mules, even dairy cows. Lenora June reined her mount around an old woman who rode a graying mule, her legs demurely ensconced on some Confederate lady's side saddle.

Soon the column of marching troops and freed people thickened at its head, slowly pooled and spread from the road into fields on either side. Apparently Wheeler's cavalry had burned the bridge over a little river. An Army engineer company with a train of wagons had almost finished replacing it. Bluebacks unfolded the last of a set of wooden frames, which they were turning into boat-like pontoons by lashing on canvas covers. Other soldiers unloaded pre-built lumber road sections that would cover the pontoons, tied to hempen ropes that already crossed the river.

The crowd pushed down to river's edge. The water was murky, stippled with floating leaves and twigs. Bundling coats and blankets tight about them against the falling rain, they looked yearningly toward the shelter of juniper trees on the far bank.

Two Negro women waded into the water. Lenora could see the danger and, indeed, people near the women called warnings. But they lifted their skirts high, carrying their shoes. They were wading knee deep, talking loud one to the other, and laughing about crossing the river. Then they sank from sight.

"Oooooooooooo!" rose the cry from the crowd.

Several men ran down the bank, glancing out toward where the women might be. In a moment they did appear, bobbing, thrashing with their arms. On the half-built bridge, soldiers began jumping from pontoon to pontoon, gathering in two little groups near the west bank. As the women passed under, a dozen hands groped down and hauled them up. This time the crowd's cry was, "YEAAAAAA!"

But the women had lost their hats and shoes. They stood streaming water amid the knot of soldiers. One man grinned and hugged the prettier woman snug against his chest. She mock-slapped him and turned to crawl to the next pontoon, and the next, working her way toward shore. Soon both were back on the river bank where they had started, except shivering violently now, their clothes sodden.

Even under her rubber waterproof, Lenora June could feel drips wetting her uniform. She leaned forward, lay a hand along the neck of her roan gelding, felt his heat come out even through the damp. The animal had stretched its neck down, was briskly tearing mouthfuls of lamb's quarter from the pasture's edge. Behind her she heard the little clicking, like *tchick-tchick-tchick*, with which Billy urged his horse forward. The animal pulled up beside her, sagged toward her own mount, thumping Billy's leg against her own. His mount instantly dropped his head to pluck big mouthfuls of the weeds. Billy glanced at her and then nodded to the growing crowd on the river bank.

"What-all you reckon gonna happen to these folks?"

"I don't know."

She wondered, in fact, what would happen to Billy and herself.

"I mean, gettin these people out here on the road, in this weather, are we doin the right thing?"

The bill of the forage cap sheltered his face but let water run down from his hair, from ears to whiskery jawbone to the point of his chin, from which it dripped steadily. His blue eyes shone on her, earnest and troubled. Even though he was riding with them, Billy didn't yet seem to know whether he was Union or Confederate. So far, though, he had seemed to relish the job of freeing slaves.

"Billy, it took Master Sherrow with his cats and chains to keep them back there. We didn't get'em out here on the road. They came on their own." She waved a dripping hand at the crowd of men and women huddled on the river bank, heads bowed against the rain. "They think this is better."

Irritated with him for being so thick headed, she tightened the reins to pull the roan's head up and spurred away toward the nearly-completed bridge.

That cold night the squad again slept spooned seven in a row, waterproofs and blankets piled on in what this time proved a vain attempt to get comfortable. This time the night was colder. They lay there wet and shivering, Lenora feeling Billy's feathery breath on her neck. He lay a hand on the pocket of her uniform pants, tapped lightly and whispered into her ear.

"I mean, gettin this squad, getting you and me and the rest of us out here on the road in this weather, are we doing the right thing?"

If she couldn't see it, she could imagine his sly grin. She flung off his hand and reached back to sharply spank his hip.

12

We want no Confederate government without our institutions....The
soldiers of South Carolina will not fight beside a nigger—to talk of
emancipation is to disband our army...Falter and hack at the root of the
Confederacy—our institutions, our civilization—and you kill the cause
as dead as a boiled crab.
   —editorial against enlisting black soldiers, January 13, 1865, by
        Robert Barnwell Rhett, jr., of the Charleston Mercury

KNOWING THIS GROUND WELL, THEY came at the Hunnicutt plantation
from the back side, riding in through frost-rimed trees, in among
the slave cabins just at dawn. The woman glanced up from her
cookfire, eyes alight with terror as Negro bluecoats cantered toward
her like mounted ghosts, horse nostrils gushing gouts of steam. Then
the single white soldier swung down from a creaking saddle and stood
at her fire.

"Yo, Martha!" he said. His narrow face could hardly contain its
grin.

She swallowed once and drew a deep breath.

"Billy?"

"Who you think?" He hugged her. "Guess who I brought."

Her eyes searched the faces of the other six, and she shrugged.

"Who-all?"

"This here's JOHN MARION Moffat," Billy said. "HE's a Union
Army sergeant now. See there them stripes on HIS sleeve."

Lenora dismounted and approached Martha, whose eyes searched
up and down the sergeant's uniform, lingering at the face.

"Haw!" Martha yelled. "Ain't I told you, Billy? Ain't I? Haw!" She
paused to think a moment, her eyes lighting with her recognition of

the problem. She said: "John Marion, HE ran to Sherman just like I say, that's where HE run!"

Martha and Lenora June hugged, rocking back and forth. After a moment Martha stepped back for a better look, eyes roving the whole squad.

"Billy, you a bluecoat now, you a traitor to the CAUSE."

She had emphasized the word in jokey fashion. Still, he looked at the scuffed toes of his boots, feeling the flush heat his face. He felt himself so close to being a traitor that he didn't like being called that. Back at Highland Forge his ma and paw might call him traitor, the very thought curdling in his gut.

"I ain't no bluecoat," he said. "Just I'm for Georgia."

Lenora June's hand closed around his forearm.

"Except he frees slaves," she declared.

Billy felt such a rush of gratitude he put a hand up to hide his face. Martha smiled.

"Sure. Time before when he walked in here, he was a-carryin Lovage, and I knowed what he was." She patted him on the shoulder and began to yell. "Ezra! You, Ezra, get outa that bed! Get wood for the fire. We got break-fess to cook for these folks."

Thanks to the squad's liberal foraging of the previous day, the meal was better than Martha might have dreamed, preserved peaches to start, day-old lightbread, chops from a purloined hog sliced thin and fried relay after relay in her big skillet, finished off with chunks of three gooseberry pies taken from a plantation pie safe. Their army-issue coffee depleted, they drank the Confederate substitute brewed from roasted acorns. Billy raised his tin cup in a salute.

"Right good!" he lied.

As winter sun broke over the horizon, striping them all with tree shadows, other slaves gathered and stood big eyed around the fire, a dozen, then two and then more, grown-ups and children, their chilled breath sun-bright in the air around them.. Martha rose and emphasized to Lenora's old friends that now she was Sergeant JOHN MARION Moffat. Billy was afraid Lovage would betray the secret by using Lenora's real name, but the child had other concerns. He sat on the log beside Billy and looked pleadingly up.

"You gimme another penny?"

Billy sighed and fished a tarnished one from his pocket, scrubbed it against his pantleg and gave it to the boy.

"Ain't none of your Confederate stuff, neither. This here's Union coin."

Lenora called her slave neighbors by name, inviting them to sit. Half starved on their plantation diet of corn and sweet potatoes, they ate everything the squad had hauled in on their pack mules. After the meal Lenora delivered her little speech about freedom and its dangers, telling them they could stay or go. They could take the carriages and wagons and any food they needed for the journey. Reluctant in the face of her offer, Ezra shook his gray head.

"Savannah paper say Richmond Congress gonna let niggers enlist. We get to be grayback soldiers. Paper say General Lee, he wants it too. Master say Congress BUY us if we go. Richmond Congress pay him money for us. Then after fightin we gets freedom."

Billy knelt beside him.

"You free right now, Ezra. Lincoln done freed the slaves."

"Oh yeah, but it ain't *leee*-gal."

"Lot more legal than this rickety damn Confederacy." Billy was surprised to hear himself say this, but it was true. Even that Mississippi corporal he'd marched with outside Atlanta had known it: This Confederacy's *DY-ing* of gaw-damn State Rights. He only hoped his Georgia was not dying with it. Ezra turned his white-whiskered face soberly to Sergeant Moffat.

"I got that Savannah paper. You read what it say?"

He hustled into his cabin and returned with a frayed single sheet. On one side were headlines and tiny black letters, on the other a vivid floral print. Lenora held it up for all to see.

"This is your *leee*-gal Confederacy," she said. "They're down to printing the news on the back side of wallpaper."

Quickly she found the article. With one finger, still greasy from the pork, she searched out a key paragraph and read aloud.

"We propose that we immediately commence training a large reserve of the most courageous of our slaves, and further that we guarantee freedom within a reasonable time to every slave in the South who shall remain true to the Confederacy in this war. As between the loss of independence and the loss of slavery we assume that every patriot will freely give up the latter."

"See?" Ezra cried. "I told y'all. Richmond give us freedom if we fight for the South."

Billy took the paper from her and looked for the catch. He soon found it.

"Them words in this, they're from General Cleburne. He wrote that last January. You bet, that Richmond Congress talkin about it. They ain't took no vote."

Hearing this, Ezra sagged back against the log where he sat. Beside him, smoke rose straight up from the fire but clotted in the treetops and spread wide through the branches, seasoning the air with a hickory tang. Far away a rooster crowed.

"Got them cows to milk," Ezra sighed, "stalls to muck out. If we don't get quick up yonder, master gonna be down here."

Billy felt a tug at the paper in his hand. Lenora took it from him and read eagerly to herself for a moment. Then she looked around at the others and spoke.

"This says General Hood just days ago won a great victory at Franklin, Tennessee. He ordered his army to assault the Union breastsworks. They even broke through at one point. It says their gallantry is proven by their losses. Sixty-five Confederate commanders were killed, wounded or captured. Thirteen of them were generals. *Thirteen generals!* It doesn't say how many soldiers were killed."

A murmur rose from the crowd, but nothing more.

"One of those killed was General Pat Cleburne," Lenora told them. "He's the one who wanted slaves in the Confederate army. I have to admire the man, because he didn't call us 'servants'. He called us what we were, slaves."

A clangor of cowbells, and then the steady, repeated bawling of a single cow came down to them through the woods. Nobody moved. They sat watching the colored sergeant once again study the Savannah paper. Again Lenora summarized in a strange mechanical voice:

"This report says General Lee's Army of Northern Virginia has made a strategic withdrawal to fortifications around Richmond and Petersburg, which better positions it for future offensives that will bring victory in defense of Southern Institutions."

"I got to get yonder, see after the milkin," Ezra said, starting to rise. "Martha, they gonna need you in that kitchen."

Martha pushed him back against the log.

"Set right there." Her brow was furrowed, her face frowning thoughtfully. "Thirteen generals lost in one battle. That ain't no victory. And ole Gen-ral Lee is possum-treed up at Richmond. The South is losin. It's a-losin this war."

"And the Union is winning," said Lenora.

They sat quiet for a moment. Then Billy heard a rhythmic beating— Martha's brogan on the packed dirt—and what started as a groan or moan somewhere else in the crowd. Now all of them, even the children, began singing.

> You got a right, I got a right,
> We all got a right to the tree of life.
> Very time I thought I was lost
> Ole dungeon shook and chain fell off.
> Oh Brethen,
> You got a right, I got a right,
> We all got a right to the tree of life!

Billy didn't know the hymn, but Lenora did. She sang with her friends, barely able to shape the words through her grin. Martha pranced close, touched fingertips with her, and both danced as the crowd sang another chorus. It ended in a burst of laughter, over which Lenora shouted.

"The Union's winning! We should have a party. There's a ballroom in the big house. We could have it there."

Instantly, the shouting and merriment died.. They looked in wonder at the Union sergeant.

"That the MAS-ter's house," Ezra croaked.

The sergeant shrugged.

"You all built this place. You did the work. Just once we could have a party there."

Billy rose from his seat beside Lovage and, staring at the ground, paced thirty steps to the tethered, grazing horses, swung around and came back. He looked up at Lenora.

"Sure, the Union's winnin, but we're long ways out from Sherman. Nobody to help if we're dawdlin here and Wheeler's cavalry pops up. We run off their horses. Now they got a par-TIC-ular grudge against us."

But in her eyes he could see how much she wanted it.

"So-o-o-o-o," he sighed, drawing it out long enough to let him think. "Gonna have a party, cain't wait till dark. First get these people loaded up, every damn wagon and carriage on the place, ready to haul out, them that wants to leave. After that we post pickets and have a party." Billy sighed again, even more wearily. "Of course before any of that, we got to get Master Hunnicutt under control."

Worried that they would recall the Union sergeant as their former slave, Billy himself handled the confrontation with the surly Master Hunnicutt and his irate wife.

"What a hell of horrors the people of Georgia must endure to win our liberty from you black abolitionists!" she raged.

"No, maam, I ain't black, but reckon you're right about the other. We *are* emancipatin."

Flush faced, the Master himself stood with her near the barn. They'd come out together to see why the unmilked cows were complaining so. The Master was wearing what seemed the same broadcloth coat he wore the evening he ordered Ezra to shoot a certain Georgia Guardsman. Yet didn't recognize the bluecoat lieutenant as that man.

"Emancipating!" Master Hunnicutt shouted. "Emancipating the spawn of Ham and Canaan after Noah cursed them! Cursed be Canaan! A servant of servants shall he be unto his brethren! Sir, y'all are defying the will of almighty God!"

Billy had heard much pulpit preaching about Ham's sin, how it supposedly damned colored folks to slavery. Always it seemed dumb to him, but to keep slaves people need such arguments. He prodded Master Hunnicutt with the carbine muzzle and briskly marched the couple out to an empty corncrib. This was one the Hunnicutts had used as a punishment cage for their slaves. It contained the usual equipment, manacles, cats, chains. Billy just herded them inside. On this door, as on so many plantation doors, hung a huge padlock. On smokehouse, kitchen pantry, grain bins, tack rooms, fruit cellars, even bureau drawers, locks were necessary to keep property safe from the "servants." He didn't use this padlock, figuring Hunnicutt might have the key in one of his many pockets. Billy just nailed the door tight shut.

Coming back through the barn with its rich cow smell and its horn-gnawed lumber stalls, he saw Ezra with his gray head tucked into a Guernsey's flank. Both his hands rhythmically squeezed her bloated teats, milk hissing into a wooden pail already half full.

"You ain't gonna stay here, are you, Ezra?"

"Nawsir, leavin today. Just milk these cows one more time, because they all swole up. Hate to see'em suffer."

Between barn and house, men were loading wagons and a carriage and some old two-wheeled carts mostly with food from the kitchen pantry and smoke house. The squad's own mounts, still saddled but unbridled, gratefully munched oats in a corral beside the barn. In the first-floor den of the Mansion, Billy found the 10-gauge shotgun that had wounded him near the turnip patch, along with two revolvers and six old muskets, a real collection. He gave one revolver to Corporal Densmore, saved one for Lenora and gave the other weapons to the Hunnicutt "servants." It occurred to him that today once more slaves were becoming free people, that the guns were in different hands now. But he had to show them how to load and prime. He posted Ike Spears to watch the road for danger.

Then, to reach the third-floor ballroom from the basement, Billy had to climb three flights, which made him uneasy. It would take awhile for a crowd to climb down from here. The room seemed huge, thrusting up with its many windows to stand above other roofs of the building. By now the house servants had a ladder erected, lighting already half-burned candles in a crystal chandelier—not that they were needed. The room was bright with sun. Still, the candles seemed to delight Lenora, who stood steadying the ladder with her head thrown back, smiling up.

There was a pianoforte, but nobody knew how to play it. The people were bringing their own instruments, drum tambourines, a harmonica, a fiddle, a mandolin with cow-gut strings and a body carved from a calabash gourd. The musicians gathered on a little bandstand, their instruments already jingling, plinking, groaning tunelessly as they tried them. Hardly an hour before, the people had eaten breakfast, but women carried in food, laying it out on a darkwood table. Sighting Billy, Lenora June grabbed his arm and dragged him toward the stairs.

"Come on! I need a dance partner."

She led him down one flight into a large room off the hallway, its canopied bed curtained with mosquito netting. She slammed the door and threw the bolt. Already she'd rifled the open wardrobe that stood against one wall. Laid out on the counterpane was a fancy gown of rich brocade, its hoop petticoat inflating the skirt, making it stand up like half a balloon. Instantly, Billy took a keen interest in the proceedings. Did she want him to help her dress? Could this be his long-awaited chance to see once again her walnut-brown butt—regrettably concealed from Billy since childhood? She spun him around to face her and began unbuttoning his coat.

"What you doing?"

"Stand still." She tugged the coat first off one arm, then the other, letting it fall to the carpet. She started on the shirt buttons. "This would go quicker if you'd help," she said, a little sharp with him. She dragged the shirt off, then caught the tails of his long john top and began jerking it off over his head.

"Hey! Hey!"

It came off and was flung into a corner. When she went for the top button of his breeches, he grabbed her wrists.

"No! No, now, Lenora June, you ain't gonna do it!"

Through the floor above, down through the bedroom ceiling, came the fiddled strains of *Listen to the Mocking Bird*. Fists clenched, Lenora hopped up and down on the carpet before him.

"Oh please, Billy! I want a real dance partner, and I can't dress like that. The squad would find out I'm a woman."

He refused to take off his breeches, which would be hidden anyhow under the gown. He tried to refuse the whole damn thing, but she wanted it so much. When she began to dress him, he relished her every touch. Soon his skinny frame was swallowed in the folds of the plantation mistress's low-cut gown. Lenora stuffed the bodice with handkerchiefs and draped it with a silk scarf, as if the righteous wearer had tried to conceal its bounty. From a blue ribbon around his neck, she hung a cameo carved with a pretty woman's face. Still her eyes, staring into him as he sat before her, looked troubled.

"The whiskers!" she groaned.

There was water in a white porcelain pitcher, a basin beside it, on the table. She soaped him up and shaved him with the Master's razor, as she had many times shaved her father. She daubed him with rose petal perfume from a dresser top. With a feather puff she powdered the freckled paleness of his shoulders, rising bony from the brocade gown. He should hate every minute of this, of course he should. Her hands were all over him, combing his curls, patting here, tugging there, straightening and primping. Her quick breath brushed his face. He breathed it in with the rose scent, drunk with pleasure.

Under the full skirts, inside the uniform breeches he had refused to trade for pantaloons, his pecker began to crawl down the pantleg, slowly stiffening. Here he was becoming a woman and lusting after one, right at the same time. What would stern Leviticus say about this? She held his face between perfumed hands and studied it keenly.

"You're just beautiful!"

He grabbed for her, felt her narrow waist under the bulky uniform jacket, sensing how her body widened upward toward a woman's bust, downward toward a woman's hips. She backed away and dragged him from the chair.

"Time to dance," she said.

Still he held her, squeezed tight to her, both of them panting as if in flight.

"Billy, we can't!"

Still panting, she took one hand, led him to the door and then up the stairs, Billy catching up the skirt with its hoops to avoid tripping. On every step with one hand he pulled her into his side, feeling her sink warmly to him and then push away. The ballroom rang with fiddle and banjo, a different tune now. The floor whirled with jigging dancers, Ben and Leon among them, facing off against the prettiest women. Ezra and Martha stood at the side, clapping and singing.

Billy and Lenora stepped full into the ballroom just as the music ended. The chatter and clapping died. Heads turned in a ripple that ran across the room. Suddenly everyone was looking at them, this brocade-bundled Southern Belle with her colored soldier beau, a sergeant no less, slim in dusty Union blue. A look of shock and then fright ran across those faces, as if they'd been ambushed in their wild slave revel by a suddenly youthful Mrs. Hunnicutt.

"Just stand quiet," Lenora told him.

Leon Duffy stepped out of the crowd and marched over, his eyes raking up and down the figure of the Belle.

"Who-all done that to you? Sergeant Moffat doll you up? Well, ain't you CUTE, Loooo-tenant Ludwig!"

A quiver of laughter ran through the people. They clapped and hopped till Lenora June waved them silent. She looked at the mandolin player who always lead this group.

"Buford, will you play a waltz?"

This grayhead among the musicians nodded and hugged his instrument close over his belly. The music started, stately and regular, proving Buford's long experience in playing for the master's parties in this same ballroom. Eagerly Billy reached with his right hand for that delicious waist under the uniform coat, but she caught it with her left, extending both those arms straight out. Her right hand went to *his* waist, and she plopped his left onto her right shoulder. He stood amazed, paralyzed, a male in the female waltz posture.

"Just follow my lead," she commanded.

He tried, murmuring to himself, one-two-three, one-two-three, moving his feet in mechanical squares. It was she who'd taught him to waltz, and he was good, yet confused and slow until, abruptly, she forced the pace. The squares rounded off into circles, then rolling spirals, Lenora propelling him across the waxed pine floor as a jockey drives a racing sulky. They whirled amid that sea of faces, the hoops of his skirt swaying wide, Lenora laying her head back to grin at the chandelier.

"Isn't this is grand!"

Balancing her weight against his, spinning with her, Billy himself lay back to see the chandelier, glittering with its hundred smoky candles, the ceiling smudged above it from candles of bygone years, of gay plantation parties played for, served by, these same colored people, who now for the first time began joining the waltz on this floor. They were dressed like tramps but danced well. The waltz went on, he trying to pull her close, but foiled because his hand was not at her waist, Lenora steadily holding him away and smiling with her lips and her clear eyes. They waltzed and panted and looked into each other until Billy felt a tapping on the perfumed and powdered skin of his shoulder.

"May I cut in?" said Leon Duffy.

Billy and Lenora came apart, stood panting until Lenora bowed.

"Most assuredly, sir," she said deep voiced and, with a generous sweep of her hand, offered Leon the Southern Belle.

"Thank you, Sergeant, sure 'nuff, but it's *you* I want."

He took her, caught her unawares and danced away with Lenora in the female posture, his right hand on her waist, hers on his shoulder. Well, Billy sighed, he needed a rest anyway. He sent Hubert to relieve Ike Spears at the sentry post on the road. Then he hitched up the bloated balloon of his skirt, aligned the hoops and set sail for the table of food. Suddenly the woman Leon had danced with earlier stepped in front of him.

"I'm Ophelia," she said. "You right cute in that dress. I wanna dance!"

So, he danced with her, and—after her—several more. All the squad members were popular. Billy was the rage. Women shyly asked the Southern Belle, and—in accord with the old courtesy of the dance—he never said no. They were not so standoffish as Lenora. In the waltz some would cuddle close, his handkerchief-stuffed bosoms brushing their genuine articles. He saw Lenora June watching him over the shoulder of her newest waltz partner.

After the waltzes came a Quadrille and *Pop! Goes the Weasel.* In these flowing line dances he got to hold her hand—if briefly—and pass close in front to see the smile she gave him. Then Buford struck up a fresh jig on his mandolin, singing as he played.

Harper's creek and roaring river,
There, my dear, we'll live forever,
Then we go to the Indian Nation.
All I want in this creation,
Is pretty little wife and big plantation.

A boy standing on a chair behind Buford reached around with steel knitting needles and drummed a cadence on the fiddle strings, the bow sawing away, the needles ringing joyously as the people jigged. It was too much for Billy. In his slope-heeled cavalry boots, he limped to the stairs, descended two steps and sagged down to sit on his hoops. He was worn slick. From tree shadows seen through the stairwell window, he judged it was getting on toward noon. Maybe he should go out to relieve Hubert as sentry on the road. With the jig grinding on in the ballroom, he heard a heavy tread behind him. Leon Duffy plopped down beside Billy on the step.

"Right good dance."

"Yah," Billy said.

"What-all's her real name?"

Billy looked at him.

"What?"

"Sergeant John Marion Moffat. What-all's her *real* name?"

Billy looked at his own clasped hands, washed clean as Lenora could get them for the dance but still dirty in the cracks. Leon's question didn't surprise him. He'd halfway expected somebody would figure it out.

"Name she uses, John Marion Moffat, it's her daddy's name. Hers is Lenora June."

"That's right purty."

"Anybody else in the squad find out she's a woman?" Billy sighed.

"Don't reckon. Believe they'd foller her anyways, even if they knowed."

"Better they don't," Billy said. "Cause trouble with the army if it gets out."

A cheer rose in the ballroom as one jig jerked to a stop. Instantly another started, and with it the beating of feet on the floor's sounding board. Leon's pink palm ran slowly up and down the walnut stair rail, idly polishing it.

"I like her," Leon said. "I saw you together at that millpond. You like her too?"

"You bet," Billy said. "Been liking her all my life, all I recollect of it."

Billy found himself staring into Leon's eyes as Leon stared back, neither gaze flinching, the eyes neither friendly nor unfriendly, only curious on both sides, Billy wondering whether Lenora June might consider him equal to this man, whose skin was nearer the color of hers. He'd never really known Lenora as colored, from childhood had accepted her first as girl and later as woman—nothing more. Only now did he realize that all along he'd seen Leon as colored, the full sense of him as a man arising only when he became a rival But now Billy had even more urgent worries.

"Leon, how about you come out with me, relieve Hubert on the road?"

"I do it."

They went down the broad oak stairs, Billy detouring to retrieve his carbine and cartridge box from the bedroom. He came out on the portico in front, blinking in a flood of sunlight. With Leon posted on the road, Hubert came rushing back into the house, eager to reach the dance.

After a frosty dawn, the day had warmed. Sunlight bathed one wall of the Mansion, which was set between farm fields to the south and woods on the north. He heard a bluejay call. Billy looked west on the road a half-mile and saw nothing except red-clay ruts stretching out a good half-mile to a turn. Eastward, he saw a horseman appear at the turn and then disappear, riding into the woods—strange. Billy circled the house, noticing a track, just a horse trail, coming in from the woods. This he hadn't seen before—a third direction from which an enemy could approach. He walked that way, down toward the old corncrib.

Master Hunnicutt stood inside it, fingers clasped on the boards, like a black-bearded jailbird holding the bars of his cell. His head was scratched, his ear and neck dripping blood.

"That's my wife's ball gown!" he roared. "Gaw-damn Union vandals!"

The woman was not there with him.

"Where'd she go?" Billy demanded.

"You will soon find out."

"I said where IS she?" He leveled the Spencer at the man, who stepped back and raised both hands, palms forward.

"She's gone, you can see she's gone."

Of course. She'd gone to round up help.

"How come you ain't?"

"I kicked off a board. She got out but I couldn't squeeze through."

Billy started for the house in a rush, only to be stopped by a shout.

"Hey, you, VANDAL!" Hunnicutt yelled, and Billy swung around. The Master's eyes burned at him above the black beard. "You, sir, you a white man, but you brought outrage to us here. One thing that stirs Southron blood to heat is Nigra soldiers. Nigra *soldiers!* Who that is not dead to every sense of honor will never submit to your Nigra soldiers. This day every tree on my plantation will bend with Nigra meat. And your own! May God pour out his wrath on you!"

Billy gripped the gown at the bodice and yanked, popping the line of buttons down the front. Then he stepped on the hem and walked out of it, leaving the brocade, pearl buttons, handkerchiefs, ribbons, cameo broach and all splayed in the dirt behind him. Bare chested, bare backed, he ran for the Mansion door, yelling to Leon.

"Prime your musket. Get the horses ready. We leavin right quick."

Billy took the steps three at a time, hearing as he climbed Lenora June, her alone, singing in her clear voice the final lines of a hymn.

We mourn not that man should toil.
Tis Nature's need, tis God's decree,
but let the hand that tills the soil,
be, like the wind that fans it, FREE!

The crowd had no chance to cheer, nor Billy to sound his warning. At that instant glass in the ballroom's north windows shattered. A hailstorm of Minie balls and buckshot crashed into the ceiling and the south wall above his head, raking the chandelier, sending its crystals and candles flying. People screamed and ran for the door, though the shooting was high, gunmen on the ground outside aiming at third-story windows.

13

The fate that befell the army of the French Empire in its retreat from Moscow will be re-enacted. Our cavalry and our people will harass and destroy his army, as did the Cossacks that of Napoleon, and the Yankee general, like him, will escape with only a bodyguard.
—Confederate President Jefferson Davis' prophesy for Sherman's army, September, 1864.

BILLY RAN FOR THE NORTH wall, hugging close to a bricked section between windows where the slugs couldn't come through. He swallowed spit and swallowed again, as if that could choke back the panic that rose in his throat. Lenora June slid in beside him.

"Who's shooting?"

"Beats me. Ole lady Hunnicutt, she got loose. Ran for help, I reckon."

From outside, just audible above the sputtering of muskets, came the high piping of a woman's voice, raging, screaming.

"Stop! Stop! Don't shoot my house! Kill the Nigras, but stop shootin my house!"

With gunfire slackening, Billy and Lenora peeped around the window edge, staying clear of jagged glass. Where the woods started not eighty yards distant, and fully exposed, stood a ragged line of roughly-dressed fellows, mostly old men and boys. The woman stood behind them. They seemed to flinch at the wrath she poured out on them.

"Idiots! Go in after'em! Shoot the Yankee Nigras instead of my house!"

As Lenora tugged the Spencer carbine out of his hands, Billy realized the rabble at wood's edge was not Wheeler's cavalry.

"Don't!" he said. "Don't shoot'em. They just a mess of Peckerwoods."

Her right hand rose to slap her own forehead.

"Your precious Peckerwoods!" she hissed. "Master Hunnicutt keeps'em half starved, but he's got them involved in slavery too. Your Peckerwoods make it work for him." She pushed so close he felt her breath on his face. "Now here they come, ready to fight so he can keep his slaves!"

"Well, I did it my own self," he said. "I fought for the South." Not very hard, he admitted to himself. "Anyhow, there's about fifty of'em yonder to our seven."

She lay the carbine barrel on the window sill and levered a cartridge into the chamber.

"I'll just move'em back."

She fired, POW, changed her aim and fired again, POW, went on quick-firing POW POW POW until the gun was empty. Above the men her slugs clipped branches. which fell on them, cleaved bark from trees behind them. They stared amazed at the one window from which so much gunfire had erupted. Then a musket roared near the Mansion's front door, probably Leon taking a shot. The ragged battle line collapsed, men and boys fleeing into the woods as Mrs. Hunnicutt raged, running behind. Lenora handed back the rifle. Groping with shaky hands for a fresh magazine to reload, Billy said:

"They's a stone wall at the edge of the yard, between them and the house. We can form a line there, try to hold'em."

As they crossed the ballroom toward the stairs, he noticed that candles from the shattered chandelier had melted into a pool of wax, now flaming at the edges in a widening circle. He'd always made such a fuss against the practice of burning houses. He considered stomping this fire out but then thought, hell, we didn't start it. They paused in the bedroom, grabbing haversacks and weapons. He saw Lenora at the bookcase picking up, of all things, an old blueback speller and an arithmetic book.

Minutes later Billy was pulling on his uniform coat, sheltered by the stone wall where the squad had deployed. Behind them rose the cliff-like wall of the Mansion. Ahead were a cow pasture and woods, which rattled with gunfire, buckshot and Minie balls ricocheting from the stone. Three colored men from the plantation armed with muskets had joined them there. The other freed people had found shelter beyond the Mansion with, by now, horses harnessed and ready to leave.

"There's so damn many of them Peckerwoods," Billy said. "They can flank us outa here if they try." The gorge of panic was rising again in his throat.

It was Mrs. Hunnicutt who suggested the answer as, once again, she began wailing from the tree line.

"Fire! My house is on fire!"

Billy rolled over to look. Where ballroom windows had once been, there were now only holes, even the mullions in some windows blasted out along with the glass. Sure enough, he could see the flicker of flames on the ceiling inside, smoke crawling from window tops.

"Put it out! Oh, SOME-body, put it out!"

By now the woman, defying danger, had advanced into the no-man's-land between the two forces—a chubby, distraught figure raising her hands prayerfully. To Billy's amazement, Lenora jumped to her feet.

"Hey, don't!"

He caught her left hand and tried to pull her down. Leon heaved himself half above the wall and grabbed her coattails. Gun smoke gushed from the tree line, a volley of slugs rattling against the brick house wall, shattering yet more windows, this time on the first floor. Lenora flinched and threw her right hand up as if to shield her face. Again Billy yanked at the hand, tried to drag her down, but she shook him off and jerked free of Leon. The two women faced each other across thirty yards of cow pasture. All firing stopped.

"Your people can put it out," Lenora yelled. "We'll let them put the fire out. First stack your weapons. Make your people pile 'em right where you're standing."

Mrs. Hunnicutt turned to face the woods, raised her arms and dropped them in limp surrender. Then Billy saw him, Master Hunnicutt there behind a tree. So they had freed him from the corncrib and here he was. He'd dodged the Confederate draft with the twenty-nigger law. Now it seemed he'd sent his wife to save the house.

"Get moving! Move!" Hunnicutt yelled at his Peckerwoods. "Stack your weapons! Put the fire out!"

Three old men came shyly from the trees to lay down their muskets. With Hunnicutt threshing after them through the brush, more came, the stack growing steadily. Billy suspected some, loath to give up their weapons, were sneaking home through the woods. But most of the guns got stacked. As Master Hunnicutt and the others rushed inside to fight the fire, Billy passed some of the weapons along to freed slaves who wanted them. Then he busied himself ramming the remaining gun muzzles into pasture soil, stuffing the barrels with dirt. He drew out all the ramrods---some metal, some wood---lay them in groups against the stone wall and stomped them. Without ramrods, they'd spend awhile getting the weapons clean enough to shoot. Finishing, he turned and saw Lenora thoughtfully fingering the cuff on the left sleeve of her uniform coat.

"They got my pretty brass button," she said.

More than that, the slug had cleanly sliced the woolen fabric just inside her wrist. One inch of difference would have severed blood vessels there. Two inches would have shattered the bones, requiring amputation. Billy didn't breath for a moment. He reached for her hands but she stepped back, holding the flat of her palms up to him. Then he saw Leon with blood draining down his face to drip from his chin. Lenora moved quickly to him.

"Ain't nothin," Leon muttered, "slug knocked a chip off them stones. Cut me." He fingered his scalp where the blood welled out. "Sum-bitches keep takin little chunks off me." With her cotton neckpiece, Lenora wiped his face and then folded the cloth, pressing it to the wound.

"Hold it till you stop bleeding."

Soon the squad and former slaves were formed up on the road ready to leave. Mrs. Hunnicutt appeared at the door of the Mansion, smoke wafting out around her body. White men hurried past her, carrying water buckets into the house. She stepped between two of them and headed straight for the line of wagons. She rushed up to a carriage on which Ezra sat holding the reins, with Martha beside him.

"No! No!" cried Mistress Hunnicutt. "Y'all cannot steal my cook!" She looked pleadingly at Billy, already mounted and ready to go. "I beg you, sir, you must not steal Martha. I never cooked a meal in my life. I simply cannot. Mr. Hunnicutt, he loves Martha's pies. He loves her chicken. Y'all must make her stay!"

Billy shrugged.

"Up to her."

That a question so vital could depend on the will of her slave seemed to baffle Mrs. Hunnicutt. She looked up at the woman on the wagon.

"Martha?"

Martha looked straight ahead. Ezra made a clicking noise with his tongue. The mules jerked forward into their collars. The carriage rolled out onto the road. The squad followed on their mounts, Billy spurring ahead to ride beside Lenora June.

"Ain't it funny how them Peckerwoods shot the winders out?" he said. "'Course they's all *involved* with slavery. They just *love* these rich plantation owners. But they musta knowed shootin from down there they wouldn't do nothin but knock hell outa the lady's chandelier, maybe set the house afire. Shot them winders out anyway. What for you reckon them Peckerwoods did that?"

Lenora June sucked her upper lip down in a frown.

"Billy, you who read so well, you can speak better English than that."

Billy, always at least one step behind this woman, could only sigh. Seeing Master Hunnicutt peering from a vacant window square, Billy saluted him. He yet recalled what the master had said about getting vengeance on Nigra soldiers, so he broke into song, to be joined by the others in a verse Billy had only recently learned.

Father Abraham has spoken and the message has been sent,
The prison doors he opened, and out the prisoners went,
To join the sable army of the African descent
As it goes marching on. Glory, glory hallelujah...

Finishing the chorus, Billy understood, of course, that this was yet another verse celebrating Lincoln's famous proclamation. Maybe it was just this grand melody. For some reason Union didn't sound so bad to him anymore, but was he, Billy, yet a *Yankee?* As Martha had said, he was damn sure a traitor to the Cause. But Yankee too? On his Georgian tongue the word savored of moldy farmer cheese.

14

While in Richmond I was told that 'the passage of the enemy through the country was like the flight of an arrow through the air,' that 'overrunning was not subjugation.' Well, this may be true in some sections...but it is far different here. Our people are <u>subjugated</u>—they are crushed in spirit—they have not the heart to do anything but...recount their losses and suffering.

—letter by Confederate Congressman Thomas C. Fuller of North Carolina, January, 1865.

THEY HAD STARTED EARLY THAT day, but their party at the Hunnicutt plantation delayed them, letting the 179th Illinois slide ahead on the march toward the sea. Under cloudy skies they rode in its wake and before noon found a once-prosperous village of a hundred or so homes. What had been the general store, a blacksmith shop and a cotton gin still smoldered on the main street, the blacksmith's big anvil standing isolated amid that ruin.

In the alley beyond the gin, a two-story stack of cotton bales burned furiously. Smoke towered above the ruins, melting into the cloud layer above. Three houses on the main street had been torched, and others on other streets. People clustered at the ruins. Now and again someone would dash in and, with gloved hands or a folded cloth, drag out an iron tool or pottery vessel, fired now for the second time. The squad had pulled up, hidden behind a juniper hedge where the street curved. Standing high in the stirrups so he could see over, Billy looked troubled.

"How come Yanks burn so much?" he asked Lenora June. "What good's it do?"

She sighed inwardly. Here it was again, the perpetual issue with this man.

"The Confederacy sells ginned cotton," Lenora said, "buys weapons with the money. That's how they get those English rifles. The blacksmith, he can fix any weapon made of iron."

"How come them to burn houses?" His voice had tightened almost to a whine.

"Billy, you walked right by that fire in the Hunnicutt ballroom. You didn't put it out. You know very well I burned a house."

"Sure, but the Bossman back yonder chained them folks to a tree, didn't feed'em, let that ole woman die on a chain. You got mad, that's how come you to burn it. These people in this here town, what-all they do wrong?"

Would he never stop this?

"I don't know. I count six burning houses here. That's all. Maybe somebody shot at our troops from those houses. Why do soldiers burn houses? Jubal Early burned Chambersburg, Pennsylvania, burned it to the ground. The Atlanta papers were real proud of that." She was almost yelling at him now, as if Billy himself were responsible for Chambersburg. "They fired on Fort Sumter. To keep my family as slaves, they started this war. All they have to do is STOP IT!"

She spurred her horse around the hedge into the open, heard the others coming behind. Clumps of people near the ruins abruptly dissolved. Women hiked their skirts up and fled down side streets, men only walking behind but glancing anxiously back. Halfway through the village an elderly man in a grease-spotted dress coat moved timidly into the street. As they approached him, he looked up at Billy and said:

"Please. *Please.*" He let his body sag, and stiffen, and sag again, almost genuflecting.   Billy doffed his hat.

"We just passin through," he told the man and rode on.

Leaving the village they crossed the Georgia Railroad, or what had once been that. Union soldiers had ripped rails from the roadbed, started bonfires with the crossties and melted the iron into snarled sheaves. Under dim light from the clouds the ruin stretched westward a good mile where a turn in the tracks closed off her view. It stretched eastward between cleared fields—straight and far, as far anyhow as she could see. Again and again she had read the Atlanta papers as they rejoiced when their generals rushed troops back and forth on rails like these, winning battles as they bolstered threatened points in their defenses. The Georgia Railroad would haul no more Confederate reinforcements, no more cannon from the arsenal in Macon.

A rush of triumphal fervor stiffened her back, tilted her chin up. She spurred her horse to a canter and tasted the freshness of the wind. We're winning! Then those old Quaker doubts, like stomach cramps, afflicted her. Winning what? What will be left when it ends?

At mid-afternoon they overtook a ragged column of former slaves toiling along the road, and, ahead of them, the 179th Illinois. Slowly passing the regiment's triple file of marching infantry, they heard a few catcalls, nigger this and nigger that. Then came a roar from a burly Irish sergeant:

"Pipe down, you id-jets! Them's the niggers saved our bacon." So the word had been passed down by Colonel Langley.

Billy now rode well ahead of Lenora June. He seemed wary, as if feeling the strain his earlier questions had created between them. They had nearly reached the head of the infantry column when a marching corporal fished into his haversack and extracted a weighty treasure. The long chains were wadded into his fist, the gold watches—a half dozen of them—swinging under it like a string of fat perch, his catch of the day. The gold shone dully in hazy light from the clouds. He held the watches high, inches from Lenora's face.

"Looky what I got! Forage liberally! Ha!"

From the men around him rose a chorus of protest.

"Shuddup, Johnson!"

"Quit your stupid braggin!"

"Thievin sum-bitch!"

They passed the head of the column and then passed three vedettes, mounted scouts riding ahead of the regiment. With the vedettes behind, Private Duffy urged his big Belgian into a lumbering trot and came up beside her. He nodded politely and tugged at the brim of his cap, his lustrous eyes looking out under it, straight into her own.

"How you doing?"

"Just fine."

It was the first time he'd ever asked that question of her. Billy had told her Leon now knew she was a woman. Is that why he was suddenly so attentive? She had noticed this morning that Leon troubled to shave his scraggly whiskers, using a full well bucket as a mirror. Then he had wetted a rag to scrub at dirt spots on his uniform.

"Sergeant Moffat, I got a question."

Worried he was about to make some amorous overture, she sighed.

"Sure, Private Duffy...."

He cleared his throat.

"Well now, you let us take food from these places. We take hosses and guns, all we want. But you ain't lettin us take no gold—I mean, like that Yank back yonder did. How come we don't get no gold?"

She sighed again, this time with relief. It was a question she could answer, or so she thought.

"The food and guns and horses, they're contraband, spoils of war. We need them to win. We don't need the gold. And we're not thieves. We're better than that, Leon. The rest of our lives, we have to be better than that."

As he rocked forward on the plodding Belgian, Leon seemed to be fighting back a grin. He spoke out then in exaggerated patois.

"That's right PEE-cular, cause best part of my life people were tellin me I was just a nigger. Get off the street, you dirty nigger! Get to the kitchen, you lazy nigger! Worthless damn nigger, split that stove kindlin! Now just sudden-like, here's ole Leon Duffy, too good to steal. How you reckon that happen?"

After her debate with Billy, she wondered why Leon also had begun trying her in argument. She didn't need another like that. One advantage that mounted infantry has over the walking kind, she decided, is that you can abruptly spur your horse and ride away from annoying conversation. That's just what Lenora did, leaving Leon to contemplate her mount's receding rump.

15

Here were four lovely creatures from the tender but precocious girl of 13 to the mature but fresh and blooming woman nearly 19 each contending for my love...all of them rushing on every occasion into my arms and covering me with kisses, lolling on my lap, pressing their bodies almost into mine...Is it in flesh and blood to withstand this?
>—diary entry of James Henry Hammond, later U. S. Senator and South Carolina governor, describing liaisons with his nieces.

SHE SEEMED REAL IRRITATED. BILLY couldn't figure out why. Even as they made camp that night, she kept her face turned down, busying herself with sewing a tear in her uniform coat. Then it was cleaning her musket, washing spare stockings and drawers. She wouldn't look at anybody.

He still carried *Romeo and Juliet* in his haversack. That he'd told Martha he was searching for Lenora June just to give her this book—the lie yet embarrassed him, though Lenora had never heard it. He unbuckled the flap, fished out the little volume, then walked over and laid it in her lap.

"I brung that from the Forge for you."

Her brown hands flew to it, folded back the leather cover to the title page.

"Oh, my!" Her fingers riffled the gilt-edged pages to the end, where she proved to herself the entire play was there. "*Romeo and Juliet!* Oh, my, that's wonderful!" At last she looked at him, full at him, the smile stretching her face wide. Threads of gold laced the bright brown of her eyes. She didn't ask why he'd withheld the gift so long, why for that matter he was even giving it. She just said:

"Thank you, Billy!" At the sound of her voice, Leon turned and looked at them there together. That's all. He just looked at them, his eyes taking in the gift Billy had bestowed. The squad had camped in woods where a huge spring welled from the base of a cliff, forming a blue-green pool from which the spring branch rushed fifty yards to join a creek. The spring water tasted like air. It was the best water they'd found. To keep it clear, they tethered the horses fifty yards downstream, on long leads so they could drink and also graze on vetch that grew there. It was a reasonably secure camp, walled off by the cliff on one side, protected by the creek on the other.

The night before, and without awakening the resident farmer, Ike Spears had filched three sleepy chickens from a crowded henhouse. He had roasted them on an iron spit over slow coals, was sliding them off now, cleaving the dripping flesh for the squad's supper. The sweet potatoes had scorched black outside but were velvety inside—so Billy discovered when they settled down to eat, the circle of faces lighted by Lenora's two lanterns. Beyond bare tree branches above them the sky had cleared and darkened. Ben Densmore chewed thoughtfully at a chicken thigh, spat the bone into the fire and then, around the meat in his mouth, choked out a question.

"Ike, how you catch them bird so quiet-like? I see you sneak in that henhouse, after awhile slide out carryin chickens, necks wrung good. Didn't hear not one cackle."

The question caught Ike at a crucial point in his meal. He'd split a sweet potato and laid back the two sides. Mouth open, he was ready to bite into the steaming flesh. He set the potato down, sucking his fingers clean.

"Plantation we live at, master for long time didn't give us no meat, not for colored. Not even goat. Just corn pone, corn grits, corn porridge, and not mucha that. Master eatin good. We don't get nothin, we all hungry, so my daddy showed me how."

With his audience interested, Ike used his bayonet point to pry out a section of sweet potato. He speared it, popped it in and mouthed it slowly.

"Showed you how WHAT?" Ben said.

Ike swallowed. "How to catch them chickens."

"Get to hell on with the story!"

He wouldn't be rushed. He set the potato aside and wiped his mouth on his coat sleeve. He looked keenly around at the circle of faces, assessing their interest.

"First thing after you slip in, chickens gonna croak and chirp some. So just set still, and after while they kinda relax. Run a hand slow along that roost till you feel a chicken leg. So chicken lifts that leg up. Put your hand under, he sets his foot down on it. Move a hand to the other foot, he lifts that one too, sets it down. Now he got both feet on your hands. You swing him slow up against your chest, friendly like. Then wring his neck and tighten up so he cain't flop. After while he just sag, so stuff him in your sack and go after the next one. If you just take two-three chicken at one time, master think the fox get'em."

"Ha!" Ben crowed. He held a frayed drumstick aloft in celebration.

The squad went back to eating the fruit of Ike's craft, chewing slowly, now and again glancing up to look contentedly across the fire at one another. They heard the soft stutter of the spring branch over the round stones of its bed. An owl called from woods across the creek—not the big hoot owl this time, instead something with an almost human, complaining voice. As if prompted by that complaint, Leon Duffy abruptly spoke out to the night and his fellows.

"I don't hold with race mixin."

He looked straight at Billy as he said it. They all looked at Leon, at his sober, handsome face with its ginger-gold complexion. Nobody said anything.

"I mean all this mixin colored blood with the white." The rustle of the spring branch seemed somehow louder. "Bible speaks against it," Leon said.

Billy dropped his eyes from Leon's and stared into the fire. This was one debate he didn't care to join, since it damn sure grew out of the rivalry between himself and Leon.

"Bible? Where in Bible?" asked Ben Densmore.

"Ezekiel. Prophet EEE-zekiel. Our ole preacher sermoned on it, about our sins. If he don't preach Leviticus, he preach Ezekiel. This old-time woman, A-ho-LI-bah, she whored with them Babylonians, and they defiled her with their whoredom. She played harlot in the land of Egypt, she bruised her tits with them Egyptians."

Leon nodded apologetically to Sergeant Moffat.

"Beg pardon."

Ben, Ike and the Smallwood brothers glanced back and forth among themselves, clearly wondering why a mention of tits would offend their sergeant. Leon said:

"A-ho-LI-bah, she DOTED on them Egyptians, whose flesh is as the flesh of asses, and whose issue is like the issue of hosses."

When he fell silent, nobody spoke up. Ben leaned to the fire and with thumb and forefinger plucked a little oyster of meat from a chicken back. He popped it into his mouth and swallowed it whole. Turning to Leon again, he said:

"Leon, we ain't no Hebrews, like A-ho-li-bah was.. WE the ones from Africa, where them Pharaohs lived. WE the Egyptians. Damned if MY flesh is like the flesh of asses. Damned if MY issue is like the issue of hosses."

Sitting cross-legged, leaning back against a log, Leon seemed to shrink into himself. He rested one elbow on a knee and with that hand clenched into a fist, supported his chin as he stared into the fire. Lenora June leaned sympathetically toward him, her eyes warm with lamplight.

"There's nothing wrong with mixing blood, not if the people love each other," she said, and Billy felt the heart jump inside his chest. "The children are just fine. Look at you, Leon, you've got more white blood in your veins than any of us—except maybe Billy. You're strong, you're a good-looking man."

Maybe? Billy thought. What's she mean, *maybe* I got more white blood than Leon? But then, Southron bred, he wasn't sure what a search back among the kin on his Georgia mother's side might turn up.

"No," Lenora said, "what's wrong is only that people won't accept it. You won't accept it, Leon. Lovers who do that, they get shunned. They live miserable lives."

Well pleased, Leon turned his smile on Billy. Billy liked Leon, hoped he would keep on liking the man. From darkness beyond the fire, a voice spoke out.

"They don't ACCEPT it, but they DO it where we come from. Mixin blood, I mean."

It was Hubert who spoke. He and his brother, Aaron, sat together on a limestone ledge well back from the fire.

"When me and Aaron just kids, Master Hammond, he start messin with his nieces, five young white gals. Long time before that, he visited crost the waters, brung back two ebony statues, carved like they dressed real fancy. So he suit up me and Hubert like them statues. He make us guard like statues outside the door of his office. We just kids then. But we seen through the crack what he do. He goin down them gal's dresses, he goin up their dresses, all them fancy under-drawer, two-three gals at once. One them gals thirteen year old.

'They was HAMPTON chil-rens. WADE Hampton chil-rens. Biggest dang family in South Carolina. After while the gals tole on him, tole Master Hammond's wife. Master runnin' round scared Wade Hampton gonna call him out for one them DUELS, shoot him dead.. Didn't happen, though. He got away with it.

"Master Hammond, if he get a chance, he stick it in a knothole yonder in them woods," Hubert said, nodding to the forest across the creek. "Raise hisself a bunch of Hammond oak, maybe Hammond chestnut tree."

A few smiles shone on faces around the fire. Aaron sat scowling into the coals.

"Ain't funny," he said. "None of it funny."

Hubert rose, stepped forward to the fire and plucked out a burning twig. He sucked the flame into his pipe, breathing out a plume of smoke to be brightened by firelight.

"That's right interesting," Ike Spears said, "but it ain't no race-mixin."

Hubert returned to his seat, gesturing to his brother.

"Aaron, you tell'em."

Aaron stood up and coughed, then sat down again and started.

"Master Hammond, he got a wife, he got eight chil-rens outa her, but his wife Miz Catherine and them Hampton gals, that ain't enough for the master. He bought Sally, too, paid nine hunnerd dollar for Sally. She eighteen year old. Sally already had a baby name Louisa. Master Hammond got hisself four more chil-rens outa Sally. Then he start on Louisa. He took the mother, then he took the daughter."

Aaron put a hand to his forehead, squeezing it between his thumb and bunched fingers, as if he had a headache. Aaron said:

"You tell it, Hubert."

"Naw, you doing all right. Go on."

"Well," Aaron sighed, "we same age Louisa, we all raised up with her, all time play with her. We *knowed* Louisa. I *like* Louisa. Here Master Hammond put us to guardin his door again, keep ever-body out. He in yonder with Louisa, she sayin 'no, please, no, please, Master Hammond...'" She twelve year old, he forty three. I never forget that.. He gray whiskery, turkey neck, all wrinkly. She squeal in yonder, she yell, 'ouch, ouch, oh!' We knowed how it happen, it wasn't her fault, but after that she don't associate with us no more. She just shamed. She twenty six year old now, same like me and Hubert. Time we run off to get in this war, Louisa had three of them Hammond babies. She cain't help herself. Ole Master keep after her."

"Master Hammond?" Lenora June said. "Which Hammond?"

"James Henry. Master James Henry Hammond."

A twisted smile broke out on her face..

"The United States senator?"

"Sure, once he was governor, he senator too from South Carolina."

"He's the King Cotton Man," she said. "He's famous for that U. S. Senate speech. It was in every newspaper just when the war was about to start. He said you dare not make war on cotton. Cotton is king. He's the Mud-sill Man. He said every society must be built on a mud-sill, like us slaves, to do the drudgery. Otherwise, there couldn't be a higher class of people like him to build a refined civilization."

Still she smiled, but Billy saw her hands had clenched themselves into fists. Leon chucked a big log on the fire, sending a column of sparks up into the night sky.

"What I was saying in the *first* place," Leon sang out, "shouldn't be no mixin colored blood with the white."

16

*If one Confederate soldier can kill 90 Yankees, how many Yankees can
10 Confederate soldiers kill? If one Confederate soldier can whip seven
Yankees, how many soldiers can whip 49 Yankees?*
    —from "Johnson's Elementary Arithmetic," published in North
Carolina for young patriots.

B EFORE LEAVING, THEY FILLED THEIR canteens and three empty jugs
with sweet water from the big spring. Lenora had reached up to
the saddle cantle, preparing to mount, when Leon ducked under the
big roan's neck and faced her.

"Sergeant Moffat?" She released the cantle and turned to him. "I
brung you somethin," he said, his breath a bright cloud in the chill
air. "Thought you maybe like it."

In his pale-pink, outstretched palm lay a fat pocket knife. She
glanced up into his eyes, which shone with so much hope Lenora felt
her own face warm with embarrassment.

"Leon, I don't want your knife."

"Naw, see, now, it's real good." With the fingers of his left hand,
he began snapping out the tools. "Got a can opener, got a awl for
hole-drillin, got big blade and little blade. Looky here now, got a
screwdriver too."

As a gift *Romeo and Juliet* would have been useless to anyone
else in the squad—except perhaps Billy, the giver. But the pocket
knife would be cherished by any of them, perhaps most of all by Leon
himself. She shook her head.

"I can't take it, Leon."

Beyond him, at the creek bank, Billy had just pulled the headstall
over his horse's ears and was fitting the bit between the animal's teeth.
He lifted his eyes to Lenora June and said:

"Leon wants you to have it. Why not just take it."

She shrugged and took the knife, her cold fingers sensing in its bone grips the warmth of Leon's palm. She hoisted herself to the saddle.

"Thank you, Leon."

She was the first to mount, inspiring action in the others. They began crawling into their saddles. The sky was pure blue, bare of clouds, an omen that the day would warm. This was lucky Indian Summer weather for a march through Georgia. Lenora saw Leon swing around and nod politely to Billy, a thank-you gesture. Billy smiled, flipped a salute and climbed onto his horse. They had barely taken to the road when, from the southwest, they heard the faint crackling of musketry. It went on awhile, punctuated now and then with the "whump!" of artillery. Far behind them, almost on the western horizon, a pillar of smoke boiled up.

"We way ahead of the army," Billy told Lenora. "Gotta keep a sharp eye."

But all morning they saw little except shack after shack occupied by white families. Most were just one log room, shingled with planks of lumber, set amid a few tilled acres. Here what crops had ripened were long harvested. Smoke rose from some chimneys, but no one appeared until, at a turn where a dirt path met the road, Lenora surprised a woman with three children. They stood on the path beside a sagging gate in the rail fence. Instantly, Aaron smiled, checked his horse and swung toward them. Lenora followed. Barefoot, the woman wore a soiled and ragged Nankeen dress, and nothing else against the morning chill. She set down the wooden bucket she was carrying and hugged herself with folded arms, standing stolid as the gate post. Two little girls and a boy clung to her, faces twisted in terror at the approaching soldiers.

"Y'all may as well get on," the woman said, "get on yonder down the road. They done already took it, them Wheeler men, them cavalry. We ain't got nothin."

The statement was so bleak Lenora wished it could be mended.

"You have this good land," she said.

The woman clicked her tongue behind her teeth.

"We just share-croppin here. I was born and raised in this state and never owned a foot of land all my life."

"I'm sorry."

"Ain't nothin to be sorry for, just how folks get by. Only ones worse off around here is the niggers."

Niggers. Lenora wondered how this woman felt about the war, whether she might provide a bit of military intelligence.

"Can you tell me when Wheeler's cavalry came through?"

"Hell yes! They ain't no kin to us. Come through yestidy dinner time. They come once afore, but that time I hid the shelled corn under the bed. Yestidy they come after it again. I was ready for'em—pot of water a-boiling on the fire. I throwed that water on'em, scalded two of'em good, but another one crawled up under the floor. Pried up a plank and got it. Last we had."

Lenora shook her head pityingly, a gesture the woman shrugged off.

"What they told me, soldiers gotta eat too. Anyways, we ain't got nothin for y'all to take. Ain't got supper tonight for these youngins."

A cloth sack hit the ground in front of her, raising a wisp of dust. The children screamed and flinched back, but she stood rooted like a tree. Aaron doffed his forage cap.

"Didn't mean to scare y'all. That ain't hoecake. That's good cornbread, baked in a stove. Got hen eggs in it. We took lotsa stuff outa that Hunnicutt plantation, back west a ways. Got bacon, got ham, got peach compote in a jar."

He looked questioningly at Lenora June.

"Sure," she said. "Bring up the pack mules." Given what ordinary life, and now war, had done to these people, ham and peach compote was sorry recompense.

On the road again, Lenora heard a new burst of musketry to the southwest, still a skirmish going on back there. Wheeler's men had taken the woman's corn only yesterday. His patrols would be close. With the little farms behind them now, woods thick on both sides of the road, she sent Ike Spears to ride as a vedette a hundred yards ahead of their column, alert for ambush. The morning chill had surrendered at last to a sun that warmed the road. This brought out gnats to rise and hang in scattered clouds above the wagon ruts. The riders reined their mounts back and forth, detouring around the bugs. Lenora urged the roan to a trot and caught up with Billy.

"Maybe we're too far out from the army," she told him.

"Shhhhhhh!" he hissed, pulling up his mount. He raised a hand to stop those riding behind them. "Y'all hear that?"

She did hear it, a chorus of voices singing, a few muddled words and then, faint but understandable, "...hurrah! hurrah!" Cupping his hands at his head, Billy made elephant ears as he searched for the source. He pointed at woods to the south.

"Thataway, maybe a mile. Must be another road yonder."

Ahead of them, Ike had spun his mount and now thundered back, the animal's hooves scattering clods. He reined up before them.

"Y'all hear?"

"Yah," Billy said. "Sound like they headin same DI-rection we going."

"All right," Lenora said, "we just keep on for a ways. See if we can figure it out."

She signaled for quiet, and they rode on, the trees becoming few but taller as they moved. For awhile they heard no more of the voices. Then the chorus rose again, closer now and quite clear.

We are a band of BROTH-ers, and na-tive to the soil,
A-fightin for the proper-TY we gained by honest toil,
And when our rights were threatened, the cry rose near and far:
HURRAH for the bonnie Blue Flag that bears a single star!

"They talkin about savin their property," Billy said. "Reckon them Peckerwoods actually own some?" He pointed into the woods. "Lemme go scout'em out."

There was no point in telling him to be careful, but she did. Only after he'd ridden off through the trees did she recall that he had asked to go. Perhaps, despite his lieutenant's bars, he'd finally acknowledged her as leader. The thought made her smile. The squad rode slowly on, listening as the Confederates paused, then spiritedly sang again..

Hark honor's call, summoning all,
Summoning all of us unto the strife.

Sons of the South, awake! Strike till the brand shall break,
Strike for dear honor's sake, freedom and life!

The Rebs were so far ahead of Sherman's army they thought it was safe to sing. A good thirty minutes elapsed before Billy reappeared, his horse struggling up an incline to reach the road. His face was flushed as he pulled up beside her.

"It's a coffle of slaves," he breathed, "two hunnerd of'em, maybe three hunnerd."

He was panting harder than his mount. The other squad members spurred up to join them. Their horses, infected by the agitation of Billy's, stamped and circled, forcing the riders to turn this way and that, following each others' eyes as they talked. Billy caught a breath and said:

"They got them slaves lined out marchin on one long chain, runs a good quarter, maybe two quarters, down that road. Never seen so many slaves. But the ones singin, they Wheeler cavalry. Ain't none of them old men and boys like at Hunnicutt. Anyhow forty Wheeler cavalry."

"Slave coffle!" Corporal Densmore boomed. Lenora put a finger to her lips, and with an effort that squeezed his eyes shut, he muted his next words. "I was in a coffle once, got sold from Kain-tuck to Georgia. Made us walk in a coffle. Men and women together, never get off that damn chain. Piss in the road, shit in the road. Three of us DIE on that road. They drive a mule herd right behind us, none them mule die. They treat mule good."

Lenora jerked the reins of her roan, dragged his head around to turn so she could see Billy. "Why have they got slaves out on the road?" she asked him. "Why now?"

Billy shrugged his skinny shoulders.

"If they kept'em where they was, Sherman's army gonna free'em sure. Them Wheeler men are refugeeing the slaves. Get'em out the way of Sherman."

The chorus of voices was closer now, even clearer.

War to the hilt, theirs be the guilt,
Who fetter the free man to ransom the slave.

Up then, and UN-dismayed, sheathe not the battle blade,
Till the last foe is laid low in the grave.

Lenora June felt her own face burn, even as the flush was draining
from Billy's.

"You thinkin about trying it, ain't you?" he said. "Us seven fightin
forty Wheeler cavalry. More than that. There's three-four more white
men with'em, maybe overseers, one wagon teamster."

"Three *hundred*," she said. "A coffle of three *hundred*!"

"I didn't say three hunnerd, I said maybe three hunnerd. But there
ain't no maybe about it's more than forty real fightin Rebs against
seven U. S. Colored Infantry. I hid on a rise above that road and
watched'em pass."

"Low in that grave!" Ben hissed. "That's how we gonna lay'em!"

She was commander, she knew that, but she wouldn't order it if
Billy said no. She didn't ask. She just looked pleadingly into his face.
He glanced away, off into the sky above the trees, and began talking
tactics.

"That other road, it's a wide main road—way better'n our road. It
follers down a creek, all time gettin closer to this road. Probably ours
is gonna come down to meet theirs at a bridge where it crosses the
creek.. We got to get there afore'em, set up to bushwhack'em."

Billy lifted his forage cap and combed thin fingers back through
his hair, staring gloomily down at the flaxen mane of his chestnut
mare. The other soldier heads were up and alert, eyes shining, eager
for it.

"Keep quiet and follow me," she said.

From the singing voices that still came through the woods, Lenora
judged her squad was already a little ahead. She started at a trot for
a half-mile, then spurred her roan to an easy canter. Now there was
no way to detour around the gnats. She rode through clouds of them,
feeling their faint pit-pat against her lips and cheeks, on her eyelids.
Glancing back, she saw Billy with his sour face and, behind him, five
other riders grinning like crazy men as they ducked and jerked their
heads about, trying to dodge the bugs.

A long mile ahead, their road angled abruptly to the right and
sank away down a slope, emerging from woods into a pasture that

bordered a creek. Their road joined the wide main road, which ran to the left down into the creek.at a ford and came out on the other side. No bridge here, just a ford. Leon's big Belgian came thumping up on her left, crowding her, his brogan and stirrup banging hers.

"Whoa up! Just whoa up here!"

The whole squad slowed and slid into another whirl of horses and mules.

"Don't cross that ford, Sergeant Moffat," Leon told her. "Cross below, so them Secesh won't see fresh track."

"Good I-dee," Billy said. "We muddy that water, them Rebs catch on."

They searched downstream, finding one place deeper than the ford but still so shallow they didn't have to swim the horses. The animals were thirsty. They waded in until the water touched the stirrups, then paused to drink. Emerging on the far side, they struggled, plunging, up a steep clay bank and then onward up the hillside. Lenora studied the ground, wishing for stone walls. The only good cover here was a partly-finished barn, four walls ill constructed, the top logs already fallen.

They dismounted and, holding the reins of their horses, huddled close. They were less eager now, eyes roving the scattering of boulders among blackberry bushes on the slope down to the creek. Sunlight shimmered there on shallow water where the road crossed at ford. She saw the others were looking not at her but at Billy. She shrugged and said:

"What do you think?"

His blue eyes seemed darker now, brooding.

"Kinda hate it, but reckon we got no chance unless we kill a few of'em in the first volley, afore they see us. That would even the odds a little, maybe scare'em."

Kill a few in the first volley—terrible words, she told herself. But these men were dragging three hundred slaves along that road, intending to keep them forever in chains.

"We can do that," she said, feeling the eager tingle at the base of her brain..

He shrugged. He was looking up the road where the coffle would appear. But when he turned to her, the others followed his eyes as she instructed them. Lenora June told them to make the first shot count, just squeeze the trigger slowly until the musket fires. Nobody should shoot until she does. Be careful not to hit slaves in the coffle. She sent Aaron and Hubert to tether the animals well back in the woods, using the link straps on their bridles. When the brothers came hustling back, she deployed her soldiers ten paces apart, two in the unfinished barn, the others concealed by boulders. Their line was pitifully thin but perhaps long enough to make them seem a larger force.

Behind her own boulder, on a big wood chip, she laid out five musket cartridges, paper cylinders stuffed with powder. The Minie balls that tipped them were .58 caliber, an inch long, fat as her thumb, heavy in the hand. They would break any bone they struck, break a rider's thigh and shatter the spine of the horse under him. She plugged a percussion cap onto the primer nipple and looked out over the field.

The air over this slope, over the creek and woods, seemed utterly still, sun heating the back of her uniform coat. There was plenty of bird song, bluejays and scolding wrens. A yellowhammer woodpecker flapped across, rising and falling with every wingbeat. As minutes passed, she blinked and caught herself nodding, fought back the sleepiness that enwrapped her against all good sense. A little whistle brought her back. Stretched out behind his own boulder, Billy had rolled onto his side to look at her through a veil of brown grasses. He spoke almost in a whisper.

"What Aaron told us about that little gal, Louisa, did it ever happen to you?"

"No. Not to me. I was afraid of it, but my pa, he's too important around that Forge. It would hurt'em if he started pounding bad iron. Remember the Forge Master and Rachel? He blamed her, called her his Bathsheba. Anyhow, she never complained. Wouldn't help her if she had. But Rachel kept the Forge Master busy enough."

He lay looking solemnly at her.

"I'm glad nobody done it to you."

The gloom of the moment lifted a little. He flipped her his salute, then rolled to his belly behind the boulder. Already, she saw, he had laid out two Spencer magazines, brass tubes that shone in the noon sun. When the singing started again, it was close. This time she knew the song, "Riding a Raid." She'd heard it before when Confederate units marched past the Hunnicutt plantation.

> There's a man in the White House with blood on his mouth!
> If there's knaves in the North, there's braves in the South.
> We are three thousand hosses, and not one afraid.
> We are three thousand sabers and not a dull blade!

Where the road emerged from woods beyond the creek, a lone rider appeared, clearly a vedette. Slim and well set in his patched gray uniform, a turkey feather jaunty in the band of his slouch hat, he searched the slope ahead of him with interested eyes. Lenora feared he would quickly cross the ford and detect the ambush. Indeed, he tried to cross, but the horse fought the bit, hooves churning the mud. The rider had to slacken the reins. The animal nickered and plunged its nose into the water. It drank long and deeply. Out of the woods burst a whole squad of Secesh, also struggling to check their scrawny mounts, hauling back on the reins as the horses plunged toward the creek. Lenora counted eight of them. Their horses splashed in and drank thirstily.

The riders were a hairy, raggedy lot, one in bib overalls, a couple wearing blue Union jackets to finish out their gray or butternut uniforms. Tobacco passed back and forth among them, five or six pipes being lit from a single friction match, smoke clinging around them in the still air. Lenora could almost hear jokes passing among them as they joshed each other, slapped shoulders, laughed aloud.

Ye have heard that it hath been said, an eye for an eye, and a tooth for a tooth, but I say unto you, resist not evil. At least this is not murder, she thought, this is ambush, like the ridgetop ambush some of this same regiment sprang on the 179th Illinois. Except we don't have cannon. We cannot fire cannister like that which tore those blueback soldiers. *I say unto you, love your enemies, bless them that curse you, do good to them that hate you.* Mere Peckerwoods the graybacks might be, as Billy keeps insisting, but these hold captive three hundred hungry, dirty, exhausted people. Three hundred slaves.

Even now she could see the coffle, a jostling snake of human flesh with its backbone of chain. The slaves, thirsty as the horses, came at a half run along the road toward the water. She clenched her teeth against those crippling words of Jesus. *Pray for them which despitefully use you and persecute you, that ye may be the children of your Father which is in heaven, for he maketh his sun to rise on the evil and on the good.* So this is not murder. It's not murder.

Now she'd waited too long. With his mount's thirst satisfied, the vedette broke away from the rest and rode lightly up the slope, leftward across the battle front. He veered closer to her hiding place. She turned her face down to dirt behind the boulder and tried not to breathe. The click of iron horse shoes on gravel passed from right to left in front of her. When at last she dared look, she was amazed to see first his horse, then the vedette himself, sink into a swale on the hillside.

She hadn't noticed that any such battle cover lay so close to their line. She'd allowed the vedette to escape. Quickly, Lenora laid her musket foresight on a sergeant among the cavalrymen in the creek. As Billy had taught her, she held the aim, squeezed and let the actual discharge take her by surprise, the buttplate kicking back into her shoulder.

She saw nothing of the immediate result, veiled behind her own powder smoke. Muskets erupted around her, huge BOOMs echoing through the valley along with the POW! POW! POW! of Billy's Spencer. She bit the paper of a fresh cartridge, stroked it down the barrel with the ramrod and primed. When she threw the musket up to aim, she saw all the riders were down, one dragging through the water, his foot lodged in the stirrup. Spooked, the other animals fled crazily away, bucking and kicking.

A wounded man sat at creek's edge, bracing a revolver between his knees, blasting away at their puffs of powder smoke on the slope. A slug whined off the boulder where Billy sheltered. Lenora aimed and knocked the man back with her second shot. Still another wounded man, abandoning his musket carbine, crawled jerkily away toward the woods. That man kept people bound up in chains. Fiercely, she wanted him killed, but at last the gorge rose in her throat.

"Cease fire!" she called, her hands working furiously to load.

The slave coffle recoiled from the shooting, bending on itself and tangling as it fell back, until it could move no farther. Packed together in a knot, the people stood with manacled hands thrown up, as if that could protect them. The crawling man reached the trees, where white hands lifted him, dragged him into the woods. A vast silence settled over the valley. No birds sang. The bodies stirred in the current of the creek, dyeing the water with their blood. One floated free and, face up, drifted idly downstream. Once more Billy put his hands up, palms forward, making elephant ears. Lenora could hear the enemy too, even without big ears.

"They're going wide through the woods on both sides," she told him.

"Gonna hit us on both flanks," Billy said. "Big mess of'em comin on the right towards that clay bank where we crossed the creek."

So her squad had killed or wounded eight of them. That left thirty two soldiers and some overseers coming against her squad's seven. She understood better now what she'd led them into.

"We could back away," she said, "go for our horses and run."

"Hell no!" Through the grass stems she saw his face redden. "Then all this killing be for nothing. They's three hunnerd slaves yonder. We gonna get'em off that chain."

She was surprised to feel tears burn in her eyes. That he wanted what she wanted—why would that make her happy? Had he become at last a Union man? Billy said:

"I'll take Ike off to the right, meet that one bunch at the creek where they ain't lookin for us. Best y'all move too, meet these comin on the left. Bushwhack'em again if you can."

He grabbed up his Spencer magazines and began crawling away. Then, strangely, he swung around in that odd posture, on hands and knees, his head raised, his eyes shining into her.

"Lenora, I love you. I want you. For-EVER."

Love *forever*? When in five minutes both of them could be dead? She shook her head violently at him, at the hopelessness of it. When he turned and crawled away, her breath came in something like a sob. She watched him go until, well back in woods to the left, she heard horses splashing into the creek, probably swimming. That was the force she would meet and would kill, given the chance. Her teeth were set for it. She followed the clatter of hooves around to her squad's left front, where it ceased. She saw threshing in the brush at wood's edge down the hill, no doubt the horsemen dismounting. Long before, cavalrymen on both sides had learned that a mounted charge against emplaced infantry is seldom profitable.

Gunfire erupted on the right, POW! POW! BOOM! POW! POW! That was Billy and Ike, bushwhacking the other force. Then came a sputter of musketry and shotguns as Confederates there answered. This too-early burst of firing seemed to surprise the people Lenora faced. They came out of brush at wood's edge, casting puzzled looks at one another. She counted sixteen men. No doubt the two wings had been ordered to attack simultaneously. That their plan had gone awry was proven again with a fresh eruption on the other battle front, Billy keeping the Spencer hot. But she had her own batch of Secesh to fight and now, suddenly, one idea.

"Squad," Lenora ordered, "shoot at those Confederates!"

They fired a ragged volley. There was little hope of hitting anything at this range. The volley did spot their own hillside with black blooms of powder smoke, marking their positions. She saw a saber go up in one Confederate's hand, go up and come down pointing directly at her. Just as the Union line had advanced toward ambush by cannon in the battle at the ridgetop, the Confederate line now swept forward, all those throats yip-yip-yowling with the Rebel yell. Lenora herself caught one breath and yelled to make herself heard above it:

"Squad, reload!" Not that they needed to be told.

She had called out such formal orders in practice drill, but never so far in real action. She squeezed a Minie-ball tipped cartridge into the muzzle of her own weapon. With her ramrod she stroked the load down the barrel and plugged a percussion cap onto the primer nipple.

She glanced up to see the Rebels coming not at a run, but at the quick step that offers long endurance. The swale in the hillside had been deep enough to hide the vedette. Now she saw the legs of sixteen Confederates sink into that wrinkle of the earth, followed by their torsos. Then the soldiers vanished altogether into the swale. She jumped to her feet.

"Squad, stand up!"

Again, the stagy sound of the order embarrassed her. But the squad did as she said, did it fearfully, looking bewildered around at her. Why were they standing upright in the face of a charging enemy?

Would she now order them to flee the field? She struggled to smile, hoping to reassure them.

"Squad, maintain your formation facing the enemy. To the left oblique, march!"

Ben Densmore, on the left flank, was first to remember his drill instruction. Blindly, he did as she said.

"Follow Corporal Densmore!" she ordered. "Quick time!"

At a half-run, they slid forward and leftward across the invisible enemy's front. Lenora pushed them onward, weaving among the brambles. A blackberry cane caught her ankle and sent her sprawling, the jagged branch of a juniper raking her forehead. She scrambled up and saw Leon stopped, waiting for her.

"Go on!"

She followed him fifty yards farther and then, fearing discovery, shouted:

"Halt and take cover!"

There was little cover to take, just widely-scattered shrubs and scraggly juniper, but they hit the ground. There would have been more time. A good minute passed before the first rebel slouch hat grew up out of the earth, his musket muzzle and the rebel himself rising from the swale. Now other heads and bodies appeared, all converging on the positions the squad had just abandoned. Lenora feared the man on the Confederate right flank would see her, she being out of place, too far forward. She squeezed the stock of her musket to stop the trembling in her hands. The Rebels jogged blindly left to right across the front of her squad's new position.

The yip-yowling rose in pitch as they dashed in for the assault. Beyond the foresight of Lenora's musket, they formed a moving line along her axis of aim, sixteen men almost in a row. She fired, figuring that if she missed one, she would hit another. Four muskets boomed around her. At this short range the raking shot tumbled three men. Lenora drew her Colt revolver. Steadying it in both hands, she took aim at the closest man—he was a slave-keeper, she knew he was—and fired down that line, which now showed many gaps. The Colt was a poor weapon for shooting at long range, but this was short. She fired shot after shot.

The soldiers had halted in place, some firing blindly into the squad's former battle line, others searching dazedly for the source of the slugs that were killing them. Her own gun smoke obscuring her vision, she couldn't see the ones she hit, and by then, in her rage, was sorry not to see those fall. One dropped his musket, bent forward over his gut and staggered away down the hill. Somehow he kept going.

The Confederates sighted the squad's powder smoke and tried to fight back, but they were in each other's way. They got off one sputtering volley, which plowed dirt and clipped branches along the Union line. Frantically, they began reloading—too late. Corporal Ben Densmore jumped to his feet, charged toward them extending his own Colt before him as he ran.

"Re-MEM-ber Fort Pillow!"

Lenora ordered everyone up to follow Ben, but he was already among the Confederates as they struggled to reload. Running headlong toward them, she saw one man try to draw his pistol, only to be shot down. Another had just primed his reloaded musket when Ben saw the danger and killed him. Ben swung the pistol around to a third, who turned, ran and was shot in the back. Several just threw down their muskets and ran toward the creek.

"Keep firing!" Lenora said. "Keep'em away from their horses."

Indeed, three turned in that direction, racing straight back down the hill. When a fresh volley felled one, she was glad for that—yet another slave-keeper killed. The other two veered off and followed the general rush to cross the creek. Now Lenora heard echoes of that last volley, coming back from surrounding hills. They all reloaded. Though quiet again settled around them, they were wary, glancing cautiously around.

"Anybody hurt?" Lenora asked, afraid of the answer. The squad members looked down, amazed at the wholeness of their bodies. Leon moved toward her, studying her face. He raised fingers to her forehead and came away with blood.

"You're cut right good up here."

She waved him away. Ben, looking dazed, stood amid the human wreckage of the battle. Nine of the sixteen Confederates had fallen where they stood, a single cavalier among them. Handsome in his belted wool coat with its captain's bars, he lay with his saber clutched in one hand, a revolver in the other. Here was an aristocrat who hadn't escaped war through the twenty-nigger law.

Flung randomly down around him were a Peckerwood corporal and six privates, only the corporal still alive. He'd been shot through the upper right arm, the slug shattering bones there. Wounds in the front and back of the arm pulsed with blood. Lenora found the dead ones not so hard to look at. The live one was different, wide-eyed and astonished, like a run-over hound she'd seen years ago on a town pavement. Above his graying beard, the man's face was starch white, lips drawn back from his teeth in a grimace of pain. Still, he managed to smile up at Lenora.

"I be gaw-damn if it ain't a bunch of nigger Yankees. That were right cute, how y'all got on our flank. Never thought the nigger had brains for it."

He was just a slave-keeper, dragging people down the road on a chain—so she told herself. Seeing him hurt weakened her. She pulled off his wool scarf and bound it tightly around the arm, making it press on the wound, entry and exit.

"You need to keep it tight and stop the bleeding. You should live through this."

He shook his head.

"Wound no worse than this was plenty enough for Stonewall at Chancellorsville. Killed him daid."

His canteen had been punctured by a slug. She gave him a drink of sweet spring water from her own. His brown eyes looked up into hers as he swallowed. He pulled his lips away, sucked in a breath and said:

"Thankee."

She took a nearly-full canteen from a dead Confederate and placed it beside the wounded man. But Lenora had forgotten where they were, what was happening. Remembering Billy, remembering the assault he had faced on the right flank, she rose and looked up the hill. She saw horsemen there, as in a nightmare she saw horsemen coming over the crest toward them.

"Squad, form a line!"

There was quick movement from the others, but only indolence from Leon, who, sheltering his eyes, stared keenly up the hill.

"Them's Billy and Ike, bringing Secesh hosses home."

Ike was smiling as he rode up, Billy as somber faced as before the battle, a blood-soaked neckerchief wrapped tight around his right hand.

"Look like y'all done good," Billy said. "Easy for us over yonder too. Caught'em crossin the creek. Couldn't get their hosses to climb that bank with us shootin at'em. Reckon the ones that got away gonna give it up."

With Billy and Ike now among them, the seven stood close gathered, all the eyes roaming all the faces, where grins were beginning to break out. Their pink lips were smudged black with powder from bitten cartridges, white teeth showing between them. Lenora felt herself grabbed and lifted, her brogans flailing air. Ben Densmore shook her back and forth, hugged her like a precious morsel.

"Ha!" he yelled. "Bedford Forrest, he say niggers cain't stand up to them Secesh, but we beat'em! Ha! Re-MEM-ber Fort Pillow!"

He set her down and picked up Billy, twirling with him, Billy's legs swinging out like a scythe blade, which caused the others to back away, laughing. Far beyond the spinning men she saw a figure's head, then quickly shoulders and torso rise from the swale. The soldier was carrying a musket. He was running toward them.

"Look out!"

Lenora ran at him. He was so close and already stopping, beginning to throw up his weapon. As she rushed in, she saw his eyes waver between his intended target and this attacker rushing down on him. Gun smoke burst past her as she reached him, knocked him backward. He was surprisingly slight. She yanked the musket out of his frail grip, slammed the barrel down across the man's throat. He wheezed air in through the choked windpipe. Because of its chin strap, the slouch hat still clung to the head. The hat band held a turkey feather. This was the vedette who'd escaped the first ambush, who'd saved them by revealing to Lenora the existence of the swale, and who now had attacked them using that same swale as cover.

Lenora glanced back to see Billy rushing toward her, and somebody else back there on the ground. She bounced on the musket, and the grayback's wheezing stopped. Feebly the soldier struggled to lift it, and Lenora let him. He sucked desperate gasps, scared eyes looking up at her.

"I'm a woo-man."

"What?" Lenora said.

"I'm a *woo*-man."

That's all she said, and Lenora instantly believed her. Standing beside them, Billy said:

"She saying she a woman?"

"Yes."

"Well, she gut-shot Ben, that's what she done this day."

The woman sighed out a breath, took another and sobbed:

"Look what *y'all* done this day. Killed about half of us. I seen it all. Wasn't fair, way y'all done it."

They jerked the Reb to her feet, marched her back to where the squad had gathered around Ben. He lay on his back with one hand centered over his abdomen, blood rising between tight-squeezed fingers. When she knelt over him, he looked up confidently, as if to ease her mind.

"Nawsir, just kinda knock the breath outa me, catch me surprise like. I get movin here right quick, get down yonder, let them people off that chain. First thing, get them people off that chain."

She had led them into this, she had let the vedette escape, she had failed to remain alert against further attack. It was hard to kill the enemy, and a thousand times worse to suffer the death of friends. Soberly, Ben studied their faces, as if he worried for them.

"Just lemme catch my breath here. Gonna get myself up quicker'n a hiccup. Y'all hear that? Quicker'n a hiccup." Though nobody else did, he smiled at his joke, then commenced singing, though with little melody.

"We are done with hoeing cotton, we are done with hoeing corn.

We are colored Yankee soldiers now as sure as you are born...."

He talked a while longer, making less and less sense. Then the blood stopped rising between his fingers, and he took a deep final breath. Lenora watched it and thought of the lie Tom Paine had told, the lie she had repeated in teaching Ben to read:

The mind once enlightened cannot again become dark.

17

...the poor wretch [a Polish immigrant] was so disheartened by suffering that one day he deliberately stepped over the dead line and stood there till the guard was forced to shoot him. But what I can't understand is that a Pole, of all people in the world, should come over here and try to take away our liberty when his own country is in the hands of oppressors. One would think that the Poles... ought to sympathize with a people fighting for their liberties.

—Eliza Frances Andrews in her "War-Time Journal of a Georgia Girl" describes a Union soldier killed by a guard at the Confederacy's Andersonville Prison.

H IS HAND TIGHT-WRAPPED WITH THE neckerchief, Billy wielded the mason's hammer and cold chisel, cutting bolts that secured the manacles. The squad had captured a big kitchen wagon accompanying the coffle. Shuffling forward in a long line, the slaves one by one would lay the manacle up on the iron wagon tire. Usually a single sharp blow with hammer on chisel, PING!, would snap the bolt, the black circlets falling free of the wrist.

"Praise the Lord!" a woman shouted, raising her liberated hand to heaven. "It's the truth done made us free!"

"AND the U. S. Colored Infantry," Billy told her, unable in his present condition to manage a smile.

The line stretched far down the road between the trees. As the slaves were freed, Lenora armed the most able looking with musket carbines and shotguns scavenged from the battlefield. Leon taught them to load and prime, then took them out with Ike and Hubert to form a picket line against the possible return of Wheeler's men.

Clustered close about Billy, craving his service, the slaves reeked of soured sweat and dirt and the bowel filth that spattered their lower bodies. He figured anyhow half of them had that awful soldier's quick-step. When the shackles fell off, most kicked off their shoes, if they had shoes, and walked straight into the creek above the ford. That Confederate bodies floated just downstream didn't seem to bother them. The freed people ducked and squealed at the cold and laughed at one another, enjoying this one more than all their previous baptizings. It was warm for November. Still, they came out shivering to strip off their wet clothes and stand in the sun, staring, amazed, at one another.

They were naked and were not ashamed, though this was no Garden of Eden. There were strong young men and women, some with children, and old women whose deflated bosoms, Billy noted with surprise, hung lower than their belly buttons. He'd never known his own grandmothers. Lenora June passed out chunks of slab bacon and weevily hardtack from the wagon, which the people ate hungrily. Some troubled to tap the biscuits on a handy stone, flushing startled weevils from their holes.

"Where y'all come from?" Billy asked one man who stepped forward to the wagon wheel.

"Forty mile south," he answered. "Three day on the road, this the fourth. No water 'cept from creeks we cross. Three womens die on that chain."

Billy placed the manacle clasps firmly on the wagon tire so its iron, and not the wrist, would bear the impact. The brown flesh there showed purple bruises, which the man shielded with his other hand. The sledge came down, PING! The shackle fell away.

"Great Jesus God!" he shouted. "Ole whale done cough up Jonah!"

And Billy felt such a surge of pleasure in emancipating that he forgot for a moment the pain in his own hand. It lightened also the shadow that had befallen them with Ben's death. As Lenora June had said, Union or not, Billy loved this work. To speed it, he tried to develop a rhythm, encourage teamwork. Slaves in the coffle move two steps forward, slave in the lead places the manacle on the wagon tire, PING! And a free man or woman walks ahead to take a food ration from Lenora.

Even before the shackles came off, most of them were smiling, but a bushy-headed fellow seemed to scowl darkly even as he was freed,

PING! He turned and waited for the next in line, a girl about twelve. With her, but unshackled, was a tiny boy. When the girl was freed, PING, he swung the boy up into his arms and started back along the coffle, back down the road.. The girl ran alongside.

"Where y'all going?" Lenora yelled, and he swung around.

"My woman back yonder ten-twelve mile. She sick, cain't walk no more. Yestidy they throwed her off the coffle."

"Wait!" Lenora searched in the wagon to find a canteen, abandoned in the Confederate teamster's haste to flee, but nearly full. She carried it, along with a sack of hardtack and bacon, to where the man stood. He said nothing, just took food and water and turned back to the road.

"Pa, I'm HUN-gry," the girl groused.

"Eat while we walkin." He passed her a biscuit from the sack. "We going to mama."

Billy kept knocking off the manacles. He'd worked through nearly half the coffle when bright blood started dripping from the hammer handle. Lenora saw it. She took his right hand, picked at the knot in the neckerchief and unwound it, clotted blood pulling out in strings as the fabric layers came apart. The hand kept twitching away from her all on its own, as if it didn't want to be seen.

"You hurtin it worse," he said as the cloth fell away.

"Oh, Billy, Billy..."

"Hell, it's just one finger. Ain't anyhow my trigger finger. Slug glanced off the forestock, or it woulda took more. Sure glad it didn't bust the Spencer."

He hadn't felt the bullet strike, didn't even notice when it happened. Only after the surviving graybacks fled did he see two joints of the second finger dangling from a flap of skin. He severed it with his bayonet and hid the finger under a stone. Idly, he wondered what would happen at the Resurrection, when all bones rushed up from the ground to be reconstructed in heaven. Would this finger find the rest of him? By then he was feeling pain, which now had dulled down to a biting ache. He could bear this work, wanted to keep going, but Lenora was merciless.

She gave his cherished hammer-and-chisel job to Aaron and led him away, made him sit, legs dangling, at the rear of the wagon bed. Three horses, blowing and stamping, were still hitched at the other end. The Confederate teamster, unable to turn the wagon on the narrow road, had cut the fourth out of the traces and ridden away on it. Lenora washed the hand with lye soap and water from her canteen. The lye stung the raw finger stump. PING! went the hammer as Aaron fell into his own emancipating rhythm. She bound the hand with clean cloth from her pack, part of the same bedsheet she'd used for her monthlies.

"Leave my trigger finger outside that wrap!"

Now it really hurt. Damn, it hurt! But the feel of her hand as it cradled his wrist, that was good. How warm it lay against the blood veins there. PING! He had told her that he loved her. Now he wanted her to look at him, just look at him. She didn't. Her eyes were downturned, focusing on the bandage.

"How y'all?" Leon said. PING! He stood six feet away in the road beside the wagon, watching them with troubled eyes. "Reckon I got to get MYself shot. Then maybe somebody hold MY hand."

She actually looked at Leon, full into his eyes.

"Be careful," she said, "don't give me away."

"Sergeant Moffat, nobody care if you a woman. We foller you straight to hell."

He stood there slack shouldered, discouraged. PING!

"I thought you were on picket duty," she said.

"Some of'em out yonder shy of musket loads," he explained, and headed for the pack mules to replenish their cartridge boxes. PING!

Billy had tied up the Secesh vedette, bound her hands behind her with rawhide strips and tethered her loosely to a big sycamore beside the road.. She had spat in his face, which just made him smile. Spit didn't bother him. She was so parched she couldn't hawk up much anyhow. He gave her a drink from his canteen. Still, he was curious about the fierce feeling that made her sass people who had reason to kill her. With his hand bandaged properly, feeling better now, he left Lenora and walked over to squat on his haunches before the vedette. Her black eyes burned out on him through a shag of hair pinched under the brim of her hat.

"You a woman. How come you to get in this war?" he asked.

"None your damn BIZ-ness!" He sagged back on his butt and sat crossed legged, imitating her posture. Anyhow, he needed a rest.

PING! A woman burst out from behind the wagon, rubbing her freed wrist, trotting toward the creek.

"That's other people's property y'all stealin!" the vedette said. "Y'all got no right." Billy sat a quiet a moment, and the prisoner sighed: "Would you wipe this hair outa my eyes. I cain't see nothin."

He loosened the chin strap of her forage cap, drew the hair back and tucked it behind her right ear. She seemed to breathe freer then but said:

"I got to pee. Untie me."

"Hell no. You done already killed one of us." Lenora June couldn't help the prisoner pee. She was lost amid the creekbank multitude, working with the people there. "All right," Billy sighed, "come on then." PING!

He helped her stand, led her behind the big tree. There he unbuttoned her breeches and the back flap of her drawers, then braced her shoulders so she wouldn't fall as she squatted. She did need to pee. It hissed out of her, soaking the leaves between her brogans, she sighing, "Oooooh....oooooh...." She had killed his friend, but now she reminded him of Lenora June as a child, pissing beside him in the woods at Highland Forge. Except this butt was fish-belly white in the afternoon sun—not the warm walnut sheen he so fondly remembered.

He buttoned up the vedette, helped her back to her place. As if it were the wild hair, the full bladder, that had stoked her anger, she seemed to relax now, sag back against the sycamore trunk. She just started answering Billy's question.

"My hus-bin got conscripted, so I joined to be with him. He helped dress me up, pretend like I was his brother. Then y'all went and killed him at Jonesboro." PING!

"I sure didn't," Billy said. "I was Georgia Guard then, I was on HIS side at Jonesboro. What killed your hus-bin was General John Bell Hood. He kept chargin us at them Union breastworks, all them field guns throwin cannister. They cut us down, look like oats fallin back of the scythe. That's when I run the other DI-rection."

PING! Under the hat her face slowly reddened.

"You a gaw-damn traitor! You run like a rabbit, left him to fight your battle."

She turned her face away, tears washing pale lines down through the dirt on her cheek. PING!

"You know better'n that," Billy said.

She did know better, she who—like so many others—had called him a traitor. After a minute she turned back and quietly asked:

"Y'all gonna kill me now?" She jerked her head toward the hill across the ford. "For that nigger Yankee I shot up yonder?"

"Reckon not. Let you go after awhile, when you cain't hurt us no more, when we get these slaves freed." PING!

She didn't brighten at that news, just looked glumly around at the land where she would be left. Billy said:

"Your hus-bin got killed, and you went right on fightin for Secesh. How come?"

Now she swapped her glumness for a hot-eyed glare.

"We fightin for honor. We fightin for liberty."

"Liberty for what?" He waved to the milling crowd on the creek bank. "So y'all can keep these folks on a chain? Drag'em crost the country, feed'em weevily biscuit, don't carry no water for'em?"

"That's cause Yankees tryin to steal'em. Y'all just leave us alone down here, nothin like this happen. This gonna be OUR country."

"Whose country?" Billy asked her. "Georgia's MY country too. As much mine as it is yourn." He threw up an arm toward the line of slaves. "How about these folks? How come this ain't THEIR country? They been here longer'n my pa. Hell, my pa come outa Bavaria."

"We fightin for State Rights," the woman said.

"Rights for what? To own slaves?"

"Sure! Slaves are in the Bible. America Constitution give us rights to own'em."

"Do you own any?"

The question seemed to discourage her.

"I never owned nothin. Nor my folks. Best we ever done was farmin on shares."

"Who owned these slaves?" He waved again at the coffle.

"Mister Homer Penick, big plantation 'bout five mile outa Gassville. That's our home town. Mister Penick, he's a friend to General Wheeler, he want us to save his slaves. He was right there, Mister Penick was, a-helpin us get'em lined up on the coffle."

156

"How old is Mister Penick?"

"He about thirty. I know what you thinkin, twenty-nigger law and all that. Nossir, Mister Penick, he don't go to the war. But somebody's got to look after them niggers. Mister Penick, he's a gent-man. And does lots for us farmin' folks." PING!

She turned her head awkwardly aside to wipe muddy tears on her coat collar, and again looked at him.

"One of these days I might own somethin. Buy me slaves if I can. I worked all my life. I get tired of workin. Don't you?"

"Sure, kinda work they got where I come from."

She leaned forward and spoke quietly to him.

"You Georgia born. How come you runnin with this bunch of niggers?" PING!

Somehow Billy had never understood that Lenora June was a nigger, had nearly forgotten that detail about the others, more and more thinking of them as Ben, Leon, Ike, Aaron and Hubert. He recalled Ben and his struggle to learn reading, Ben, still lying unburied up on that hillside, and felt his choler rise against this woman.

"YOU Georgia born!" he yelled. "How come YOU runnin with these Secesh robbers, stealin country people blind, taking all their food?" PING!

That touched her. She jerked back against the sycamore trunk.

"We don't take it all. Soldiers gotta eat too." Tears rose once more in her eyes, her face darkened again with blood and she shouted: "How come YOU pickin on me? And me all tied up. It ain't fair!"

The outburst attracted attention. Aaron turned from his work at the wagon tire. Slaves in the coffle stared at them. Behind him now, Lenora June spoke one word.

"Billy?"

"Sure, sure..." He waved blindly back to appease her. He groaned, heaving himself to his feet, and looked down at the vedette. "You right about that, it ain't fair," he told her. "Sorry. I'm right sorry."

Arms pulled painfully behind her, she stared down at her lap, tears dripping, spotting her gray trouser legs.

"I'm sorry too. He's the first one I ever killed. I'm sorry I killed that man. It's just a misery. Ain't it a misery!"

By now Aaron was back at work with his hammer PING! A girl skipped out from the coffle, raising her wrist, smiling up as she held it against the sky.

By day's end the wounded Confederate was able sit a horse. They lifted him onto the saddle of a husky Percheron culled from among the captured. Lenora boosted the woman vedette up behind him and placed the reins in her hands.

"No need to let this kill him," she told the woman. "Get him into a town. Find a surgeon for him."

The woman only nodded agreement and started the horse slowly away down the hill toward the road. They carried Ben's stiffened body to the hilltop, where the view was good to the curving creek and what would soon be a sunset. From there Billy could see peeled white forms of the Confederates on the slope and on the creekbank below, where freed people had dragged them from the water. They had stripped them first of shoes, then other garments to wear against the cold. Most of the former slaves had already left, walking south toward the protection of Sherman's army. The wagon, loaded with those too weak to walk, was just now rolling out with their column.

Together Billy and Aaron dug all the grave they could, about three feet of one, before they struck rock. Over Ben in his grave they laid a Union overcoat, reclaimed from a dead Confederate, who himself no doubt had taken it from fallen blueback.

Of course they all wanted to hear the Twenty-third Psalm. Billy held Lenora's Bible open before him but spoke the passage word by word from memory, looking down the slope, wondering whether the poem's comfort counted not only for Ben but also for those stripped Peckerwood bodies. When he finished, Lenora took the book and flipped through to a different page. With the blue of the eastern sky behind her, she squinted against blazing sunset yellow and read:

"This is an evil among all things that are done under the sun, that there is one event unto all. Yea, also the heart of the sons of men is full of evil and madness is in their heart while they live, and after that they go to the dead. For to him that is joined to all the living, there is hope, for a living dog is better than a dead lion. For the living know that they shall die, but the dead know not any thing, neither have they any more a reward, for the memory of them is forgotten, also their love and their hatred and their envy."

The words, like a stone in his chest, made it hard for Billy to breathe. He could hear the labored breathing of others around him. She turned the page to another passage and read again:

"And desire shall fail, because man goeth to his long home, and the mourners go about the streets. Or ever the silver cord be loosed, or the golden bowl be broken, or the pitcher be broken at the fountain, or the wheel broken at the cistern. Then shall the dust return to the earth as it was, and the spirit shall return unto God who gave it."

If the Psalm had comforted them, Ecclesiastes broke them down. Embarrassed, they turned away from each other, walking out through the brown grass, blowing noses, wiping eyes. Broke them down and made them weep at last over Ben's death,and begin to get past it. After awhile, after much breathing and sighing, Leon swung around on them and said:

"We got to get this man under the ground."

18

Should We the youngest and brightest nation of all the earth bow to the traters and forsake the graves of our Fathers? No no never never.
—letter by Union soldier Joseph Fardell to his Illinois family, July 11, 1863.

THE MIND ONCE ENLIGHTENED *CAN* again become dark. It *can*. These words, echoing in her thoughts as the squad rode away from Ben's grave, infected her with an unaccountable fever to teach reading. Could reading roll back the shadow that swept Ben from life? Of course not. But teaching it to her fellow Negroes would at least transgress Georgia law. There was that to say for it. After supper that night she lighted the two lanterns, swept a patch of dirt free of litter and called them around. They came reluctantly.

"We right tired," sighed Hubert Smallwood.

"Hubert, you can be first. Write your name for us."

This he did easily with a sharpened stick, H-U-B-E-R-T. They could all write their names now, would never again have to sign with a mark. They could write each other's names, knew all the letters in each one, and how those letters fit into the ABCs. She lay one hand on the pyramid of their stacked weapons and under Hubert's name, aligning each letter, she wrote M-U-S-K-E-T.

"That's musket!" Ike shouted. "How come that U don't sound the same, like HU-bert?"

"It's just English," Lenora told him. "Same letters can sound different. Got to put up with it."

"K sound just the same," Ike said, "same as in IKE."

She went around the circle asking for words beginning with the letters scrawled in the dirt. She heard "hosses, trees, money, Union, invade, robber, thief, blood, kill," and, from Billy, "slay." The grim word choices daunted her a little, made her drop the question-answer method. She got out the blueback speller and worked with them awhile from that.

Wary of vengeance from Wheeler's cavalry, they had camped on a hilltop with wide views in every direction. Their balloon of lamplight pushed up into a vast sky, which the waning moon brightened only a little. Great drifts of stars shone through. Yet compared to that sky, the dark land southward was starred more densely with the campfires of Sherman's army, fueled by the fence rails of a hundred farms. After one chapter of the speller, Lenora saw Billy yawn. Aaron said:

"That's enough teachin. Now read us somethin good."

She had actually seen *Romeo and Juliet* performed as a play in Pennsylvania but never before had read it, or owned it. She dug the limp volume from her haversack. She relished the feel of its suede front cover but was daunted a little by the gilt face of Tragedy imprinted on it. Of course, she recalled the play's action. She'd forgotten the prologue, which took her by surprise when she read it as poetry.

"Two households both alike in dignity,

in fair Verona where we lay our scene,

from ancient grudge break to new mutiny,

where civil blood makes civil hands unclean."

She paused, struggling to understand it, and then read on.

"From forth the fatal loins of these two foes,

a pair of star-crossed lovers take their life,

whose misadventured piteous overthrows,

doth with their death bury their parents' strife."

They all looked at her, confused but wanting more. Robber, thief, blood, kill, slay, now finally death and bury. Two families, black against white? Union against Confederate? Star-crossed lovers in misadventured overthrows. She cleared her throat, took a breath, meaning to give them more. Instead, she croaked:

"I'm tired too. Let's stop for tonight."

She was very tired, yet lay a long time awake, turned on her left side, looking out across a dim landscape where Union campfires were burning low, beginning to wink out. The moon had crawled halfway down the western sky. When they were little, she and Billy often watched the moon, discussed the features of the man in it, pointing out what might be his nose, his eyes. They would sneak out at night, creep into the flat-bottomed work boat and, with an oar, skid it down onto the millpond. They lay side by side on a bottom grid of boards, their feet thrown up across a thwart, the boat turning slowly on the dark water.

"Thass the Drinkin Gourd," she told him once, pointing out seven bright stars hanging well down in the northern sky.

"Ain't neither," he said. "You know it ain't. Thass the Big Dipper."

"Drinkin' Gourd," she said. "If you foller the Drinkin Gourd, you gets freedom."

"Freedom from what?"

Well, if he didn't know, she wasn't going to tell him. But, tunelessly, she sang the song:

When the sun come back and the first quail call,
Foller the Drinkin Gourd.
For the ole man's a-waitin for to carry you to freedom
If you foller the Drinkin Gourd.

"How come you waitin till the sun come back?" he demanded. "If it's daylight and all, you cain't even see them stars."

"You can see'em at night. Then, when the sun come back, you walks towards the Drinkin Gourd. You just walks North. North!"

Beside her in the boat bottom, he heaved a mighty sigh.

"Don't you be follerin no dang Drinkin Gourd. Ain't it nice right here? Ain't this fun?"

It *was* fun, that part of it. Even now, even through the woe of a savage day, the recollection made her smile. Billy, tight wrapped in his blanket and rubber waterproof, lay within reach of her hand, though she did not extend it. She saw the moon glint on his open eye.

"Billy?"

"Uh huh," he answered.

"You can't sleep either."

"Must be I was waitin for you to sleep."

His wispy beard was coming back, cobwebby now where moonlight struck it.

"Billy, if we went away together after this campaign, where could we go?"

His form heaved up, dark against the starry field of dying campfires. He rested on one elbow, his face inclining toward her.

"We could go up into them north Georgia mountains, maybe on into that Blue Ridge. Up yonder they don't like this damn Confederacy."

"They don't like colored, either."

"Lenora, we can find a preacher to marry us, all them preachers cain't be bad. Or jump backwards over a broom, way so many of'em do. Damn if I care how. I *want* you. We could get up yonder in them mountains, pretend you my con-ke-bine. They don't mind colored con-ke-bines."

"I don't want to be a concubine."

"You know you ain't gonna be that to me. Or we could go to Kansas. They's abolitionists out yonder."

"They don't want slaves because they don't want colored," she said.

"No! Some of'em good people. You told me about bleedin Kansas, them abolitionists fightin to make it a free state. Get out yonder, we plant us a vineyard and grow them tender grapes, like Solomon talked about. Grow them pommer-grannies, too."

"Pomegranates, Billy," Lenora June sighed. "They're *pomegranates.*"

"Sure! That's what I was sayin. We can grow'em yonder. Kansas is a good place. Ain't no place perfect."

She felt a smile grow again on her own face.

"You're right, Billy. It sure ain't perfect."

His left hand flew to his mouth, covering it as Billy mimed his dismay.

"Oh, Lenora June," he said, "you who read so well. You can speak better English than that."

Beyond him, another form rose from the earth to blot out yet more of that starry campfire landscape.

"We goin' to KAN-sas, is we?" said Leon Duffy. "Oh yeah, that's fine by me!"

19

Let every man fly to arms. Remove your Negroes, horses, cattle and provisions from Sherman's army, and burn what you cannot carry. Burn all bridges, and block up the roads on his route. Assail the invader in front, flank and rear!
—1864 declaration by Georgia's delegation at the Confederate Congress.

Uneasily, Lenora noted that this plantation house had the look of a fortress—a two-story cube of heavy squared logs, surrounded on three sides by deep porches. The solid porch railings alone could conceal a squad of crouching sharpshooters. The noonday sun, casting deep shadows under the porch roofs, made it doubly threatening. The many windows on first and second floors could provide firing embrasures for a platoon of infantry. If her squad were caught in the house yard, they could all be shot down

After Ben was killed, among themselves they had discussed tactics, dividing the squad into two parts, first part being Ike and Billy with his rapid-firing Spencer, second the musket-armed group including Sergeant Moffat along with Leon and the Smallwood brothers. Minutes before, they had tethered the horses in a thicket. Now, crouched behind a holly grove at roadside, Sergeant Moffat told them they would advance by units and at quick time. The part held back would be ready to cover the other's advance with gunfire.

"Go!" she ordered. Billy and Ike scurried fifty yards forward and took cover behind a derelict platform wagon, missing both wheels on one side. "Now us!" she hissed to the others, leading them at a hard run to the scant concealment of a low-branched magnolia, the ground under it littered with huge stiff leaves. She signaled another advance by Billy's group. Soon they were all together, crouched close under the front porch railing, Billy struggling to whisper through his puffing.

"What-all you reckon is that noise?"

His hearing had always been acute, but Lenora also began to hear the slow beating rhythm.

"Pat----pat----pat----pat----pat..."

He crawled forward through a bed of dormant flags, crawled to the stairs and rose to his knees, staring up onto the porch floor. Instantly, the tempo picked up, grew louder.

"PAT-PAT-PAT-PAT-PAT..."

Billy rose to his feet and waved her forward. She kept her musket leveled as she reached the stairs and saw a fat old black-and-tan hound stretched out in the sun on the porch floor. Billy's appearance had brought forth nothing more than the faster tail tempo, but, sensing Lenora, the hound troubled himself to raise his head and glance good naturedly at her over his scabby shoulder.

"PAT-PAT-PAT-PAT-PAT..."

She went slowly up, at the top stepping over the dog onto the boards. To her right, suspended on chains from the ceiling, was a porch swing well padded with cushions. In it lay a white man, grizzled and gray whiskered, asleep on his left side under a light blanket, pillowing his cheek on an open hand.

"Sir," she said. She moved close and touched his denim jacket. "Sir."

He cleared his throat and coughed. He sat up, rubbing his eyes. He seemed just a little surprised.

"Well, I thought y'all would come, heard all about Sherman coming, supposed to be only a matter of time. Dang stupid anyhow, them startin this war. I just didn't expect Nigra Yankees, that's all."

"Yessir, " Lenora said. "We've come to free your slaves."

"Well, sure. They're right close," he said, "a-nappin yonder in the Quarters. Except Sundays, we work from sun to sun, but we all take a little nap after dinner."

He stuffed his stockinged feet into high-topped shoes placed below the swing and began tugging at the laces, tying them. A white woman appeared in the house door, of ample frame but not fat, nowhere near as fat as her hound. Her face was wrinkled somewhat by age but more by folds of the sheet on which she'd been napping. She lay the back of her hand to her forehead and stared out under it toward the Nigra bluebacks who now inhabited her front porch.

"Francis, looks like we got company. Why didn't you call me?"

He waved her question away and posed one for Lenora.

"Speakin of dinner, y'all get any yet? Reckon y'all will take it anyhow. We may as well just serve it up. Throw some kindlin in your stove, Milly. We got that roasted mutton quarter, and let's fix a mess of biscuits for these folks. Little sorghum syrup on'em, some of that clover honey."

It was the first meal in months any of the squad had eaten at table, not to say at a table like this one. They washed at the pump in the back yard, then took their places as if initiates at some sacred rite. Among them only Lenora had ever sat at such a table, and her single previous experience had come at an abolitionist home in Philadelphia. The thick linen tablecloth was white, the China pale blue ringed with pink roses, the flatware elegant but only silver plate—so said Millicent Forcheveaux, perhaps hoping they wouldn't take it with them when they left.

Such hospitality from a Confederate household seemed too good to be true. Lenora considered the possibility that they would be poisoned. She dismissed it and sent Ike to the pack mules for what would be the squad's only contribution, a pound of coffee beans from federal kitchen wagons. Master Forcheveaux's horny hand trembled as he held the dainty cup and slurped his first genuine elixir since the Union blockade stopped the import of such frivolities. It was a magnificent meal, astonishing in its contrast, Lenora realized, with those being set on sharecropper tables not a mile distant.

The plantation slaves—all fourteen of them—flooded in, yawning and stretching, to help their mistress serve and to admire the U. S. Colored Infantry. Male and female, they fluttered about the table, placing full dishes and removing empty ones, refilling water glasses, repeatedly touching the squad members as they dined. A man plucked a bit of straw from Lenora's uniform sleeve, letting his hand trail up her arm to caress the gold sergeant's stripes. A woman leaned in to set a drum of sweet cream butter on the table, steadying herself by laying a hand at the collar of Leon's jacket. He smiled up at her, but she was already gone, petting this one and that one as she moved around the table. Lenora felt honored that merely seeing Negro American soldiers could make them proud and happy. They were not so pleased with their master.

"You had your dinner this noon, Master Francis," a woman server said. "Now here you go, piggin that mutton down. All this fat meat ain't good for your puky gizzard."

"He knows it, of course he knows it," said the young man who stood behind the master's chair. "He do it anyway."

The man stepped forward, reaching for his master's plate. Francis gripped the pink-rose rim with both hands and looked pleadingly up at him.

"Now, Jules, she roasted one fine haunch of mutton, Lucille did, and I want two bites. That's all."

"You mean two *more*," Millicent said from across the table, "because at this sitting you already had about ten."

But when she shrugged, Jules stepped back to his place behind the chair. Master Francis forked in a bite, touched the napkin primly to his lips and changed the subject.

"I see by the Savannah paper that President Jeff Davis is hollering for us Georgians to pile onto Sherman's army. Now you Union boys are down here, we supposed to assail y'all front, flank and rear, like the peasants did Napoleon in that Russian winter. Get y'all surrounded in the wilderness. We supposed to starve out Sherman's troops and utterly destroy'em. In all of your travels, have you boys seen any sign of your troops starving?"

Lenora, who had just bitten into a hot biscuit dripping with butter and honey, was in no shape to answer. Billy swallowed down a bite of mutton and spoke up.

"Nawsir, don't seem much like we surrounded. Nor destroyed. Don't seem like we starvin, neither."

"Of course this Georgia winter is nothing like that Russian winter," opined Master Forcheveaux. "Maybe that's the reason."

Lenora June replaced her napkin on the table and rose.

"Mr. and Mrs. Forcheveaux, we thank you for this marvelous dinner. Please take care that it is not your own last meal. Sherman's whole army is a half-day's march behind us. They will eat out your house and your smokehouse and your barn. I suggest you hide some stores of food in the woods."

For all their pleasure in meeting the U. S. Colored Infantry, the Forcheveaux slaves didn't seem to want the freedom being offered. After dinner Jules struggled to explain it to squad members as he sat on a sagging wicker chair outside the door of his cabin in the Quarters.

"Naw, Master Francis, there was a few times he tried to be like them other masters. Them other masters round about, they all the time whoopin the servants, throw'em in stocks, leave'em outside a week at a time, sell'em to some damn slave speculator. From what I hear, Master Francis' daddy do that too, he was just mean. And Master Francis *tried* to be like his daddy."

He sat forward, looking down at the dirt between his knees, a chuckle rumbling in his chest. Others among the dozen slaves standing with the squad grinned, more at Jules himself than the story he was telling. They already knew the story.

"Here ten year back, I got real bad, all time fightin, sneakin off from work, stealin stuff. Once I stole Master Francis' pig, traded him for a jug, got drunk, didn't go out to the field when he blow the horn. Master Francis decide he whip me, like them other masters do."

A woman stepped into the light at the open cabin door behind Jules, her long skirt swinging, two children shyly pressing their faces into it, then beaming smiles at Lenora and Billy.

"That time you sure need it," the woman said. "Whoopin do you good."

Without looking back at her, he raised his hand, waggling it before her face.

"Ruth, let me tell my story."

"It my story too." But she shut up and let her man talk.

"Well, Master Francis, he hit me once kinda easy with that buggy whip. I howls, I jumps, I squalls. Hit me second time, I just swoons to the dirt. My eyes wide open, me kinda jerkin on the ground, then I close eyes and get real still. And Miz Millicent, she say, 'Francis! Francis, look what you done, you killed our Jules!' They carry me straight to the couch in that dinin room, right where y'all had dinner today. I laid yonder two weeks a-gettin well real slow, didn't chop no cotton, didn't milk no cows, never ate so good in all my life."

"That's where I came in," Ruth said. "I was the one fed 'im. How we got to know one another so well." She lay a hand on Jules' close-cropped head. "Start of all my troubles."

A ripple of laughter ran through the people, who stood warming themselves on winter sun reflected from the bricks of the cabin. An old grayhead, squatting with his back against the bricks, jabbed a finger at Jules.

"That youngin, he took the worst whoopin Master Francis ever put out, the first, last and only."

Amused, the slaves eyed one another, well pleased.

"So, Master Francis doesn't whip you," Lenora said. "Is that reason to be a slave?"

Her question drained Jules' story of its enjoyment, flattened the smiles on their faces. Ruth stepped forward to stand beside her husband, lay a hand on his shoulder.

"Naw, now, what I liked was the way Master Francis get us married," Ruth said. "With these other masters, it's jumpin backwards over a broom, that's all it is. Or maybe preacher say the words, but not all of'em. Then when a speculator come down the road, master might sell the wife one DI-rection, husband goin different way, chil-ren somewheres else. Never see each other again. When the white preacher come to marry me and Jules, he didn't read all them words. Master Francis open the book way back, he say, 'Read *all* them words.' So preacher did, he read'em, 'What God has joined together, let no man put asunder.' I never forget them words."

Jules' left hand snaked out of his chair and smacked his wife lightly on the rump. Then the arm hugged her ample hips. Lenora marveled that they didn't see the problem.

"But everything depends on Master Francis," she said. "If he changes, if he has to sell you, or if he dies and leaves you to someone else in his will..."

Old grayhead shook his head discouragingly.

"These niggers runnin off to freedom, they think they gonna be richer than white folks. They think freedom make'em that way, cause they stronger and know how to work, and whites don't. But it ain't like that. Freedom make folks proud, but it don't make'em rich."

Leon, who had been standing far back, now shouldered forward through the crowd. With a flattened hand he slapped the breast of his uniform.

"A good master owned me up in South Carolina," Leon said. "Good as masters get anyhow. My paw was a tanner, tanned hides to make saddle, harness and like that. Even make shoes. Master Jack, he paid pa good for overwork, when daddy worked nights and Sundays. Master let daddy BUY me outa slavery. I didn't have to run away. I was seventeen year old then, might sell for a thousand dollar on the market in Columbia. Master Jack, he's a good man, he charge my daddy four hunnerd for me, and I was free. I went to DE-troit. That was 1858. Been free ever since. I ain't rich, but got good wages tanning hides up yonder, toolin leather for saddles."

Grinning, the old man pointed a finger at the brass buttons on Leon's chest.

"How come you back down here, and a-wearin that blue coat?"

Leon stood shaking his head, frowning at the ground.

"Just take any old animal, bluejay, rabbit, possum. Treat it good and feed it good—then open that cage. He'll run right out, run back to them woods. Animals got sense. I come down here to free the slaves. If I get the chance, I free my daddy and mama, I free my sisters."

Lenora thought it a powerful argument, but it only seemed to provoke Jules. He jerked up from the wicker chair, grabbed his wife's hand and tugged her back into the darkness of the cabin, their children trailing after. Maybe Leon's words had offended him. Certainly it made the others uneasy. They milled around, murmuring among themselves, beginning to drift away. Billy sidled up to her and spoke under his breath.

"Good dinner, but I reckon that's about it. We ain't makin no headway here."

The other squad members had already slipped away to feed the horses on rich grain stores in the barn. By now the sun had a pretty good slant. She wanted to find decent water before they stopped for the night. She and Billy had started toward the barn when Jules popped out of the cabin door. They turned back to him as he addressed Lenora.

"Sergeant, that Private Leon, he said what he's doing down here. Are the rest of y'all doing the same?"

"Yes. We came to free slaves."

Good humored and grinning before, Jules was now grim faced.

"I ain't no bluejay," he said, "I ain't no possum, I don't care for that runnin-off kinda freedom anyhow, like just runnin off in them woods. But I want join up with y'all, do what y'all doing. I want join the U. S. Colored Infantry."

Behind him in the cabin door stood Ruth, tears striping her cheeks in gleaming lines.

God may have joined them together, Lenora thought, but man—and man's war—could cleave them asunder. Master Francis would not give his Enfield musket to Jules; he wanted Jules to *take* it.

"Won't go down good with the neighbors if I start arming the U. S. Colored Infantry," he explained.

Jules, of course, didn't want to take it. In the plantation house front hall, Billy reached up to the gun rack and pulled it down—a standard rifled musket, but embellished with inlay and silver fittings on the walnut stock, quite beautiful. He lay the musket in Jules' hands.

"Thankee, Master Francis," Jules breathed.

"Jules, we about past the master stuff by now. Have been for some while. Wish I'd seen it quicker."

Millicent stepped forward to lay a hand on Jules shoulder.

"We gonna look after your Ruth. Just take care of yourself." The woman's bright blue eyes then stared into Lenora. "He was raised on our place. Don't get him killed."

"Maam, we do our best to avoid that."

Still lying on the front porch, the hound had heard their discussion through the unlatched front door. He nosed the door open and ambled down the hall toward them, swaying side to side with his tail wag, claws clicking on the waxed oak.

"Francis, you get your dirty ole hound outa my clean house!"

Master Francis raised a commanding arm, pointing at the door.

"Romeo! You get back yonder to that porch. Hear me? You GET now, Romeo!"

Encouraged by the sound of his name, the grinning hound came on, wagging more enthusiastically. Jules looked apologetically at the mistress of the house.

"I catch'im, Miz Millicent." He laid a hand against the hound's muzzle, turned him and, carrying his musket at shoulder arms, marched him back toward the door. He grinned down at Romeo. "You just a damn ole fool," he told the animal, wagging his own rear in imitation of the hound's. "You ain't nothin but a fool!"

Billy stood in the hallway smiling after the departing dog.

"Don't old Romeo look like a slave hound?" he said. "Reckon we ought to shoot him?"

The squad spent that evening in camp teaching Jules how to load and prime his musket, struggling to decide for themselves how well he filled the breach left by Ben's death.

20

The power of the master must be absolute to render the submission of the slave perfect...The slave, to remain a slave, must be made sensible that there is no appeal from his master; that his power is in no instance usurped; but is conferred by the laws of man at least, if not by the laws of God.
—Justice Thomas Ruffin of the North Carolina Supreme Court in the case of State *vs.* Mann, ruling against indicting a master for battery on a slave.

SOME BAND OF FORAGERS, BUMMERS, bandits, thieves—whatever they were—had gone ahead of them through this stretch of country. The squad rode into what had been a prosperous crossroads village of a few dozen houses, finding three of the biggest burned, still smoldering. A covey of hissing housecats fled at their approach. When they dismounted, a skinny feist dog made furious barking charges at their ankles, forcing them to dance away.

A postoffice there had been kicked open and stripped. Doors of most houses hung wide. Windows were broken, curtains streaming on the wind. What looked to be the finest of the houses still stood unburned. Against one wall of its parlor was a pump organ, the porcelain knobs above its keyboard proclaiming the qualities they had evoked in its music, Trebel Forte, Dulcet, Melodia, Celeste. But no more. Someone had smashed the organ with an ax. There was no food in the houses, no people and, to Lenora June's relief, no dead bodies either.

Under gray morning skies, hunkered on their mounts against a fresh wind from the south, the squad rode southeastward on a road marked with a single set of wagon tracks. Weed-choked fields lay on both sides, no crops, just broken, rotted cornstalks left from the year before. This year, the fourth of the war, these fields had gone unplanted. She saw Billy lean down from his mount to study the dirt of the road.

"Must be some people in the wagon," he told her. "Maybe five or six more ridin horses ahead of it."

Soon she saw a torn white envelope on the red clay between the wagon ruts, then another. She rode awhile before noticing the third. The interval between envelopes became twenty yards, then ten, then five. Someone in the wagon had opened letters from the postoffice, perhaps searching for money, and tossed them out. Riding beside her, Billy drew his bayonet, leaned far down from his mount and speared one. Using his left hand rather than the bandaged right, he offered it to her on the bayonet point.

The envelope, plastered with three Confederate stamps, was addressed to "Corpal E. R. Gist, 49 Georgia Inf Reg, Richmon, Virginny CSA" It still enclosed the letter, a single page written on the lined backside of a old grocery bill.

> Dec 5 1864
> Emmanuel
> Cum hom plees Liz get dipthera Yu ma die They tuk the hawgs, kilt ole Jers an butcher her No milk now for youngins I got no help Cum hom
>
> Maybelle

"What's it say?" Billy asked.

She handed the sheet across as they rode. Reading it sentence by sentence, Billy seemed to take on Maybelle's woes, sagging bodily in the saddle.

"Oh boy," he sighed, "when's this gonna be over!"

"When the Confederates quit," she said. She glanced again at Billy. That he could be so distressed at the plight of his precious Peckerwoods—it made her like him better. The trail of letters on the road seemed endless. The pages rattled in wind, some blowing off to hang in bushes at the side. Toward noon the wagon track, with its wake of letters, turned off the main road onto a rocky trail. Jules, now riding the best mount in their little herd—a thoroughbred offered by Francis Forcheveaux—followed the tracks onto the trail.

"Whoa!" Lenora said. "Jules, where you going?"

He reined his mount in, letting it dance sideways. In his slave cloth garments, he looked like a civilian and was acting like one.

"Gonna foller that wagon," he said.

"In the U. S. Colored Infantry," she said, "you don't follow wagons. You follow orders. Or you ask. You *ask* me before you go."

Listening to her own words, she was surprised at their tone. She'd heard this before at Highland Forge and the Hunnicutt plantation. Master Lenora June, is that what she'd become? At least she didn't whip her subordinates. And Jules didn't seem offended.

"Can I foller that wagon?" he said.

Well, it wasn't a bad idea.

"We'll all go," she told him.

She sent Billy ahead as vedette and they rode warily on between twiggy, low-hanging branches, once again smelling smoke on the wind—not the tang of firewood but instead the rank odor of painted wood burning. Not a quarter mile along, peering ahead down the road, they found the source. It was a clapboard farmhouse apparently abandoned. The fire was fresh, licking up from the windows, chewing at the shingled eaves above. Whoever set it was not far off. She ordered the squad to dismount, leaving Aaron to hold the horses. They went forward, weapons ready. The road widened into a clearing, house on the right, a big barn on the left with weedy farm fields spreading out behind.

The wagon that had made the tracks, its horses still in harness, heads down, stood in front of the open barn doors. Its bed was piled high with booty—fancy chairs and tables, rolled carpets, oil paintings, tapestries, parlor lamps and more. Six horses, tethered beyond the wagon in a persimmon thicket, raised their heads inquiringly at the squad's approach. From the barn came two clearly-shouted words:

"No! No!" Then a muted, plaintive murmur Lenora couldn't make out.

She signaled for the others to hold back while she and Billy advanced. They went quietly to a rough hole cut in the siding, where a weathered shutter hung open on rusty hinges. Just inside was a milking stanchion and stall, rich with cow smell. Beyond it, in the center aisle of the barn, stood several men variously uniformed. Lenora counted three blue, four gray. An elegantly-gowned young woman stood on a hay mound, backed up against a timber supporting post. In one hand she held a spike bayonet, pointing it at gut level toward the encircling men. The youngest of these, a peach-cheeked young Reb, was pleading with her.

"We done left your auntie's house a-standin back yonder," he said. "We didn't burn it like them others, cause you *promised*. Now you got to show us somethin."

"I kept my promise," the woman hissed. "I showed it to y'all. I did!"

"Got to be more'n one damn ankle!" shouted an older fellow wearing Union army corporal's stripes. "We see more'n that with you just walkin around."

"Do you think me a harlot? You think I would dis-HONOR myself like some Delilah, some Bathsheba or Jezebel? No! But I will keep my promise."

Defiantly, she thrust out a leg and lifted the hem of her skirt, revealing a button-top shoe and four inches of black-stockinged calf. As if in despair, the yankee threw his arms out, swung around and walked away.

"Been two year since I seen anythin under woman clothes," said a gray-clad fellow wearing sergeant's stripes. "Seem like a real Confedrate lady ought to lift a soldier's spirits. Come on now, give us a peek."

"Alas, you're no soldier!" She thrust the bayonet toward the man, who took one step backward. "You're a deserter like these Yankees. Y'all are just bummers stealing the property of honest patriots. I'd expect that of these blue Lincolnites, but y'all are from the sovereign state of Georgia. You defile the HONOR of the South!"

This seemed to discourage the whole lot. They looked at each other, shrugging shoulders, stuffing hands into pockets. Peach Fuzz stepped forward again.

"Sergeant Ebbert, he did see a woman two year back. He's actual *seen* one. I ain't never in my life seen anythin under woman clothes.

You promised us back yonder in that town. I been hopin on seeing somethin."

Her pale, long-fingered hand fluttered to her throat, sliding downward then into lace at the cleft bodice of her ball gown.

"Well...." she sighed. "Just for you then. But the rest of y'all must avert your eyes."

The others didn't avert their eyes. Neither did Billy. Lenora could hear his coarse breathing. His head was thrust forward through the window, gazing on the scene inside. She socked him on the shoulder and gestured for him to follow. The Confederate lady had reached only the third hook and eye from the top when the U. S. Colored Infantry appeared at both ends of the barn's center aisle. The bummers noticed the intrusion only when the hammers of seven weapons snapped back to the cocked position. The Confederate sergeant's fingers hovered briefly over the revolver at his belt, then floated upward to scratch the back of his head. Peach Fuzz jerked spasmodically toward a musket leaning on a barn post, only to be blocked by the older Yankee.

"No, no, son, don't be foolish." The Yankee then turned and smiled at the newcomers.

"Howdy!" he said. "We sure glad to see them blue coats. But us Union men"—he gestured to the two Yankee privates—"we just about got these Rebs under control."

Seconds later the bummers, blue and gray alike, lay face-down on the dirt floor, being searched in detail. Neglected for the moment, the Confederate lady still stood on the hay mound, taking it in. One hand flew up to cover her mouth.

"Oh, no! Oh, God, Nigras! Nigra Yankees! God pre-SERVE me!"

The searchers found wads of money taken from the mail, Confederate shinplasters that by now would purchase little. On the men and in the barn they found a wealth of weapons, savage-looking Bowie knives, another Spencer repeater, which Lenora took for herself, and enough revolvers to give every squad member at least one repeating firearm. The pockets of the Rebel sergeant yielded five gold watches. Lenora passed them out to her privates, saving the fattest to dangle on its chain before Leon Duffy's shining eyes. Leon swung his hands back, clasping them behind him as if renouncing temptation.

"Nawsir, Sergeant Moffat, we ain't no thieves. We better than that. Rest of our lives we got to be BETTER!"

She couldn't help but smile stupidly back at him.

"We're not stealing, Leon, we're recovering stolen property." She drew the watch slowly away from him. "Still, by refusing, there's no question but what you're doing the right thing."

His hands jerked out to grab it. He took the watch reverently, shook it, held it to his ear. With the bummers divested of their property, she ordered them to stand and take off their clothes.

"All of'em?" inquired the Yankee corporal.

"ALL!" Lenora shouted. "Get to it!"

They began to shed garments. Lenora threw the blue corporal's coat to Leon.

"With Ben gone," she said, "this squad could use a corporal. But don't count on getting corporal pay."

With coat and trousers and shirt stripped off, the Confederate sergeant stood shivering in his long Johns, looking down at his feet.

"Y'all ain't gonna steal our shoes?"

"Those are federal shoes," Lenora said. "You took'em off a Union soldier."

"Naw, now, y'all CAIN'T keep our shoes."

"Take your clothes off! Take'em off! Other people need them more than you." Again she heard it in her own voice, Master Lenora June, equal to any plantation overseer. Billy lay a hand on her arm.

"Now, Sergeant Moffat, we got to let'em keep their drawers."

"Sure," she sighed. "They are Peckerwoods, after all."

Reduced step by step from their previous state of wealth, the bummers seemed relieved at the long john decision.

"Oh, dear Jesus, take me from this place!" the Confederate lady wailed. "Jesus, take me home!"

Lenora had forgotten all about the woman, still on her hay mound, who now extended a beseeching hand to the bummers.

"Help me," she said, "y'all must save me from these Nigras!"

"How we gonna do that?" asked the Confederate sergeant.

Now the woman looked right past Billy, the white lieutenant, looked straight into the eyes of the colored sergeant.

"You Nigras will not rape me!" she cried She turned the bayonet, laying its point just under her breasts. "I will die first. This dagger will rescue me, as the asp did Cleopatra."

"Nobody wants to rape you, miss," Lenora said. "As for me, I wouldn't touch you with the far end of a black locust fence rail."

Since their own uniforms and shoes were showing wear, the squad members took for their own the best the bummers had to offer. On his first full day with the U. S. Colored Infantry, Jules won a complete Yankee uniform, taking it from a Union private. Everything else, every scrap, went into the wagon. The Confederate sergeant asked Billy if they could warm themselves at the burning house.

"Sure," Billy said. "Kind of a shame y'all burned it. You coulda used a few things outa there."

In stockinged feet they trotted across, Billy and Lenora walking behind them to prevent any mischief. Heat stopped them ten yards back as the fire crested the shingled roofpeak, throwing gouts of ash up into the gray sky. The men stood shivering, first facing the blaze, then turning to warm their backsides. Billy said:

"How'd you boys meet up, anyways, Secesh and Yankee?"

The Confederate sergeant shrugged.

"We was all out foragin for grub. We start talkin to these Yanks crost a creek. They had real bean coffee, and we had tobacky plugs. Made a good swap. We was tired of fightin anyhow. We larked around together right nice for awhile there. Looks like y'all done spoilt our fun."

With everything else ready, Ike Spears climbed onto the wagon seat to drive. His own mount and the entire string of bummer horses trailed behind it on leads. Now the Confederate lady emerged from the barn. She gazed woefully at the long-johned bummers sunning themselves before the burning house. Lenora had just whistled the column forward when the woman's hand hooked Billy's boot in its stirrup.

"Y'all can't leave me here!" She stared pleadingly up at him.

Billy looked at Lenora, who shrugged.

"Sure!" he said. "Climb up on that wagon seat."

Though she lowered her voice, Lenora heard.

"Beside that *Nigra*?"

"His name is Ike. You sure welcome to walk."

Ike must have heard it too. Still, he reached a hand down and hauled her up, a perfumed heap of cameos, pearl-buttoned taffeta, ribbons, ruffles and Maltese lace—this day, luckily for them all, without the hoop petticoat under her many skirts.

21

The Southern people come of that race...recognized as Cavaliers...directly
descended from the Norman Barons of William the Conqueror, a race
distinguished in its earliest history for its warlike and fearless character,
a race in all times since renowned for its gallantry, chivalry, honor,
gentleness and intellect
> —the Southern Literary Messenger, June, 1860.

HER STORY GUSHED FORTH AS the wagon rolled. Her name was
Desdemona Pierpont. She'd been visiting at her aunt's house
in Spotswood, the little town with the postoffice, when the bummers
appeared on the road to the west. The town was half abandoned
anyway. Others, including her aunt, fled in carriages or on horseback.
But Desdemona refused. She donned every stitch of clothing in her
luggage to defend it, and perhaps her own body, from violation.

"I did not fly," she said. "No more was I daunted by those savages
than was Eleanor of Castile by the Saracens. I faced them down. And
they dared not burn Aunt Willa's little home, though they did, I'm
afraid, destroy her lovely organ."

Where a major trail joined it, the road improved, picking up a good
surface of river gravel. With Lenora and Billy riding horseback on
either side, the wagon rolled on between bottomland fields—all of them
planted this year and not all harvested yet, spindly ears still hanging
on many cornstalks. The Confederate lady looked across Lenora into
Billy's face and smiled.

"You are an officer, sir, a Union officer, are you not?"

"Reckon so, maam. Close enough, anyhow."

"Once before I met a Union officer, a captain, impeccably uniformed
in blue and gold. Two months ago he beckoned me as I awaited a train,
the last to leave Decatur before Sherman's vandals destroyed the

Central of Georgia line." Desdemona lay two fingers across her glossy lips and looked off into the sky above Billy's head, as if struggling to recall that moment. She spoke again. "The captain pointed out a girl on the platform, a queenly being, tall and lithe in figure and willowy in motion. Her beauty and nobility of manner imprinted itself on my memory, never to be effaced by mortal alchemy." Desdemona sighed. "She was a typical Southern girl, who gloried in that honor."

Lenora saw that Billy had let his reins go slack, giving the horse its head, so he could stare raptly at the Confederate lady.

"Right purty, was she?"

"Oh, beyond that, far beyond. The captain asked, but I was unable to tell him her name. Then he said: 'I shall learn it; and if she has not already become the wife or affianced of another, I shall offer her the devotion of my life.' That Union captain—like yourself—is part of Sherman's horde, but he was a true gentleman. You, sir, are you also a gentleman?"

Even through the weathered tan, Lenora could see the blush rise in his cheeks.

"Kinda hard for a farm-raised feller, maam. I try."

She rewarded him with another smile.

"I *knew* I could count on you." She leaned off the wagon seat toward him and spoke, as if confidentially. "You were listenin, weren't you, before y'all rushed in there to save me?" Lenora gritted her teeth. So the Nigra rapists, after all, had saved her. But Billy, the idiot boy, just grinned.

"Reckon we did," he said.

Desdemona blushed.

"When we get to my folks' plantation, I sure hope you don't tell them what you heard. I was only playin with those mongrels, but my father wouldn't understand."

Lenora cleared her throat.

"Miss, when we arrive at your home, Lieutenant Leidig will indeed keep his mouth SHUT."

So Billy kept Lenora's promise at the Pierpont plantation. Desdemona rushed weeping into her old father's arms, met Aunt Willa with word that her home still stood back in Spotswood. The reunion was wreathed with smiles and tears. The squad off-loaded the booty in the wagon, setting it out for return to its rightful owners in Spotswood.

This was the last of the good news for the Pierpont dynasty, as the squad went about its business of freeing their slaves. There were more than forty, two of whom sat, chilled to the heart, with their heads and hands clamped into stocks in the Quarters—an example Master Pierpont had set before his other servants who might misbehave. Hubert took a double-bitted ax to the hickory apparatus, making chips fly past the cringing captive heads while he cheerfully sang.

A cold frosty mornin
The nigger's mighty good,
Take your ax upon your shoulder
Nigger, TALK to the wood!

"Stop singing those slave songs!" Lenora yelled.

"Ain't no slave song. This makes me FEEL like singin." And he kept right on, defying Master Lenora June. With the top panel cut through, the stocks fell apart. The prisoners rose up, massaging their necks, sighing and groaning. Aaron found all the other prison equipage, shackles, fetters, gags, chains, whips, and—making sure no one saw the hiding place—sank them in the pit latrine used by the slaves.

The Pierponts had oats for the squad's horses, plentiful supplies of food the freed slaves could take along. Lenora saw that they were equipped with all the plantation's buggies and several wagons, with horses to haul them, as well as every firearm on the place. The slaves also took the bummers' remaining weapons, clothing, horses and their wagon. The house slaves stayed behind, but the rest set out to march in the wake of Sherman's army.

The early winter evening was coming on. With a Pierpont smoked ham and two rhubarb pies added to the larder on their pack mules, the squad itself was ready to leave. Lenora marshaled them in front of the Mansion, their horses balky by now, weary from the day's ride. The eastern sky was dark, but there was sudden light from the west as the sun broke level from under the cloud layer. The house with its Ionic columns, the mounted riders, the long aisle of glossy-leaved magnolias—all was starkly illumined as if by the limelight Lenora as a girl saw once in a Philadelphia theater.

Down the steps then came Desdemona Pierpont, still wearing the ball gown. She swept along the flagstone walk to stand at Billy's right stirrup, her blue eyes blazing up at him.

"I befriended y'all," she said. "I trusted y'all as fellow Christians. I invited y'all to my ancestral home. I took y'all to my bosom. Now you have robbed us and cast out our servants to the perils of the road. Judas, betrayest thou the son of man with a kiss? Et tu, Bru-tay!"

Billy's puzzled glance rose from Desdemona's eyes to Lenora's. Apparently he couldn't recall kissing anyone. Lenora considered whether she should correct that, though this was not the time. As they rode away, Billy turned an earnest face to Lenora June.

"Way she spoke about Judas, I reckon I know what that means. But what's the 'et tu' stuff?"

"It's Shakespeare," Lenora sighed, "something you haven't read."

22

I cannot believe Providence intends to destroy this Nation, this great asylum for the oppressed of all other nations and build a slave oligarchy on the ruins thereof
—letter from Union Private John Hamer to his wife, Aug. 5, 1864.

JUST AT DAWN ONE DAY they rode down toward the 179th Illinois's Ohoopee river bivouac, which adjoined the camp of the next regiment and the next and the next of William Tecumseh Sherman's great army. Billy watched sun break over the surrounding low hills, shining into a valley where woodsmoke swirled and settled. The troops had bedded down mainly along the water. It was freed people who bent over those breakfast fires on the slopes above, thousands of them waking now, readying themselves for the next day's march behind the army.

Colored people they knew called to Sergeant Moffat's squad as they rode past. Mary Etta, she who desired a man too small for good slave breeding, ran over to walk beside Lenora June's horse. Walton, the offending bantam, came with her. They talked happily up at the Union sergeant who'd brought them together. One man whom Billy had freed from the slave coffle came quietly out to walk beside his horse.

"That day I didn't give y'all no thankee," the man said. "I was worryin for my woman, she got sick like that, got throwed off the coffle. I figure she lost. Found her ten mile back on that road. She yonder in the camp now with the chil-ren." His face turned soberly up to Billy. "I thankee."

The hammer blow that broke the man's shackle bolt had required but a second's work. It amazed Billy that the pleasure now flooding his body could arise from so trifling an effort.

"You sure welcome."

The road ran a half mile through the freed peoples' camp, then turned to follow the river as it entered the 179th Illinois bivouac. Some soldiers still lay rolled in their blankets. Others were up cooking breakfast, frying mush with bacon strips in little skillets, sunny side eggs, split hardtack dropped inward side down into sizzling grease. Smelling the bacon, Billy felt spit rise under his tongue, readying his mouth for breakfast, though he'd already had his breakfast, a poor one.

"Yonder comes the nigger squad," said one smudged-faced blueback. "How come that lieutenant cain't get him a white squad?"

Billy spat on the ground at roadside.

"Try to beat this one!" he snapped back.

"Damn right!" said a fat little corporal. "Look at'em, seven of'em, they whooped a whole platoon of Joe Wheeler cavalry. Killed half of'em, run the rest off. Them's fighters, they are. And they freed a bunch of slaves."

"Oh, yeah, and just look what's happenin to them slaves." Smudge Face waved an arm wide at the freed peoples' camp. "What we gonna do with all these niggers? I ain't fightin to free niggers. I'm fightin to save the Union."

"You gaw-damn id-jet!" the corporal yelled back. "We fightin for all of it."

"Amen!" Billy sung out.. "We fightin to make this Union *worth* savin!"

Billy had no idea how that notion came into his head, but it felt good rolling off his tongue. Even better, just then Lenora June smiled, edged her mount closer to his and socked him lightly on his left shoulder. As the corporal and Smudge Face wrangled, the squad rode on. They found the regiment's quartermaster wagons ranged through a cottonwood grove on the river bank. They waited their turn and were issued coffee—only two pounds this time, since it was running out at this stage of the march. They got all the corn meal and ammunition they needed, plus the side of bacon Billy wanted. The pack mules were loaded, and they were ready to leave, when Colonel Langley came briskly down the road. After an exchange of salutes, he smiled through his beard.

"Hello! I heard you were in camp. You know, your 'nigger squad' is acquiring some notoriety in our part of the army. Last week this long column of freed people came pouring in to follow us. They told quite a tale about your tussle with Wheeler's cavalry. I congratulate you."

He shook Billy's hand—not the bandaged right hand, but the other. Billy waited, fearing he would not also shake Lenora's brown one. He did shake with her, vigorously, pressed her hand between both of his own and held it. Billy said nothing, offering Lenora the chance to answer.

"Thank you, sir."

"May I ask, sergeant, whether you were educated by the Quakers?"

"Yessir, in Abington, just outside Philadelphia."

"So was I," he said, "but in Hartford. They gave me my religious awakening, the light within, growing into goodness, the peace testimony—those sweet, sweet feelings. Sadly, I've fallen away from it."

Billy had always believed colored folk, with their brown faces, could never blush. Now Lenora seemed to, her cheeks glowing as she looked into Colonel Langley's eyes.

"Many of us have had to fall away," she said, "with this war."

He released Lenora June's hand and stepped back to study the two of them.

"Against slavery," he said, "against the people who started this war to defend it, what else can we do but fall away from peace? Think about the slaves. What would the Good Samaritan have done if he'd come along earlier and seen the thieves in the act of wounding the wayfarer?"

"Reckon he's gonna pitch right in," Billy said. "Ain't gonna stand there and watch that man get whooped."

"Yes!" the colonel said, and laughed.

But to free three hundred slaves, would the Good Samaritan have bushwhacked those Secesh cavalrymen, shot them off their horses at midstream? That vision rose in Billy's mind, bodies adrift in the water, coloring it with their blood. If the Union was winning, wouldn't those slaves soon be free anyhow? Then he'd been hot to kill the Rebels, even Peckerwood Rebels. Now the question gnawed at him.

The colonel moved between Billy and Lenora, placed his hands on their backs just at waist level.

"Would you walk with me?"

They moved down an open aisle between the wagons, then along a sandy trail through the grove. White sycamore trunks, brown flecked, towered toward the sky, twigs at the top lighted by the rising sun. When they were well away from the wagons, the colonel turned to them.

"There's something you need to know." He stood looking at the ground, pulling at his beard with one hand. "The Fourteenth Corps of Sherman's army has a general named Jefferson Davis. Hard to believe, but he shares the name with the Confederate president. And our Yankee Jeff Davis holds the same feelings about Negroes as the Rebel one. He thinks this great Exodus of freed people is slowing our army. He wants it stopped."

"Wants to stop freeing the slaves?" Lenora said, frowning.

"He doesn't say that. He wants them to stop following the army. Which amounts to the same thing. If they stay behind, they will certainly be taken back into slavery."

"What-all does General Sherman think?" Billy asked.

"He supports our Union Jeff Davis. You need to know that." Now he lifted his eyes to theirs. "I know it well enough, but my regiment will go right on freeing every slave we meet. Most of my men delight in it. I hope you continue what you've been doing. Just be aware that—like me—you're going against army policy."

"Hell yes!" Billy said. "That's the reason we here."

Colonel Langley shook his head ruefully.

"General Sherman thinks differently. He thinks we're here to tear up railroads, burn cotton gins and iron foundries and eat up their grain. Of course that's necessary to make the Confederates quit. We're destroying their property, meanwhile killing very few people. Have you noticed that Sherman is deliberately avoiding battle now, going around every force they raise against him?" He clenched his hands into fists. "But up there is what this war is really all about." With a sweep of his arm, blue clad and gold ribboned, he encompassed the camp of freed people stirring above them on the slope, people loading wheelbarrows, hefting sacks, harnessing draft animals, stamping out their breakfast fires.

"Right now twenty thousand freed people are following this army. I'll wager that on the march we've freed another hundred thousand. They're running all over Georgia, trying to reach federal lines." The colonel was getting loud. "Those runaways don't build fortifications for the South anymore. They don't load Confederate musket cartridges. They don't repair their railroads. Last I heard, a hundred-fifty thousand Negro soldiers had enlisted in the Union army—all volunteers. They turned the tide. By freeing them, we are winning the war, but even THAT'S not the point."

Billy glanced back at the wagons, wondering whether someone there might hear the colonel.

"Sherman is a great general," he went on, even louder now. "Except maybe for the Czar of Russia, he has freed more slaves than any leader in human history. President Lincoln emancipated them, but only in Rebel states where he had no power. General Sherman is actually FREEING the slaves. THIS is what he should be remembered for. He CANNOT understand that! I have told him myself, but the stupid man WILL NOT understand!"

The colonel wiped a bubble of white foam from the corner of his mouth.

"Pardon me," he said, taking slow breaths. "I'm sorry." He smiled. "I get so upset that I start raving—not at all like the Quaker witness to peace I had hoped to become. I get so angry. That's why I asked you to walk out here away from the wagons. There are so few people I can talk with. Please pardon my raving."

Rank has its privileges. As usual Lenora June strode alone into a thicket to exercise hers. Billy watched her leave, then sat back against a tree trunk, his saddle draped across his lap, and continued mending a tear in the leather of his carbine boot. They'd stopped beside the road for a noon dinner. Between bites of cold hoecake and that federal bacon cooked on a little fire, he sewed the rip closed with waxed thread. Finishing, he lifted his head just as a faint yelp rang through the woods.

"Sound like a fox bark," he said.

"Maybe that ole barred owl," Leon suggested.

"Owl ain't gonna holler at dinnertime."

Billy realized then that Lenora had not come back.

"Where you reckon the sergeant gone?"

Suddenly Leon was on his feet.

"We go see!"

"I go too," Aaron said.

"Naw, you keep watch here," Billy told him. "We go."

If anybody in the squad was going to catch this Union sergeant squatting to take a leak, Billy and Leon wanted it to be them. He grabbed his carbine and told Leon to take Lenora's Spencer, still holstered in the boot on her saddle. Not to alarm the others, Billy started at a walk. Once into the thicket, he ran between close-growing little trees along the faint deer trail she would surely have followed. Maybe two hundred yards out Billy, Leon at his heels, broke into a wide place on the path. Leaf litter there was scraped and torn. Two long tracks of scuffed dirt led eastward where the path through the thicket resumed. Then they saw it, on the dry leaves a patch of wetness steaming in the cool air.

"Secesh caught her pissing!" Leon growled.

"They know she's a woman," Billy said. "And she's a colored Union soldier. They'll do it and kill her when they're finished!"

However terrible it might be for her, he could bear finding a raped Lenora June. But Lenora dead, like those men he'd shot, bleeding into the creek—that thought split his body through the bowels. Crowding each other, banging into the little trees, Billy and Leon thundered down the path following the twin drag marks of her brogan heels. Not a hundred yards farther they found hoof prints in the red dirt of a woodland side road, saw the plowed track of a wagon that had pulled off and stopped. The team had trampled the grass there as they waited before resuming the journey.

"Listen!" Leon hissed.

Billy heard it, the distant rattle of a wagon moving fast.

"Shit! Shit!" Billy threw his forage cap against the ground. "Afoot we never gonna catch'em!"

They stood close, looking scared into each other's eyes.

"Get the hosses!" Leon said.

Billy jerked away and ran back up the path, Leon following. When they reached the road, he yelled to the other squad members.

"Secesh grabbed the sergeant! Y'all foller and back us up."

His own horse was bridled but not saddled. He leaped onto its bare back and rode like an Indian down the trail, Leon yards behind. They threshed through little trees, ducking their heads, dodging branches. A stob jabbed Billy's cheek, bloodying it and leaving that eye teary. They came out of the thicket, swung onto the wagon track and let the horses go. Their mounts seldom got a chance to run full out. Now they jumped to it, going from that jarring trot to a silky gallop. Billy felt his head loll back as air rushed into his nostrils. He wished for stirrups, the firm seat of a saddle, but he'd ridden bareback all his life.

Would some man be raping her right now in that wagon bed, maybe steeling himself to kill her? Would the first sign be a mauled body like a run-over dog between the wagon tracks? He rode, grateful for the smooth-sliding muscles of the horse under his thighs, the eager way the animal leaned into the rushing air. The horse was panting now, chest pumping, but far from winded. Billy loved this long-legged chestnut. Leon's massive Belgian was a fine animal but slow. He had fallen far behind.

Rounding a curve, he saw the wagon. Its canvas cover was tugged down by ropes at the rear into a teardrop opening, pitch black in this light. Fearfully he watched that dark, rope-pulled oval. As he overtook the wagon, a double-barreled shotgun jutted from the teardrop. The gun spat fire and smoke. He breathed the sulphurous discharge but, dumbfounded, felt no impact of the shot. The gun barrels swung upward, swung sideways, stirring about like a spoon handle in a soup pot. The gun discharged a second time, raking trees at roadside. Then from the opening in the canvas the gunman himself shot forth, arms waving, legs kicking, as if swimming through the dusty air. He landed with a crunch on the road.

Before Billy could touch the reins, his thundering chestnut trampled the man, half stumbled and then recovered to race onward. *Too damn bad for you*, Billy thought, as the toppled figure fell behind. Ahead, the wagon bounced and swayed over bumps. The noise was terrific—the clank of iron tires against the rocks, the flapping of the canvas cover, the squeal of wood against leather, the thunder of the team's hooves on the dirt.

He came up fast on the right side, saw a wagon driver on the seat. The man's scared eyes, red rimmed, opened on the rider alongside. Gathering his reins in one hand, with his other Billy aimed the Spencer point blank at the driver, hot to kill the man, until he noticed a little boy clinging with both hands to the wagon seat. Instead of squeezing, Billy jerked the trigger and let the weapon fall off aim. The muzzle blast burst across their faces. He levered another cartridge in.

"Stop!" he bellowed.

The driver hauled back the reins, stomped the wooden brake lever at the side. The horses sagged butt down, hooves furrowing the dirt of the road. The wagon slewed sideways, its right rear wheel going into a ditch. Dust fogged up around them as it all came to a stop. *I woulda killed him. I right nigh killed him.* As if an echo of his own thought, her voice came shrill to him from under the canvas of the wagon bed.

"Billy, I'm all right! Don't kill'em!"

He sucked in a fresh breath, like happiness filling his lungs. She was alive. But her command came like a chastisement. *I woulda killed that man.* Billy wondered what was happening to him, that he was so eager now to kill someone already at his mercy. Leon's big Belgian thundered up on the other side of the wagon. His Spencer was cocked, the muzzle ranging back and forth between man and boy.

"Get on the ground!" he growled.

The man poured himself off the wagon seat, took eagerly to the dirt. Not the boy. He was maybe twelve years old, standing in the road now and staring defiantly at Leon.

"I said get DOWN!"

The boy dropped to his knees, rolled carelessly onto his side. Blue eyes set in a freckled face burned up at Leon.

"Gaw-damn nigger!" the boy yelled. "You oughta be in that wagon with the rest!"

Face down on the ground, the big man squawked: "Luke, shut up!"

Across their prostrate forms, Leon grinned at Billy.

"Look like your hoss done it for the shotgun man," he said. "He laying back yonder on the road. He be crawling awhile instead a'walkin.'"

From under the canvas came that happy voice again: "Billy, get the big man's keys. They've got me manacled."

First he and Leon disarmed the fellow, shucking out of his various pockets and holsters a little pile of items, handcuffs, a leather-wrapped lead cudgel, a revolver, a double-edged dagger. While Leon kept the two prone on the ground, standing with one foot on the kid's back, Billy crawled over the wagon seat into the canvas cave of its bed. In that dimness he saw sets of manacles and leg irons bolted along both sides of the oaken frame, enough to hold eight prisoners. To reach Lenora he scrambled across the legs of two manacled and fettered captives, a man and woman whose smiles beamed on him. The man nodded toward the rear of the wagon.

"That'un, that nigger sergeant, she really somethin!"

Lenora June lay near the back, both hands manacled to the wagon side. Her feet were not fettered like those of the other two captives. Her trousers were pulled down to her knees, the dingy white drawers showing.

"I'm all right, Billy," she said.

"She is!" crowed the colored woman. "She all right! That slave guard tryin to rape her, he didn't want no fetters on her feet. Want her wide open. He took the fetters off. Then you come ridin up, we seen it, that man gonna shoot you like a dog. She kick, she kick, she kick his ass. She boot that sum-bitch right out over the tailboard. That make me GLAD!"

The key opened one manacle and, in winter light pouring through the teardrop opening in the canvas, he saw that smile pushing her cheeks up, that white smile. The freed right hand caught the back of his head and pulled him close. Her lips were chapped and flaky with strings of dried tissue. Wide and soft against his mouth, the lips drew a little apart. She breathed his panting breath and he breathed hers, Billy tasting the tang of bacon she'd eaten for dinner. He felt himself stiffen inside his pants. Delighted, also horrified, he tried to suspend his hips in midair so she wouldn't feel it through the thin fabric of her drawers. This first kiss between them had been so long in coming he wondered if there'd ever be another. But when he freed the left hand, she tugged him back again. The second time they breathed each other's breath so long he came away dizzy.

"Howdy, howdy, look at that!" sighed the male captive in the wagon.

"Looooo-tenant Ludwig," Leon called musically from outside, "oh, young Wil-helm Looood-wig, what's a-happenin in yonder?"

Billy, already busy helping her haul the trousers up, had to think a moment how to answer.

"Just a-gettin these manacles unlocked is all."

Lenora glanced at the other captives and laid a vertical finger across her smile.

"Shhhhhhh," she hissed. The man and woman nodded.

The rest of the squad rode up as Lenora and Billy crawled out of the wagon. Billy saw the white man and boy were on their feet, standing before the muzzles of four muskets and a carbine. Both wore jeans and flannel shirts and dirty sheepskin coats with the wool turned in. With a brown rime of tobacco juice around his mouth, the man was thick set and tall. Billy had to look up into his eyes. He must not be a bummer, since it seemed the only thing he and his partner stole was colored people.

"Who the hell are you?" Billy asked him.

The big man shrugged and looked off into the woods.

"They're slave-catchers," Lenora said, "like the ones who dragged my folks and me back from Pennsylvania. They catch slaves for money."

The slave catcher looked humble and fearful, but not the boy.

"Gaw-damn nigger bitch! Buncha gaw-damn niggers!"

"Luke, shut up!"

The boy's body dipped forward, as if bowing politely, and his right hand fished into the open top of the big man's left boot. It came out with a pistol, a Derringer, Billy watching amazed as the twin black muzzles swung up toward his own chest. Musket hammers clicking like castanets around him, the big man swung a heavy fist sideways into the boy's face. The pistol flung away onto the road. The child fell back howling, blood welling from his nose.

"That hurts! It hurts, Uncle Bud! I tell ma what you done!"

Uncle Bud showed his yellow teeth, his inflamed gums, in something like a smile.

"He just a little mean."

The slave-catchers had caught the man and woman runaways a few miles west. Later they had stopped the wagon at roadside and walked into a thicket to take a leak. That's when Lenora herself came down the trail to enjoy the privileges of rank. They heard her coming. Well hidden, they waited till she was finished and caught her still squatting.

Sergeant Moffatt's squad stripped the clothing off the big man, except for his drawers and the stockings on his feet. From the injured slave catcher on the road they took only a coat and high-topped shoes. These they awarded to the runaways freed from the wagon bed, along with weapons and the two horses of the team. They set fire to the wagon and left the slave-catcher and his nephew there in the road, ruefully considering the blaze. As the squad rode back toward their dinner camp to retrieve the saddle, Aaron spurred his mount up to ride beside Billy.

"You hear what that youngin say? 'Nigger bitch! Nigger bitch!' What nigger bitch was he talkin about?"

"Might be that woman runaway."

"Youngin ain't lookin at her. He lookin right at us all lined up in the squad."

"I was the one that kid was figurin to shoot," Billy said. "Maybe he was lookin at me. After all that chasin, I felt like a bitch."

"Sure, but you don't match up with the nigger part."

"Leastways I'm U. S. Colored Infantry," Billy said. "Don't that count for somethin?"

If that didn't satisfy Aaron, it was a mystery he would have to solve for himself. Billy had troubles of his own to ponder.

23

INDEED SHE HAD FELT HIS springy stiffness, struggling against enjoying her power to call it forth. During secret woodland frolics at Highland Forge, when whirling dancers slammed together, she'd felt the same thing from other boys, but never before this answer from her own body, this melting between her thighs. The blending of bloods between them would be hopeless, she knew that. People would make it impossible. So now, sitting at a dying fire many hours later, why was she so flushed, so happy, and he so sad? Billy sat staring into the coals, stirring them with a tree branch.

"What's wrong?"

He threw the stick on the fire, rose to his feet and ambled slowly across the farmyard where they were camped, looking at the ground. Presently he returned and sat cross-legged on his pallet. The tree branch crackled into flame, lighting his somber face.

"We thirty miles from Highland Forge. Recollect that dream you told me? You saw the Forge a-burnin."

"I remember."

"What's gonna happen yonder? Forge Master gonna fight us? He's got guns to do it. My pa gonna fight us? Maybe even *your* pa? I mean, he's a slave, but John Marion ain't gonna like seeing his chaffery forge tore up. He loves his damn ole forge, poundin out that iron. I don't want to fight our families."

"Better us than Union cannon," she told him. "If anybody at the Forge starts shootin at the federals, they'll bring up those Napoleons. They'll blow'em away with cannister. The Forge *will* be torn up, Billy. We can do it gentler. We'll stay around till the army passes. We can protect them."

"Sure!" He threw his hands up. "I reckon."

The Union was winning, so Billy thought. The Confederacy was losing. Still, some Confederates didn't seem to believe it. In a column of twos, with Ike leading as vedette, they rode next morning through the town of Sigman, where a few store fronts crowded the narrow street. Wanting to reach Highland Forge before Sherman's army, they were far ahead now and fearful of ambush. Even expecting it, they were jolted by the form it took.

A shower of rocks erupted from an alley between two buildings on their right—river-worn flint, round and smooth and hard. Billy threw up his bandaged right hand to parry one. It stung the hand, stung like fire. Beyond a wagon in the alley clustered a knot of boys, ten or fifteen big white boys, snatching up stones they'd stacked in the wagon bed and hauling back to throw them. Billy jerked his head aside to dodge another. He heard the click of musket hammers around him as the squad members leveled their weapons.

"Don't kill'em!" he yelled. "Aim high!"

Fierce spurts of powder smoke lashed out toward the alley. The volley of rocks stopped. People poured out of buildings on both sides of the street. With the squad reloading and the smoke clearing, he hoped he'd see no bloody corpses. Indeed, he saw none, no boys at all in the alley, but he couldn't see behind the wagon. A gray-bearded fellow popped out the door of a saddlery and rushed to the wagon, peering behind it. He swung around and yelled gleefully to the crowd.

"Didn't hit a one! Gaw-damn Yankees cain't shoot shit!"

A hoarse cheer rose from people on the plank boardwalks. They were mostly women and children, with a few old men among them.

"Dirty nigger Yankees!" somebody yelled.

Clearly, the town had been warned. Somebody had ridden in with word that the Yankees were coming—worse even than that, the hated niggerYankees. The town had made ready for them. Blood welled up through the bandage on Billy's hand, the re-opened wound now hurting fiercely. They were all bleeding, more or less, from thrown rocks. Lenora June held one hand over her right ear, a red trickle running down her neck into the uniform coat.

"Squad, move out!" she ordered.

They started forward, no slower and no faster than they'd been traveling when they were attacked. They would not be rushed. A woman wearing a faded house dress stepped into the street ahead, and, ignoring the white Union lieutenant, glowered up at the sergeant, Lenora June.

"I hate y'all! I hate your Lincoln-lovin faces! We will fight y'all for-EVER!"

The crowd cheered her. Lenora was discouraged to see that this was not the plantation aristocracy. They were poor folk, Billy's own Peckerwoods not yet humbled by the passage of an army. Their husbands and sons, fighting far away, by now understood war—as Ben Densmore had understood it after his colored comrades were murdered at Fort Pillow. These townspeople didn't. Not yet. An old man in a Prince Albert coat plucked off his hat and laid it over his heart. He started singing "Dixie." Hats flew off other heads, even women's hats, all to be held at the breast as the crowd stood at attention. They picked up the lyrics in mid song.

In Dixie land where I was born in,

Early on a frosty mornin

Look away, look away, look away, Dixie land!

Between the singers on the boardwalks, the squad rode in silence, watching for weapons. When the song wound down, the people began to look about, a few wandering off as the entertainment seemed about to end. Then, from behind Billy in their column of riders, trumpeted the loud baritone voice of Corporal Leon Duffy, belting out another version of *Dixie*.

A-way down South in the land of TRAI-tors,

Rat-tlesnakes and al-li-GA-tors,

Right away, come away, right away, Dixie land!
Where cot-ton's king and men are CHAT-TELS,
Union boys will WIN the bat-tles...

His voice was drowned by an angry roar from the crowd. A few thrown rocks thudded around them as they rode sedately on. People hustled back and forth, searching the ground for more stones to throw.

"Squad!" the sergeant yelled. "Just level your muskets at them. Do not fire."

When the gun barrels came down, the street boiled with running figures, scrambling to get inside or flee down alleys between buildings. As they reached the open road again, the squad's orderly formation broke, became a milling mass of horses and soldiers. They laughed and then, looking into each other's teary eyes, laughed again. Aaron turned back to slap Leon on the shoulder.

"I never heard that," he said. "Where'd you get it?"

"Learnt that song in DE-troit. We was singin it up yonder before I left."

They took turns patting him, then reined their mounts to swing back and pat him again. If he'd charged an enemy breastwork to capture a battery of cannon, he couldn't have won half this praise.

24

We are not only fighting hostile armies but a hostile people, and must make young and old, rich and poor, feel the hard hand of war, as well as their organized armies. I know that this recent movement of mine through Georgia has had a wonderful effect in this respect.
—General William T. Sherman report to General Henry W. Halleck,
Christmas Eve, 1864.

IN LEAFY SUMMER, LENORA KNEW, this would seem just another woodland valley, hill girded, graced by a stream of clear water glinting through dense tree cover. But the leaf-fall of autumn had revealed it as the scene of an industrial enterprise. On the valley's far side, beyond Quapaw creek, stood the balconied Forge Mansion, its five dormer windows staring down on the other three houses of whites, including Billy's parents' home. Close by were the guest cottage, the office, the stable, the store, the harness shop.

On the mansion the whitewash was fresh but on other buildings it had weathered thin, gray planks showing through. Log slave cabins stood on the near side of the creek. Wood smoke rose from the valley's many chimneys and trailed northward on a steady breeze.

Upstream along the creek stood the smoking masonry cone of Vesuvius Furnace, within which burning charcoal heated the ore to melt out its pig iron. Set near the furnace right on the creek bank, where their water wheels could draw power from the millrace, were the flour mill and the iron forge itself. Tiny compared to the whole, these industrial structures were central to its wartime uses. The flour and corn meal provisioned Rebel soldiers, and the iron kept them armed. Lenora June, sitting her horse on a hill to the west, decided they must be destroyed.

"Home," she said.

Surprised at the word, Billy pointed into the valley.

"You still call it that, after the Forge Master sold you west?"

"We had good times here."

"Didn't we!" he cried.

Highland Forge was not really high—just the highest place in an otherwise low and swampy land. She glanced at the road over her mount's raised ears and urged him forward down the shallow slope. The ambush at Sigman had made them more wary. She sent Ike out as vedette, a job he relished. He rode with head held up on a stretched neck, eyes swinging side to side. Approaching the creek, he abruptly whirled his horse and raced back toward them, nesting his face in the animal's flying mane.

She heard a shotgun boom and then a sputter of muskets, three or four. Smoke spurted from behind one of the slave cabins on the near bank of the creek. Buckshot chattered through tree branches beside the road. As in Sigman, word of their passage had gone ahead. The Forge Master was ready for them. Ike's puffing horse slid to a stop beside her.

"They's six or seven of'em yonder, three or four of'em colored. Hell, they gave muskets to colored. Colored people fightin so's they can keep on being slaves."

Lenora ordered the squad to dismount and tether the animals. She reminded them again that Highland Forge was home to her and Billy. She hoped to capture it without killing. The obvious question was, would someone in the squad be killed in taking care that Billy's father and her own were not? She was grateful none asked that question.. Corporal Duffy studied her face, his eyes a pool of light.

"We do it," he said. "Don't hurt nobody."

They deployed and advanced alternately, first three in a unit, then four, then three again. By now even Jules had learned a little drill. Stopping under cover, they fired and reloaded. The advancing unit did not fire—just ran like hell to the next cover. With a Spencer in each group, they fired fast and high but not so high they missed the cabin roofpeaks. That quick rattle of slugs in the shingles, this relentless military assault, had the desired effect. The men behind the slave cabins broke and ran for the creek. Retreating in a cluster across the bridge, they should have been amazed they were not killed. They made such easy targets. The defenders took cover on the far bank behind charcoal piled high, ready for use in the forge. The squad members reached the slave cabins closest to the creek and headed for the back doors. Lenora lifted the latch of one and ducked into the shadowy room, at mid-battle infused with a strange rapture.

"Ma? You home?"

No, she wasn't. But Lenora could smell her mother's spicy cooking, also the perfume she made by steeping the tiny pink stars of trailing arbutus in alcohol. Something simmered in a black-iron pot on the little stove. The same quilt, patched together of old coat material, lay on her parents' bed. The cabin had just one large room and the loft where Lenora had slept, her old plaid blanket spilling off the puncheon floor up there, hanging down into the room below. Compared to her log hut at the Hunnicutt plantation, this was a palace. She unlatched the single window, six precious glass panes, opened it outward, edgewise to the trajectory of any slugs that came this way. She fired one shot at the forge building across the creek, listened for the smack on thick logs. Then, in a lull, she heard Billy calling.

"August Leidig! Daddy? This here's Billy. Is that you yonder crost the creek?"

Smoke spurted from the charcoal piles. She heard slugs patter against the cabin where Billy sheltered. As the smoke drifted clear, he shouted again.

"Pa, I'm right here in ole Amos and Mary's cabin. This is Billy callin you."

"Bil-ly? MEINE Billy? Say again!"

Her squad had stopped firing, but another shot boomed out from the defenders.

"Halt, stop das schiessen! Halt!"

"This here's me, pa, it's me."

Belief and unbelief contended in August Leidig's voice.

"Vot you do dere, Billy? Mit dem Yan-kees?"

Among the defenders a musket fired, then another, followed by a shotgun, which peppered the wall of her parents' cabin. This time several squad members—irritated—fired back, raising dust spurts from the charcoal piles.

"Cease fire!" Billy yelled. "Stop shootin! Y'all gonna kill my pa!"

She saw the door of the next cabin swing open, and Billy stepped out onto the granite slab that served as front stoop. He laid his Spencer carbine and his revolver on the stone. In his worn uniform, he looked so frail. Lenora flung back the front door of her parents' cabin, stepped out and laid her own weapons down.

"John Marion Moffat?" she yelled. "Are you there? This is Lenora June." She'd kept her true name secret so long that she felt a reflex regret at saying it aloud. Now the whole squad would know. "Daddy, we've come to free the slaves."

Instantly, John Marion stood up from behind the charcoal.

"Lenora, aw Lenora June, here you into trouble *again!*"

That Lenora was here also at last convinced Billy's father.

"It's die verdammte youngins! Vot dey doin togedder noch jetzt?" But, smiling, he rose to his feet and ran toward the bridge. "Wilhelm! Mein Billy!"

A squat little figure stepped out from behind the forge building.

"August, stop! In the name of God, I tell you STOP!" It was the Forge Master, who now leveled a shotgun at Billy. August skidded to a halt on the gravel of the bridge. He raised both hands to Master Hardesty in a pleading gesture.

"NEIN, Enoch! No shoot my youngin!"

"The Lord has placed these servants under my care," the Forge Master announced. "Now these young traitors would drive them out to wander the roads like Gypsies. I will not allow it!"

A man—a big black one—jumped up from behind a charcoal pile and strode to the Forge Master. With one meaty hand he clutched the Master's neck, as a poultryman might clench an egg-stealing blacksnake behind its head, while the other hand plucked the shotgun from his grasp. There was no struggle. Only now did Lenora recognize the man as Isaac Stoneman. There was no use struggling against Isaac. Billy had learned that lesson at his first Saturday night dance. Master Enoch Hardesty strained to turn his head, to look his captor in the face.

"Isaac, let me go," he groaned. "Servants, be OBEDIENT to them that are your masters according to the flesh, with fear and trembling, in singleness of your heart, as unto Christ. Right now, Isaac, you just LET ME GO!"

Isaac gave no hint he'd heard the command, or the scripture. He marched the Forge Master, dancing on his toes, away from the charcoal piles. Billy ran to meet his father at the bridge. August hugged him, kissed his cheeks, and Billy kissed back. Her own father was more reserved. Retrieving her weapons, she had to cross the bridge to meet him on the other side. He had tried so hard to keep her straight. What would he think of her now, of these escapades? Approaching him, she dreaded his verdict. In his dirty forge overalls he just stood, staring in wonder at her.

"Look at you, look at you," he said. "We heard you run away from Hunnicutt. Ole Hunnicutt, he want the Forge Master to pay back them dollars he lay out for you." John Marion smiled shyly, and gestured to her uniform. "Look at you, just look what you went and done. You a Yankee sergeant now?"

"Yes, daddy."

That last word brought tears to her eyes. She had thought he would be angry at her. He seemed proud instead. He stood so awkward there, as if he thought this grubby soldier were now too good to embrace as his own daughter. She stepped close and slid her hands around his waist, nesting her face in the corner of his neck. Against one cheek she felt the blood pound in a vein of his throat. His arms enclosed her and squeezed. She felt his trembling.

"Where you been, little girl?" he murmured. "Where you been so long? Your mama been missin you."

25

I know...that some of the commanders of our armies...believe the emancipation policy and the use of the colored troops constitute the heaviest blow yet dealt to the Rebellion...You say you will not fight to free negroes. Some of them seem willing to fight for you; but, no matter. Fight you, then, exclusively to save the Union.
— Abraham Lincoln's August 26, 1863, letter to James C. Conkling, a long-time friend in Illinois who was skeptical of the Emancipation Proclamation.

WITHOUT BEING TOLD, THE REST of the squad emerged from cover and took control of the Forge. They locked Master Enoch, still spouting Bible verses, in a chicken house. Leaving her father for the moment, she called for Aaron, intending to post him as a picket. A huge smile wreathed his face as he approached.

"Lenora June," Aaron said, "*Sergeant* Lenora June, it's a right purty name. Remember that youngin in the slave-catcher wagon? He was lookin at us in the squad yellin 'nigger bitch, nigger bitch.' I wondered who he talkin about. Sure, YOU the nigger bitch! Only you ain't no bitch. You one fine LADY."

She wondered whether he would ever again obey her commands.

"Private Smallwood," she said, "I want you to watch these roads. Warn us if any Secesh come along."

"Sure!" he answered, instantly sobering down. Though she was a mere sergeant—not a commissioned officer—he flipped her a brisk salute and set off on his task. That's all it came to. Discovering she was a woman seemed to change nothing, at least with Aaron. Three white forge workers, recently-hired hands whom Lenora didn't know, stood together near the creek, uneasily fingering their old muskets. Passing near them, she heard one mutter:

"This here's what comes of givin guns to niggers."

They were of prime age for conscription into the Confederate army, perhaps exempted from the draft—as so many others had been—by Governor Joe Brown. Lenora spoke to Billy and called in Ike and Hubert. Together they advanced on the three men, took hold of the muskets and pulled them from their hands. They plucked the cartridge boxes from their belts.

"That's my pa's gun," the oldest grumbled, "and he got it from his pa."

"He's lyin like a dog," said another, a tow-headed younger fellow. His amused brown eyes stared straight into Lenora's. "That there musket belongs to the Forge. Ain't none of us owns a gun."

"Gaw-damn sum-bitch!" The liar shoved tow-head, who leaned with the thrust and rebounded, laughing.

"Them guns just cause y'all trouble," Billy told them. "Union army comin through here tonight. If you show'em a musket, y'all gonna die quick. Now get on home. If y'all home, in the house, then the house don't get burned."

Lenora thanked Isaac Stoneman for seizing the Forge Master and his shotgun. She gave him the three old muskets to distribute to other slaves. On her orders Leon and Jules swung open the door of the flour mill and entered. Minutes later, smoke boiled up at the base of the north wall. Soon the weathered boards caught, and fire flared to the outside. The steady south wind would carry it through the mill, which already had ground its last supply of meal for Confederate troops. From her haversack Lenora drew out her corked bottle of friction matches and ducked through the low door of the forge building.

Entering this shadowy place, she'd always felt wonder. In one corner the finery forge glowed dark red, its fire already dying. In the other the open maw of her father's chaffery forge blazed white hot. Even at this distance it heated her face. Close to the creek-side wall was the one-ton helve hammer, its head an iron block big as a washtub. Lifted by power from the water wheel and dropped, and lifted and dropped, on red-hot blooms of pig iron, the helve hammer magically turned that useless stuff into malleable wrought iron. With the millrace diverted, the face of the hammer lay inert now on its huge anvil.

Around a nearby smaller anvil were waist-high heaps of horseshoes, buckets of horseshoe nails.

"You gonna bust my forge?"

Her father's words hung in the air behind her. She turned.

"We have to, pa. Sherman will burn it anyway, and a lot more."

He gestured to the piles near the small anvil.

"Been makin horseshoes," he said. "Me, a slave, makin horseshoes for Joe Wheeler cavalry." He laughed dryly and wandered toward the chaffery forge. "Ole cottontop Hosea Reed, he taught me this.. You wasn't even borned then. Hosea, he from Guinea coast, come over on one them slave ships. Yonder is where Hosea learn it. Them Guinea folks pound good iron. Hosea, he build this chaffery forge hisself. He lay fire brick inside. I helped him, I laid that red brick outside."

She'd heard the story of Hosea the Teacher many times and never been much affected. This time she felt it. John Marion slid his hands into the back pockets of his overalls and turned to her. He stood between her and the hot mouth of the forge, shielding her from its glare.

"Honey, it don't do no good just settin fire to the building. Them forges won't burn. They fire proof. Right quick them Secesh will get some chafferyman back to poundin iron here. They can work outdoors and pound good iron."

He grabbed the helve of a sledge hammer, his twelve-pounder, and went to work on the chaffery forge. Putting his whole body into the swing, he struck beside the cast-iron doors. The first blows seemed to cause no damage. He kept pounding. At last one brick exploded, chips flying. He kept swinging. The right-hand door fell backwards into the fire, showering sparks, leaving a jagged opening across the top. A few more blows collapsed the whole brick front of the forge. Fire spilled onto the plank floor. He danced away but walked back through the coals to pound at bricks on the top, crashing the whole thing down. Fire licked upward on the log wall at one side.

He walked back to Lenora and stood, panting, mopping sweat from his eyes with a rag. He caught one breath and nodded to the other corner.

"I just get that finery forge now, and we be all finish."

When they left the building twenty minutes later, it was burning in the two forge corners, the fires eating toward one another. By now the flour mill was a flaming ruin. Walking down the slope toward them were Billy, his mother and father, and Lenora's own mother. They were smiling, every one of them, but the parents' faces seemed overcast with worry. Lenora's mother hugged her and spoke into her ear.

"Darlin, y'all both here," Reba whispered. "But how come y'all together?"

Lenora waited until the hug was finished before stuttering out an answer.

"Ma, Billy was out east of Atlanta in his Georgia Guard uniform and got attacked by a Union lieutenant. He had to kill the man. Right then my own squad came along and caught Billy. They were just ready to kill him. Then I saw who it was."

Essie, Billy's mother, cleared her throat.

"But looky here now, just look at his bluecoat uniform. Where'd he get that? The two of y'all were over yonder east of Atlanta and just come to meet accidental? Then Billy give up fightin for the Cause? He swapped sides in this war? Is that the way it happened?"

"It happened, ma," Billy told her. "It just *happened*."

It was beyond excuse, of course it was, particularly the Forge Master's charge that they were traitors. But Billy was an only child. So was Lenora June. Their parents said nothing more about their explanation, or their lack of one. Nothing at all was said for a minute or two. They stood, feeling the heat of the blazing forge building. They coughed and looked about, watched a flight of crows flap lazily across the blue sky and detour around the slanting pillars of smoke.

"Lenora June," Reba said abruptly, "I got dinner on the stove. You come home and eat. Then y'all can get on with your soldiers. Reckon me and your daddy be leavin too. Leavin with you, if that's all right."

Essie laid a hand on her son's arm.

"Billy, you come home. I had dinner all ready when this fuss start." She took up his bandaged hand and studied it. "I want to see how you hurt and bandage this right. Come home, eat with your mama and daddy before y'all have to leave."

She gripped that wrist, tugging him toward home until the arm rose to the horizontal, but he didn't move. August enclosed him with a one-armed hug, as if to escort him forcefully.

"Ve go home now, Billy. Zu hause ve go."

Still he didn't budge.

"Mama, me and Lenora June, we goin on nigh thirty days eatin rations together. We sit around that fire, talkin, havin a good time. No need to stop now. How about John Marion and Reba come home with us. We all have dinner at our house."

"Now son," said Reba, "that is UN-necessary. We got our *own* cabin. We got our *own* dinner."

"Well then," Billy said, gesturing, "how about let's everbody go yonder across the creek to *your* house. We'll all go yonder to the Quarters."

Lenora marveled at his crankiness. Wasn't this already hard enough? But his attitude somehow begat a carbuncle of crankiness in her own craw. Couldn't colored and white *ever* sit at the same dinner table? When her mother tugged at her own hand, pulling her toward home, she held back and said:

"Ma, you and pa, just go home, eat your dinner. We've got plenty on the pack mules for us. We'll eat with the squad."

Behind its stubble of graying beard, August Leidig's face slowly reddened as he looked back and forth between his son and Lenora June. Abruptly he yanked off his little billed cap and hurled it against the ground.

"Verdammte youngins!" he yelled, glaring at them. "Shit fire!" He heaved in a couple of breaths and then grew calmer. "You youngins only ones ve got. So come, Reba, John, kommst du! All in our house. Ve got plenty meat our house!"

Wondering where the rest of her command might have dinner, Lenora noticed that an admiring crowd of slaves, children hopping like popcorn among them, had surrounded the other squad members. Already they were being parceled out to different cabins for the meal. If the Leidig and Moffat families had to gather, truly the Leidig's was the better place, a hillside house with a front porch and three rooms instead of the one of her parents' cabin. Inside, though, lurked yet more agonies. At Highland Forge, Georgia, colored might serve the table, in the less strict home might even eat later at the same table, but colored *never* sat at table with whites.

Of course, there wasn't quite room anyhow for six people at the parlor table, though crowding could have achieved it. So Essie set the tiny kitchen table for the Moffats, perhaps thinking the families could talk back and forth between the two rooms. At the sideboard they all served themselves plates of Essie's beef pot roast with potatoes, turnips and carrots. August plumped down at the parlor table and patted the chair beside him.

"Billy, sitz du!"

"Now pa," he said, "that there's Lenora June's spot."

Feeling deserted, Lenora watched him march into the kitchen and sit with her parents. All she could do was take the chair August had intended for his son. She buttered a slice of lightbread and slowly chewed a bite.

"Wonderful bread," she said, and no doubt it was, though in her present distress she could taste nothing. Soon Billy and her parents were laughing in the kitchen. At the Leidig table nobody laughed.

"What you think of our son?" Essie asked.

Lenora swallowed and felt the half-chewed lump slide grudgingly down.

"You know I like him, Mrs. Leidig."

"I was afraid of that. Dancin *will* bring it on. What you gonna do about it?"

"I don't know, Mrs. Leidig. I don't know what will happen when we leave here."

The lively conversation continued at the other table. At last Essie started something like it in the parlor. She asked where they'd been, what they had done, and Lenora told them about the march across Georgia. August leaned close when she spoke of the battles, of Minie balls flying past his son. She told them how good it felt to knock manacles off slave after slave and set them free.

"Sure, I can see how you would feel like that," Essie sighed, "you being one. But don't you reckon the masters worked hard to buy all them slaves? Lenora June, right is *still* right."

August's hand hit the table, making the plates jump.

"Shut dein verdammte mouth! Woman, dese youngins home now. Ve talk nice!" In the sudden silence Lenora could hear only August's agitated breathing. Through the kitchen door she saw that all eyes at the other table were turned on them. ."Ve eat now," August said. "Ve talk nice."

Indeed they did for the rest of the meal, which was a good one. Lenora ate her fill of the tender beef and went to the sideboard for seconds, meeting Billy there. His blue eyes blazed with suppressed glee. He winked at her, which forced her to choke back a laugh. Averting her own eyes so he couldn't provoke her again, Lenora forked the meat along with turnips onto her plate. Sober as a pall bearer, she returned to the table.

Afterwards, over Billy's protest, his mother carefully unwound the bandage from his hand. The stub of the missing finger was thickly scabbed, but the hurled stone had peeled up an edge, clotted blood still thick around it.

"Oh, Billy, Billy, your poor finger..." She lay her forehead on the wrist of that arm. She drew long sighing breaths. When she rose up again, the back of his hand shone with her tears. His father stared, amazed.

"Dis finger gone! Vot happen?"

"Musket ball, pa."

August tugged agitatedly at the lobe of his ear.

"Vat you *do*, youngin? Don't you get killed!"

Of course they loved him. Lenora had long known that. It still surprised her, how deeply his pain bit into them. Could they ever accommodate the pain he would inherit in living with a Negro wife? Essie had barely rebandaged the hand with clean muslin when Aaron thundered up onto the front porch.

"Secesh on the road west!" he yelled through the closed door. "Helluva bunch!"

When she came out to the porch, Lenora saw them—what might be a battalion of riders in column, rising over the far hill to advance steadily down the road on which her own squad had approached. Standing in the door behind her, John Marion spoke up.

"Joe Wheeler cavalry. Musta seen the smoke of the mill. They gonna want them horseshoes I make for'em."

On the creek bank the Forge building, now an ashy pile within its stone foundation, still radiated heat.

"Reckon there's any horseshoes left?" Billy asked.

"Puddle of iron, that's all."

"We can run," Lenora June said, "but the Forge slaves can't. They'll never get away."

Billy rubbed the back of his neck with the freshly-bandaged hand.

"Sherman's comin two or three hours behind them Secesh," he said. "They cain't chance gettin stopped here. If we just hold'em off awhile, they'll give up and go 'round."

August lay a hand on John Marion's shoulder.

"Stay here mit uns, John. Reba also. Safe mit uns behind house."

John looked beyond August to Reba, who was standing in the open door.

"You stay, Reba," he told her. "Believe I'll get down to the creek with these youngins."

Early in the day the Forge Master himself had armed four slaves with muskets, one of them a flintlock smoothbore. Isaac had the Master's shotgun, and he passed out the other three muskets. One went to Lenora's father, and another to old Charley Broomfield, the fiddler, who seemed eager to perform on this novel percussion instrument. Billy told them all to blaze away, particularly those who had repeating weapons.

"We got plenty cartridges," he said. "Shoot'em off. Make this line smoke."

When they took up positions behind the charcoal piles at creek's edge, Lenora June sprinkled her squad members among the amateurs to help them load. Then she stood to watch the Confederates come on in a clotted column, their horses crowding each other on the narrow road. She decided this might work as another ambush like the battle at the creek. In their first volley the squad might knock down a half-dozen of the enemy. Two vedettes rode well ahead of the rest. They were still far out, maybe three hundred yards, when a Spencer carbine fired, POW! POW! In a flash of anger, she judged Billy had deliberately warned the vedettes, who whirled their mounts and spurred away. Was this more of his concern for Peckerwoods?

Now everyone else fired in a thunderous volley. Lenora worked the lever of her Spencer, shooting at the flying tails of the vedettes' mounts and cranking out copper casings to fire again. The line spurted flame and smoke. When the vedettes were far out of range, she shouted:

"Cease fire!"

Two of the beginners, who had troubled themselves to reload , fired anyway just for the joy of it. Then the line fell silent, shooters breathing the choking cloud of their own powder smoke. Ears ringing, Lenora felt her anger at Billy wane. Killing the vedettes would have enraged the rest of that battalion. They would have come on hard, as did the Rebels in the battle over the slave coffle when their comrades were bushwhacked. But these today were not forty Secesh. They were two hundred or more.

Halted by the firing, the column on the road thickened at the front, very like a snake's head, Lenora thought. She watched it, fascinated. In every previous battle she'd felt a heavy dread, and that same sense came to her now, an ache in her chest behind the heart. The squad's position could easily be flanked. If these Confederates began to file off the road in both directions, deploying, then everyone on her battle line would be forced to run or die.

She wondered whether she would tell the assaulting soldiers, as a final plea, that she was a woman. The Rebel vedette—she of the turkey feather—had blurted out that secret. She thought of Desdemona Pierpont and her fear that, captured, she would be raped. Georgia plantation ladies seemed extravagantly fearful of rape. They called it a dishonor infinitely worse than death. Why? Why would rape dishonor anyone except the rapist? It occurred to Lenora June that if she were captured in battle here, rape alone was the best she could expect—a fate much better than death, she decided. But rape followed by death was more likely.

The horsemen on the road now crowded together at the sides, opening a lane in the middle down which a four-horse team hauled a cannon. Unhitched, it was swung around. She could see the bronze muzzle. From his position on the right Billy ran toward her, crouching to keep behind the charcoal piles. He caught a breath and said:

"What's it gonna be? Too far for cannister. Maybe they'll shoot ball."

They lay side by side on a pile, heads just high enough to see over. The artillerymen were stroking a charge down the barrel. One tiny figure withdrew the ramrod, threw it down and jumped aside. Flame belched from the muzzle, which was instantly obscured by smoke. The boom reached them along with the load. The ball struck a charcoal pile and bounced over, bounced again on dirt far behind and skipped and rolled to a stop. Then it exploded with a mighty WHUMP! Fragments blown high in the air pattered on the ground around it.

"Damn, that's shell!" Billy breathed.

"What's shell?"

"Iron ball with powder inside and a fuse to touch'er off."

The cannon fired again. Its ball bored deep into the far side of Lenora and Billy's pile. A minute later it exploded, bouncing her whole body. Charcoal dust erupted in a choking cloud, which drifted over them. The balls kept coming, usually skimming over to skip away and bounce among the forge buildings behind them before exploding. One detonated against the wall of the guest cottage, which began to burn.

The cannoneers hit near the top of a pile far to the right of her. The shell plowed through and rolled to the back side. Somebody there screamed when it exploded. Could it be her pa? This sharpened the ache near her heart. The next ball landed short, right on the creek bank, but then skipped over the charcoal and thumped, spinning, to a stop at Lenora's feet. On one bulging side a fuse spat fire. She scrambled away from it, glancing back to see Billy claw into his haversack . He pulled out his canteen, jerked the cork and leaned forward to douse the shell. Hissing steam rose in a cloud around him.

"Good thing them bastards cut the fuse so long," he sighed. "They're scared it'll go off in the gun."

Lenora hadn't moved ten feet, but she was panting now as if she'd run a mile.

"Open fire!" she yelled. "Let's aim high and try to drive off that cannon."

Not that the Napoleon was in effective rifle range. Not that they could even see it, given the smoke that hid the cannon and swirled thickly through woods to the north. She fired anyway into the cloud, joining another roaring fusillade. Though the range wasn't *effective,* it was good enough. Spent slugs pinging off the rocks around them apparently alarmed the gun's crew. When the smoke there thinned, Lenora saw that the horses were hitched again. The cannon rolled off onto a woods trail to the north. And the road, far up the slope to the horizon, was empty.

"Ha!" Billy laughed. "They're going around! They thought we was a damn regiment. They hid behind that cannon smoke to sneak off."

"Maybe they're flanking us."

"May be. Ought to send Ike and Hubert yonder to check. But I don't think so."

His face, she now realized, was blacker than her own had been before the battle, his white eyes shining. She spat on her index finger and drew a pale line down his cheek.

"You look like a minstrel on a showboat," she said.

He fingered his own cheek and eyed the result.

"Reckon I'd be good at minstreling? That's a sight easier than hoeing corn."

She sent the two scouts and, dreading what she would find, walked over to visit the wounded man. It was Charley Broomfield, who still lay face down on a charcoal heap. As she approached, he rolled to one side and smiled grimly, holding up a jagged splinter of black iron.

"Nail me in that backside," he said, "but she come out easy."

He couldn't sit a horse, he told her, but he'd find a place in a wagon. Now, she decided, she wanted to release Enoch Hardesty. She'd long known there are no good slave masters, but there is a wide variety of bad ones. Enoch had been among the better of those. As she approached his little prison, he seemed more disappointed with her than angry.

"In the chicken house, Lenora June," he mourned from behind the door. "The *chicken house.* That's where you locked me, after all I did for your family."

"Yes," she said, "you dragged us back from Pennsylvania under the Fugitive Slave Act. You took all the money my father earned up there. You sold me west because I taught reading to your slaves."

"That's unjust, Lenora June. Thirty-nine lashes, that's what the law decrees for anyone teachin colored how to read. You know very well I don't whip my servants."

She leaned close to a crack between the weathered planks of the door. One rheumy old eye stared back at her.

"Promise to be peaceful, Mr. Hardesty, and I'll let you out. If you come out mad and try something, you'll get yourself killed."

His eye pulled away from the crack. She smelled manure, saw the chickens huddled, clucking, against the wall behind him.

"What else can I do?" he said. "Y'all have destroyed my authority, destroyed all civilized life at this Forge."

She extracted a wooden wedge from the iron hasp and swung the door open on creaky hinges. He stepped out, raising his knees high, rocking his torso to loosen the joints. He glanced up the slope toward the guest cottage, where flame had reached the shingles at the eaves. Yet another tower of smoke rose skyward.

"Y'all burned my mill and the forge already. Now look what y'all done!"

"Mr. Hardesty, your Confederate friends burned that one."

With one hand he waved her argument away. He'd always been such a mighty man here. She saw now that, standing level with him, she was looking down a little into his face.

"Is Parthenia home?" she asked.

"No, she's gone to Savannah, thank God. She won't have to see her old father thus served."

"Who's in the Mansion?"

"It's only Rachel."

Lenora couldn't resist saying it.

"Your Bathsheba."

"I won't speak to that." He stroked his full gray beard, stroked it repeatedly, as he might caress a well-loved pet. "I won't justify myself, no more than King David did. You know I've been a widower these twenty years."

He'd always dressed well, even on work days at the Forge. Now he wore a cutaway coat of gray broadcloth and nice wool trousers, whitened at the knees by chicken manure. He looked earnestly up into her eyes.

"You are deluding yourself, Lenora June, in this foolish quest. Some day the Almighty will ordain freedom for the slaves. But not yet. How long your subjugation may be necessary is known and ordered only by a WISE and merciful Providence. Your emancipation will sooner result from the mild and melting influence of Christianity than the storms and tempests of this war."

She listened, surprised at his eloquence. He'd read this somewhere, or heard it as a sermon in church. She opened her mouth to speak, but he raised a prophet's hand against her.

"While we see the course of the abolition of human slavery is onward," he intoned, "and we give it the aid of our prayers, we must leave the progress as well as the result in HIS hands who sees the end. He who chooses to work by slow influences, and with Whom two thousand years are as a single day."

Lenora could not quell her smile.

"Only two thousand years till you free the slaves," she said, "that's good news."

"Oh, Lenora, don't blaspheme against the God of our fathers! You do that at your peril."

She had been doing a great deal at her peril, she decided, and so far was reasonably happy with the result. She freed Mr. Hardesty to walk, stoop shouldered, up the slope toward the Mansion and his Bathsheba.

Sherman's army—the 179th Illinois, anyhow, and part of another regiment—arrived just at dusk. By that time the squad had helped provide ample food for the slave cabins and assembled the necessary mules and wagons for the freed peoples' departure. A good thing, because Union soldiers grabbed up all remaining edibles at the Forge, butchered the cows and hogs, emptied the smoke house, drew pitchers of sorghum molasses from a barrel and tipped the rest on the ground.

"How come you waste it like that?" Billy asked a sergeant.

"Keep the damn Johnnies from gettin it," the man answered. "If they hungry, they won't fight so long."

"How about these other Georgia folks? Don't they get to eat?"

"Once they quit this war, we be haulin rations in to'em. As long as the Confederacy keeps a-fightin, it's their own damn lookout!"

His interest aroused, the sergeant studied this lieutenant's charcoal-smudged face with its white streaks. "Hey, what outfit you with, anyhow?"

"Forty-fourth U. S. Colored Infantry," Billy answered.

The sergeant's eyes flashed to Lenora June, then to Billy again.

"I see," he said, as if such a unit designation could explain any strangeness of outlook.

That night every fence around Highland Forge was pulled down. Their well-seasoned rails blazed in the thousand campfires that starred the darkness of Quapaw creek valley. Colonel Langley's engineers stuffed three kegs of gunpowder into a vent of Vesuvius Furnace, touching off an eruption of hot stone that at long last vindicated the structure's name. Otherwise, the colonel was satisfied with her squad's advance destruction of forge industries. Lenora, uneasy about roaming Union bummers, stationed five squad members among the slave cabins to protect them.

She and Billy washed up in the creek, restoring him to the white race, leaving her even cleaner but less changed. They laid out pallets side by side on the front porch of the Mansion where, even after dark, they could see the black humps of surrounding hills against a paler sky. Later they watched a soldier approach. A pine knot torch flamed in his hand, lighting his clean-shaven face. He looked with interest at the building until Billy and Lenora sat up on their pallets.

"Oh!" the man cried, his breath a lighted cloud before his face. "Colonel post you there?"

"Sure!" Billy said, lying. "Colonel said keep it safe."

A snowflake spun down beside the torch-bearer. The man pointed to it.

"Looks like Michigan!" he said, and walked on.

Lenora felt rancor enough toward the Forge Master yet, like Billy, she didn't want the house burned. The torch was still moving off in the night when another flake fell, illumined by lamplight from the Mansion's windows. Then the air was full of them. The moment before, Quapaw creek valley had resounded with axes hewing firewood, babbled with soldier voices, songs and loud joking. Lenora had scarcely noticed the noise. What she noticed now was the sudden hush. Big flakes poured down from the sky and, touching earth, instantly melted. Billy stepped off the porch and looked up, letting the crystals dampen his face.

She'd seen much snow in Abington. They rarely saw it here. The air was thick with white flakes like pearled barley stirred into a clear broth—except cold. It had a lace-curtain whiteness, open and airy, yet was somehow opaque. It shut off their view of surrounding slopes. Billy returned to his pallet, pulled up his blanket and lay back beside her. Enclosed in this tight little world, their porch, their cozy blanket nests, she felt at home. But it would be the last time, she suspected, the last she'd ever feel this way at Highland Forge.

The front door creaked open. A candle glowed there within a glass chimney.

"Lenora June?" It was a woman's voice. "You out here?"

She sat up beside Billy. "Rachel?"

"Uh huh." Rachel stepped down onto the bricks of the porch. Wrapped in a belted robe of blanket material, she was heavier now, getting on toward middle age. "Look at that snow!" she said. "*Long* time I ain't seen it." Rachel turned to Lenora. "How you doing, honey? Master Enoch say you a Yankee soldier now."

Her smile, lighted by the candle lantern she held, shone on Lenora.

"I'm a Union sergeant. I'm fine. How's Theophilus?"

"Sure, he all right, he going on fourteen now. Yestidy he hitch up that ole phaeton and drive Miz Parthenia to Savannah."

With the house wall behind them and a curtain of snow in front, in this private place, Lenora thought she could ask any question and get an answer.

"Rachel, how are *you* doing?"

Sighing, Rachel sat on the top porch step, snow speckling her hair, and looked out into the white night.

"Of course it ain't what I was a-lookin to get in this life," she said, "but Enoch's a purty good ole man. Them colored down in the Quarters, they don't like it. Neither do them white folk, the ones live 'round here. Nobody likes it. But Enoch, he treat me decent."

She turned in her seat and held the light up, squinting past the candle to see them both.

"Hello, Billy."

"Hello, Rachel."

They grinned at each other, these wide, friendly, knowing grins.

"While ago y'all left outa here separate," Rachel said. "Now here y'all are back, and *together*. You two gettin about bad as me and Enoch."

26

The refugees and especially the Negroes expand in this sunlight like flowers...Their exuberant laughter may be heard for a long distance as they journey on, sometimes riding in their queer go-cars with a load of blankets, pots, etc., or when as in once instance today three little girls were at the same time astride a patient good natured old mule.

—Maj. George Ward Nichols in his *Story of the Great March.*

NEXT MORNING WHEN THEY SAID goodbye to Billy's parents, his mother clung to him dry eyed. It was August who wept. He stood wiping tears from his cheeks with the back of one hand.

"Come home. Kommst du, Billy! Zu hause. Ven you can."

"Yes, paw. I try!"

With his mother's arms around him, he reached over her shoulder to shake his father's hand. Then he pulled her arms loose and turned her to face Lenora June, who stood before Essie trembling worse than he'd ever seen her tremble in battle.

"Mama, give her a hug. Say bye to Lenora."

His ma did not look at Lenora. Wearing her best dress of gray wool, she kept her eyes on the plank floor, still wet from melted snow.

"Good-bye," Essie said, but did nothing more.

They stood on the porch of the Leidig house overlooking a valley churning with movement. The 179th Illinois was leaving, most of it gone now beyond the first hill of the road out. On their heels trod what seemed an even larger regiment of freed people, their wagons and creaky carriages and skinny livestock swarming the raw dirt of the road. Lenora June's parents were among those refugees. Lenora's squad, already mounted, waited not a hundred yards from the Leidig house. They watched with interest what was happening on this porch. His mother nodded to that little cluster of dark-faced men on horseback.

"You going off with *them*," she said. "You ain't ever coming back."

"I will, ma. Now hug Lenora."

She wouldn't. His heart pounding, Billy watched his mother stare at the porch floor, arms held rigid at her sides. August pushed past her and gathered Lenora into his arms, thumping her on the back.

"Kommst du wieder, Lenora."

Her eyes were making tears, though she did smile at last, now that she'd been embraced. When August let her go and stepped back, Essie said:

"I'm sorry, Lenora June. I just wasn't brought up that way."

As if the way she'd been brought up were the only right way. Lenora's face jerked aside, as if she'd been slapped. Billy felt a flare of anger like fire behind his eyes.

"Neither was pa!" he yelled. "He wasn't brought up like that, but Paw hugged her!"

Now his mother began to weep. Hell, Billy was weeping too, all four of them were dripping and sniffling and snuffling.

"You hate me, don't you, Billy," his mother said. "You ain't ever coming back."

He had a headache now, he ached all over his body. He pulled his mother into his arms and hugged her again, reaching around to pet the tuft of gray hair behind her right ear. The collar of her dress smelled faintly of lilac, scent left from some happier occasion.

"I love you, ma. We come back, some day we come back."

He waited, dreading what his mother might now say: "Not with her!" But thank God she didn't say it. Again he had to peel her arms away, one after the other, to free himself. Then she picked up a pair of scissors from the porch rail. Billy hadn't noticed the scissors. She moved toward him, her chest heaving, her breath coming in hoarse sighs. He stood petrified as she approached.

Once more smelling lilac, he heard the blades swish beside his ear. She came away with a lock of sun-bleached hair, which she held to one damp cheek. Billy coughed and cleared his throat and relaxed. By the time he and Lenora were mounted, riding out with the squad, everything on the porch had resolved itself. His mother and father stood there smiling, waving friendly goodbyes, like parents in an album tintype.

When the squad reached the top of the first hill, Lenora pulled her horse around to look back. Even after the long night, even after the snow, smoke still rose from the burned buildings. Through bare tree branches he could see his parent's hillside home and, on the other side of the creek, the cabin where Lenora was born.

"Billy, I can't come back," she said. "It will be a hundred years before Negro people can live decently here."

"Where? You mean Highland Forge?"

"I mean the South."

Billy wanted to come back. Some day he wanted to. But he said:

"Reckon I cain't either then. Ain't gonna be any better here for white folks, not the ones I like."

"Don't you like your mother? For your mother the South will be the perfect place."

Her words clotted around his heart. A little shiver of hurt feelings ran down through his body. He looked away so Lenora wouldn't see his face. Then he turned to her and yelled: "You don't need to SAY it! Just shut up! Shut the hell up!"

She sat stiffly on her roan, as stiff as Essie had stood on the porch. He whirled his chestnut and rode down the shallow slope toward flat land below. He cantered past Corporal Leon Duffy, who saluted smartly and called out:

"Loooo-tenant Ludwig!"

Billy no longer minded the kidding, but this time he glared at his comrade and barked:

"Shut your gaw-damn trap!"

Leon's astonished face dropped behind as Billy rode onward. The speed, the wind on his face, eased the ache. She had hurt his feelings, but his own mother had hurt Lenora's. He slowed the chestnut to a trot. She caught up on the level ground, her horse crowding his, stirrup to stirrup.

"I'm sorry, Billy."

He took a few long breaths, and the hurt was gone.

"Sure! Me too. It's a sorry situation."

Then he turned in the saddle and, grinning, yelled back at an offended Leon Duffy.

"I ain't any more a real loooo-tenant than you are a real corporal!"

Leon flipped him another mocking salute. Of course Billy *was* a Ludwig, a true Ludwig, thanks to his mother. Billy never could get over that. Mother. As she had held his lock of hair to her cheek, he ran the word across his tongue again—mother—tasting it as if for the last time.

The melted snow had left the road surface damp but not wet. This was quick-draining, sandy soil. Willows grew thick in many little ditches that laced cropland on both sides. Beyond the fields lay woods, mixed pine and oak with, here and there, tall evergreen holly trees and magnolia shining among gray branches. They rode at an easy pace until they met an army captain waiting on horseback with two aides. Billy barely got through his salute before the officer barked:

"Any more army behind you on this road?"

"Nawsir. We the last ones outa Highland Forge."

The captain seemed irritated about something.

"All right then, General Davis wants you to move along. Catch up with the rear guard."

"Is that General Jefferson Davis?" Lenora June asked.

"Correct! We're going ahead now, but we want you people to catch up. That's an order!"

"Yessir!" Billy said.

As the captain and his aides rode away, Lenora said:

"That's the general who doesn't like Negroes."

The squad spurred their animals into a trot until they reached the ragged column of freed people. They had to slow then and ride on the verge to pass a family rich in livestock. Two little boys herded five sheep and a lone hog along the road, now and again threatening them with willow switches. A woman rode astride an old Jersey cow led by her man.

"Where you folks a-going?" Billy asked her.

The woman, skinny herself but with a big belly that promised a coming birth, looked somberly back at him.

"We going where y'all going," she answered.

Her statement bothered him. Where *was* he going? Ten yards ahead trudged a young man who had rigged a leather harness for himself behind a big two-wheeled cart. He held the handles, leaning into the traces, and pushed it like a wheelbarrow. On a mound of a goods in the box sat a little boy, wrapped around with a blanket. A woman walked behind them. As they passed, she called:

"How far to Savannah?"

"Thirty mile, I reckon," Billy told her.

The man looked up at them.

"What I heard, they give us forty acre and a mule." This he panted out between breaths as he struggled along with the cart. "Forty acre! In that Carolina rice land on the coast."

"Who told you that?" Lenora June asked.

"They all sayin it. Nigger teamster, he listen by Gen-ral Sherman tent night before last. Sherman talk about it. Give us forty acre. Forty! That's rice land, that's Canaan land. Live good yonder by the sea." He nodded forward to the cart he pushed. "And I sure want that mule."

Somehow the same story had gone out to many freed people on the road. They were talking about it.

"Maybe Sherman ain't so bad about colored as we thought," Billy told Lenora.

They passed a big platform wagon, chickens pecking corn scattered on a tarp that covered the load. They were free to fly away but didn't, apparently enjoying the ride. Beside the wagon walked a middle-aged colored man and a pipe-smoking woman, whose skin was whiter than the weathered hide on Billy's hands. Maybe she was purely white—a white woman with a colored man, the backwards picture of his own hope for life with Lenora. He studied the woman with interest. She scowled back at him.

"What the HELL you lookin at?"

He caught the bill of his forage cap between two fingers and tipped it.

"I was just admiring your poultry, maam. I do love them Dorkings and Shanghais."

She pulled the pipestem from her mouth and spat on the ground.

"That ole Dorking rooster, he's trouble a-plenty. He goes in the pot tonight." She puffed out a cloud of rich-smelling smoke and softened a little. "Y'all way behind Sherman's army. You gonna catch up before evening?"

"We will," Lenora answered.

"Y'all see Sherman, tell him we lookin for them forty acre. That mule be handy too."

"If we see him, we'll tell him," Lenora said.

She leaned down from her saddle and plucked a cattail from a roadside ditch, idly laying the seedhead, the velvety cat's tail, between the ears of her horse. Billy rode beside her and thought about forty acres—ten in corn, ten wheat, five oats, maybe three in Timothy pasture and two for cowpeas, two for garden vegetables, two for sorghum cane to make syrup, three for an orchard: peaches and apples, sour cherries, maybe Seckel pears. The mental arithmetic challenged him. But that would leave plenty of land for a barn and a house, first a house of logs, to be expanded later with a big addition of planed lumber. He could see himself sitting on the front porch of an evening with Lenora June. That woman's pipe had smelled so good, he might take to tobacco.

"I wouldn't mind gettin them forty acres," he told her. "Way better'n what my pa ever got, always farmin for somebody else."

Her brows lifted as she eyed him.

"Billy, those forty-acre farms are just for colored."

"Well, ain't you colored? We could throw in together."

"So," she said, "you want me just to get my farm."

He rode on beside her in sullen silence. You couldn't talk serious to this damn woman. Only a minute later, though, she did get serious.

"Billy, nobody's gonna to give forty acres to colored. Not in the South. These plantation people will never let it go. But the government is giving away land to people in the West, a hundred-sixty acres."

"A *hunnerd-sixty acres*! Come on, Lenora June."

"They are, Billy, homestead land. Congress passed the law two years ago. At Hunnicutt's they got a copy of a Baltimore newspaper. I saw it in there."

A hundred-sixty acres. This knocked Billy's dream farm cockeyed. In addition to all the rest, he could also plant them tender grapes and pomegranates. Planting that much ground just might wear down a yeoman farmer, and make him rich. He glanced shrewdly at the woman riding beside him.

"Sure, I see now. You want me to get my farm."

She plucked the cattail up and whapped him with it, the shattered head filling the air around him with a thousand cottony seed tufts, like last night's snowfall. She spurred her horse and galloped away, raising one hand high. He wanted her, she wanted him—and for sweeter reasons than getting a farm, though they could get that too. He felt gorged on delight as he spurred his own mount after her, riding out of that seed snowstorm up the road verge to the top of a little rise. He wanted her to turn, to smile at him and prove she felt happy too. Instead, she stood high in her stirrups and pointed ahead.

"Look at'em!"

Southeastward on their own road the column of freed people stretched straight away for a good two miles, turning to enter a woodland, which closed off the view. Rolling stock was thick on the track, spring wagons, buggies, gigs, phaetons, surreys, handcarts, but there were many more walkers than riders. With the road so crowded, people and their animals spilled off into cornfields at the side. The fences were down, livestock hungrily cropping what forage remained after the army's passage. Billy saw a half-dozen broken wagons and buggies abandoned in the cropland. Most had lost wheels, sitting tilted among tattered cornstalks. The road itself crawled with plodding feet. Gaps had developed where lagging travelers slowed the procession. Others crowded past, using the road verge or cornfields to move ahead.

"Look there!" Lenora shouted, pointing again.

A mile to the right ran another road, even more choked with marchers. Colonel Langley had said twenty thousand freed slaves were following Sherman. Billy thought he might be seeing that many right here. It couldn't be. This army was advancing on a front of sixty miles, everywhere followed by the freed people. Still, here in sight were many thousands. Stretching herself high, Lenora June bobbed in the stirrups.

"That's freedom! That's freedom, Billy!"

Anyhow they're moving, Billy thought, going where they want to go, without knowing what place that is any better than he did.

"Is that freedom?"

"Yes!"

The rest of the squad raced forward to join Billy and Lenora. Their horses huffed to a stop on the little rise, hooves scattering sand. The riders sheltered their eyes and stared in wonder at the throng of freed people marching ahead of them. Somehow a Union artillery battery had let itself be swallowed up in this tide of refugees. Six cannon pulled by four-horse teams rolled far out in a pasture, double-timing it to get around. At the head of their column rode a guidon bearer with a flagstaff planted in a stirrup socket. Above his head fluttered a blue unit pennant and above that a big American flag. Aaron pointed and made a little musical noise, that's all. Next thing, the squad was singing the colored Yankee soldier song, one of many verses Billy didn't know.

> See there above the center, where the flag is waving bright,
> We're going out of slavery, we're bound for freedom's light.
> We mean to show Jeff Davis how the African can FIGHT,
> As we go marching on!

They sang the verse again, Billy this time struggling to pick up the words and sing with them. Why did there have to be a Confederate Jefferson Davis, their very president, he thought, and also a Union one—Billy's own commander on this march? *Their* president, he realized, was the way his mind had phrased it. *Theirs*, the president of the Southrons, but not *mine*. Now the song and the flag that inspired it raised his spirits, made him think there might be something better than Georgia and certainly bigger. Light headed, almost floating in his Confederate Jenifer saddle, he spurred ahead to catch up with those folks bound for freedom's light.

27

...it was all done to free the Negro; and when done by the flow of blood, three out of four of the liberators cared not a copper for the freedom of the Negro; and about the same proportion on the Southern side did not give a damn.

—Confederate Private William A. Fletcher.

THE SQUAD STOPPED FOR A noontime dinner with Lenora's parents and others from Highland Forge. Camping not a hundred yards away they found pilgrims from the Hunnicutt plantation, among them Ezra and Martha with little Lovage. The Hunnicutt folks were short of food. Lenora introduced them all around and suggested the Forge people should march with the other group.

"Sounds smart," John Marion said. "We may need extry hands afore we get outa here."

Riding onward, they found the road surface good despite the passage of the 179th Illinois and other units before them. The land on both sides was swampy, Spanish moss trailing from cypress clumps scattered among other trees. They saw rain clouds to the south. A column of smoke rose into those clouds—cotton bales burning somewhere, or a cotton gin.

They rode on ahead of the Forge people but—worried about Lenora's parents—waited for them at a water crossing. They met them downstream from a bridge the 58th Indiana had assembled from parts hauled in wagons. An artillery battery rolled onto the planks, each canvas-covered pontoon sagging as the bronze Napoleons rolled past, then bucking up again. An infantry unit followed, soldiers moving three abreast in route step. A banty rooster rode on one soldier's slouch hat, dipping and rising with his step.

Near Billy on the creek bank, a colored man stared gloomily into muddy water floating thick with twigs and brown leaves. A wad of this litter had lodged under a boat dock there. The man glanced up to address Billy.

"That ole Ebenezer creek, he mean to flood. Got rain yonder." He waved at the clouds to the south.

Muskets sputtered far to the southeast beyond the creek. The sounds died away, then took up again. The squad had dismounted, was standing among the crowd of Forge and Hunnicutt people near the boat dock when an officer rode down along the creek toward them. It was the same captain who had ordered them to catch up. Suddenly Billy wondered how well they had obeyed that order.

"Got to salute this one," he told the squad.

They stiffened and whipped their arms up. Despite this courtesy, the captain seemed to churn with some internal wrath.

"Got a skirmish going on ahead with Rebel cavalry," he told them. "General Davis wants all soldiers across now. RIGHT NOW. Rest of you folks wait till it's safe."

Surveying this out-of-place U. S. Colored Infantry unit, the captain scowled at Billy.

"Lieutenant, you people are late. Get this GAW-DAMN squad mounted and across that bridge!"

"Yah!" Billy saluted again, caught himself standing tiptoe, as if that made his obedience more emphatic.

He followed as the captain led them upstream along the gravel creek bank past the multitude of freed people waiting to cross. The crowd stretched back along the road, overflowed into pastures on both sides. They seemed patient enough about the delay. Some had built fires to cook on and speed the drying of clothing washed in the creek. Lenora's squad was the first colored fighting unit they had ever seen. A ripple of cheers, a thicket of waving arms, followed them through the multitude. Billy sat on his horse as tall as a short man could. The U. S. Colored Infantry rode among them like heroes.

Then came another volley of musketry, this time from the west, many sharp reports and a few huge booms, as from shotguns. The cheering stopped. The smiles vanished. All those faces turned anxiously to the west. Billy looked over their heads, beyond the clearing to the woods, but could see no gun smoke.

"Move, gaw-dammit!" The captain had turned in his saddle to shout at them. "Move on up to that bridge!"

Approaching the entry, they saw a square-built man sitting a magnificent horse. His narrow eyes stared out over a sweeping mustache, which itself overhung a dense black beard. He wore the two stars of a major general.

"That's him!" Lenora hissed. "General Jefferson Davis. What'll he say about us?"

Thankfully, before he even noticed them he reined his mount around and moved onto the bridge. The general rode across it, but the captain turned a sour look on Lenora's squad and yelled:

"Dismount! Walk your horses."

The captain himself dismounted to lead his horse onto the planks. The squad followed, passing through a platoon of bluecoats who stood guard where the bridge touched shore. Billy realized then they really were late. Except for the bridge guards, Lenora's squad would be the last Union troops to cross. The current had tugged the pontoons downstream at the middle, straining the ropes, so they walked a long curve toward the southeastern bank. A magnolia branch sailed down the creek and lodged between two pontoons. Its big green leaves rose and fell as the current flapped them. Billy glanced back. Beside the fishing dock maybe two hundred yards below the bridge, John Marion stood waving at them, Reba beside him. The other squad members passed ahead as Billy and Lenora turned to wave.

From the west—this time much closer—came another burst of gunfire. A ripple went through the crowd on the creekbank as all faces once more turned toward the sound. From the freed people came a low moan. Then they turned away from the shooting and swarmed down toward the bridge. That bluecoat platoon stood at the entry, their leveled bayonets barring the way. Billy heard the solid "THOCK!" of axes biting into wood. Bluecoat axmen worked there among the guards.

"What the hell's going on?" he said.

All she answered was: "Have you got a full magazine in your Spencer?"

"You bet! And one in the chamber."

Now he saw it. Above the crowd, straight along the line of the bridge and far up at wood's edge, rode a band of grayback and butternut cavalry. The horsemen wielded long staves of wood, whipping at the former slaves as they rode among them. More people fled to the creek, some wading into brown water.

The chopping of axes ceased. The axmen pulled away and, along with the guards, came running back toward Billy and Lenora. Looking along the wooden roadway, Billy saw the shore move. No! It was the bridge, of course, cut free at the west end to swing on the current like a door on its hinges.

"OOOOOOOOO!" wailed the people stranded on the creek bank.

Billy yanked off his cap and slapped his thigh with it.

"That gaw-damn Union Jeff Davis! He's leaving our folks behind!"

Beside him, Lenora June hiked her left brogan up to a stirrup and swung into the saddle.

"What you thinkin?" Billy said.

She didn't answer, but he grabbed his own saddle horn and vaulted onto his mount without touching a stirrup. Downstream near the boat dock, the people swirled in panic. John Marion and Reba were lost in the crush. A second little band of Confederate cavalry, five or six of them, drove into the crowd there, striking about with staves, driving the people like cattle.

"They're taking back the slaves," Lenora June said.

The bridge had swung so far on the current it now pointed straight at the dock where people from the Forge and Hunnicutt's had been waiting. Billy and Lenora had a perfect view of the recapture, humans being turned back into property. Billy's right hand, with the reins knotted around it, lay on the saddle horn. The left hung free at his side, until another hand took it. Her hand was icy. He looked with wonder at the place where her hand clasped his. She had lived beside him, had even kissed him, but this was the first time since they started the march that she had held his hand. Her eyes looked into his.

"I'm going."

Reins gathered in her left hand, she used her right to yank the Spencer from its saddle scabbard. At the first touch of spurs, her roan surged forward. Billy jerked out his Spencer and followed. Ahead of them on the bridge, the running bluecoats first knotted together in panic, then jumped off the roadway into pontoons as the two horses thundered past on the planks. Billy had ridden all his life, but he'd never done this—never dived a horse at full gallop into a flooding creek. Lenora's mount simply ran off the bridge into air and fell, throwing up a tower of spray.

Seeing that, Billy's chestnut faltered, half-stumbled and then leaped far out, as if trying to reach the distant shore. The animal came down upright and plunged, carrying Billy deep. It was cold! Cold rushed into his boots, around his feet. Hooves churning, the horse carried him back to the surface. Horse and man snorted water out, sucked air back in.

Billy saw Lenora's roan, head up, swimming hard for the west bank. She wasn't in the saddle. Where then? Where? Her head broke the surface, she sucked in a gasping breath and instantly sank. She was a good swimmer. Why didn't she swim? He tugged at the reins, struggling to guide his mount toward her. The animal ignored his yanking on the bit. It swam straight for shore. Billy threw his left leg over the horn and launched himself off toward Lenora.

He sank like a gravestone. Of course! Who could swim carrying a Spencer carbine, with a revolver strapped to one hip? He sank down and touched bottom. It was dark there. Moving with the current, his feet slid through mud slick as fresh-rendered lard. He let his body sag, coiling himself like a spring. He triggered the spring and shot upward, catching a breath and a quick glance. She wasn't there! Down again, coil against the bottom, up again. He saw her! She was struggling to stay on the surface.

"Drop the Spencer!"

"No!"

She was gone. He sank too and rebounded, angling toward her. A few more rounds of bouncing, and they met on the bottom. With their free hands, they groped at each other. She caught the back of his neck and pulled him to her. They held hands and shot up together, puffing like blown horses.

"Drop the damn Spencer!"

"NO!"

The crazy woman was going to drown them both. Course he didn't drop his either. Would the Spencers anyhow even shoot after being dunked in water? They were well oiled and loaded with those copper-jacketed cartridges. Billy and Lenora kept bouncing and breathing, moving toward shore. In quick glimpses, Billy saw that Secesh cavalry near the dock were still rounding up slaves, beating at them, driving them into tight groups. Looked like about a dozen Secesh here—more than he and Lenora could handle. Rising to the surface again with Lenora June, he said:

"I'll carry you!"

He grabbed some breaths and, sinking, thrust his head between her legs. He rose with Lenora on his shoulders. That pushed her head above water. He could feel her weight bear him down to a stance in the mud, which gave his feet some traction. He plodded along the up-slanting bottom toward shore. The load grew when her arms and shoulders surfaced.

"POING!" He flinched as, under water, the shot pealed like a bell. It did shoot! Soaked or not, the Spencer fired! He felt her hand pat his head, then lift again. "POING! POING!" Staggering under her weight, he pushed his own head above the surface and hungrily sucked air.

"POW!" She fired again.

On the bank not thirty yards away, a Secesh cavalryman slumped over the horn of his saddle but clung to it as his panicked horse raced away. Then he fell off. Another horse lay kicking near the creek. Lenora had shot that one. Its rider scrambled up and ran for the carbine he had dropped on the ground. Billy bucked Lenora off his shoulders and raised his Spencer. When the Secesh grabbed the weapon and turned toward them, Billy shot him in the chest, knocked him backwards. The man flopped for a moment in the dirt and lay still. *Thou shalt not kill,* Billy thought. *Not without reason.*

They stood in shallow water just upstream from the dock. The freed people had recoiled from the firing and now milled in fright downstream from it.

"We need cover," Billy told Lenora as they sloshed out, but there was no cover. Lenora had taken the first two Secesh by surprise. Now that advantage was gone.

Billy looked to the right and saw four Rebel horsemen plow toward them through the crowd. They swung staves at colored people on both sides to open a path. More graycoats had circled west of the crowd and were coming from the left. Billy cranked open the breech of his Spencer and replaced the one cartridge he'd fired from its chamber. Lenora levered a cartridge into her weapon's chamber, then withdrew its nearly-empty magazine. She slid in a full one with seven cartridges. Between them, if they fired quickly, they would get sixteen shots before being killed.

"Here we go," she said.

Billy glanced again at the four Secesh coming through the crowd. He couldn't shoot at them without hitting freed people. He was surprised when one of the four somehow vanished from his mount. The animal plunged forward, knocking people over, as a melee swirled around the place where its rider fell. The stave the Secesh had been using now rose and chopped down on that place. The remaining three spurred their horses ahead, tumbling people in the way. Their animals bucked and faltered as river rocks, clods of dirt, broken branches, thudded on the riders.

The main Secesh force, ten or a dozen horsemen well spread apart, moved downhill toward the creek. Above the beards and mustaches, their eyes fixed themselves on Lenora and Billy.

"Kneel!" Lenora commanded.

"Good I-dee," Billy said. That way they made smaller targets and could aim steady over one knee.

With three of their number down, the Secesh were angry, eager to kill the killers. Instead of dismounting, they charged on horseback, squealing and whooping. At what might be a hundred yards Billy and Lenora opened fire. A horse skidded nose first to ground but the rider, thrown aside, jumped up and ran to retrieve his weapon. Billy fired at another rider, levered the next cartridge in, cocked the hammer and fired. Horse and man kept coming. Billy took aim once more, so keenly he didn't hear the Spencer's report. The Secesh pitched from the saddle.

From fifty yards the charging riders fired a sputtering volley, carbines and shotguns. This Billy heard, and the whisper of slugs, buckshot raking the gravel in front of him, Minie balls hissing into the creek behind. Something tapped his face. It didn't hurt. The riders burst out of their own gun smoke and came on. He heard Lenora's steady firing. She was alive! As he shot and cranked the lever, he felt a wetness on his left cheek, the crawly sensation of leaking blood. Another Secesh tumbled, and on Billy's next trigger pull the hammer snapped dryly against the firing pin. That he'd emptied the weapon so quickly surprised him.

The riders dropped their empty long guns. One drew a saber but most whipped revolvers out of belt holsters. In close, with six shots apiece, they would make it a slaughter. Billy groped for the revolver at his own belt. It wouldn't come free of the holster. Loaded cap and ball with wet black powder, it wouldn't fire anyway. Wanting to die standing up, he jumped to his feet. He blinked and looked through a blood-red haze at what was coming on horseback.

From beyond the boat dock on his right, a single shaft of smoke thrust out toward the riders. Then came a barn-wide blast of it, a stuttery volley of musket and shotgun fire. Billy's glance jerked to the people there. Five or six men with revolvers—John Marion and Isaac Stoneman among them—still fired at the Secesh, running closer after every shot. Another twenty colored men with muskets and shotguns were plunging ramrods into the barrels, furiously reloading. Yes! They were firing the weapons taken from Hunnicutt's and the Forge! Twenty paces short of Lenora a horse thudded down, somersaulting. Its dazed rider rose from the ground and was instantly knocked over. Three Secesh still mounted hauled on the reins, trying to turn away. One swung a pistol around to aim at the freed people. John Marion danced close under his animal's neck and shot him from the saddle. A fresh volley from the reloaded shotguns and muskets, this one raggedly delivered, knocked down the last two.

With a throaty roar, the crowd surged over the fallen horses and men. Billy saw two hands raised pleadingly. They sank in that boil of rage. Musket muzzles rose and fell, gun butts pounding down on the wounded men. Billy wanted to stop it. He wanted Lenora June to help. She still knelt in the firing position, leaning on her empty carbine. He kept blinking, trying to see her clearly. When she looked up at him, her eyes were running tears.

"It hurts, Billy. My leg."

"Oh, damn, damn. Lie down, Lenora."

"No." She raised her hand to him. "Help me up."

When he pulled her to her feet, blood drained from her right trouser leg over the leather brogan top. He fell to his knees beside her.

"Jesus, oh Jesus...." He drew his bayonet and cut away the blue cloth of her breeches, then the clingy wool of her long Johns. This bared the muscular column of her thigh. The entry wound at the front was small, but the slug had blasted a thumb-sized hole as it burst out through flesh at the black. The exit wound bled freely. As if by magic her mother took shape at Billy's side. The fingers of both her hands circled her daughter's thigh, running up and down it.

"Thankee, God!" Reba breathed. "Bone ain't broke."

She whipped a scarf from her shoulder bag, knotted it tight around the wound to slow the bleeding. Billy stood before Lenora, reached out to steady her on her feet. She looked into his face and spoke out in alarm.

"What's wrong with your eye?"

He lay a finger on the cheek under his left eye and felt slick blood. He closed his right eye. All he saw then through the left one was dull redness and beyond it the dark blur of Lenora June.

"I still see light, but it's commencing to hurt."

"There's a little hole, Billy. That buckshot on the gravel! You caught a splinter of lead." Her two hands cupped his face. "Why did they have to hit you there!"

"They's worse places," Billy said. "Splinter's a sight better than a whole slug."

He opened his right eye and saw her face. Tears still rolled down her cheeks, drizzled into the runnel under her nose. She had sucked in her lower lip, was squeezing it now between white teeth.

"Don't hurt much," he said. "I still got my shootin eye." He pulled her hands away and began to look around. "They's more Secesh right handy here. Don't wanna let'em bushwhack us. We got to form a line."

"You wait!" Reba said. Already she'd folded more cloth from her bag to make a pad. She lay it gently on the bleeding eye and bound another swatch around his head to hold it.

He didn't expect that his lieutenant's bars would make people obey him, but they did. John Marion went ahead of him, yelling to this one and that one, urging men previously unarmed to take weapons from the fallen rebels. They grabbed up pistols and carbines and shotguns. They yanked cartridge boxes from the belts of dead men and went about reloading. John Marion caught Billy by the arm.

"She bad hurt?"

"She hurts plenty, but anyhow the bone ain't broke."

"You hurt too," John Marion said, laying a hand gingerly up to touch the bandage.

Southward a quarter on the creek bank, some grayback cavalry were still rounding up slaves. Billy saw their eyes turn toward the developing line of freed people.

"Prepa-a-a-are to fire!" Billy hollered. "Don't wanna hit colored. Aim careful at them Secesh on the left. Just fire when y'all ready."

Instantly, one musket discharged, followed by a rattling volley. Just the burst of gun smoke caused the Secesh to bounce in their stirrups. They held the hats on their heads and ducked as slugs whizzed around them. None fell. They rode up among their recaptured slaves and began whipping them higher on the creek bank, away from this new armed force, which was already reloading.

"Stand at ease," Billy called, "but watch them Rebs."

Walking back toward Lenora, he glanced at the creek and saw a half-dozen colored people flailing in the water, trying to get across. Some bluecoat soldiers had freed a pontoon from the bridge and were paddling toward the swimmers. While Billy watched, one swimmer went down and did not rise again. That goddamn Union Jeff Davis. How many people had he drowned here today, how many sent back to slavery? He hawked up a wad of phlegm and spat on the ground. America---it was better than the Confederacy, much better, and yet far from good. The boat reached the other swimmers, and bluecoats began hauling them in.

Billy found Lenora and her mother seated on the boat dock. Reba had tugged off her daughter's soaked uniform coat and was now helping her into a dry coat of patchwork quilt material. When he sat down beside her, Lenora once more took his hand.

"You're trembling," she said. "Are you cold?"

"Huh-uh. This wool coat's startin to dry."

He looked at his other hand and saw it was shaking too. He closed his eyes, felt the left lid grate against the wound. His heart beat painfully in that eye. The stump of his missing finger hurt under its soaked bandage as Lenora gently squeezed the hand. Damn near a month ago Ezra shot off a chunk of his ear, then he'd lost that finger in the battle for the slave coffle. Now seemed like he'd lose an eye. He was shot plumb to hell. He sheltered a minute in the red quietness, the calm behind his eyelids. People talked in the distance. He listened to them and drew easy breaths. He opened his eyes. In his good one the light was dazzling, but he felt better.

"Just I wasn't clear done with being scared."

Billy saw Reba staring at her daughter's hand where it was joined to Billy's. This time she just sat quiet. This time Reba said nothing against blood mixing. He squeezed Lenora's hand and asked:

"Reckon you could live with a one-eyed, nine-fingered farmer?"

"On a hundred sixty acres?" She seemed to smile at the sky above his head. Then, musically, she recited: "Let us go forth into the field. Let us get up early to the vineyards. Let us see if the vine flourish, whether the tender grape appear, and the pomegranates bud forth. There will I give thee my..."

Here she stopped, but Billy recalled the Song's next word. He felt happy. He felt happy now, even with his bleeding eye. Then, from the far side of the flooding, creek, a voice sang out.

"Looooo-tenant Ludwig! Sergeant Lenora Juuuune!"

He stood on what was left of the bridge, which the current had snugged up against the far shore. Union engineers had almost finished taking it apart pontoon after pontoon, loading it on their wagons.

"I want go with y'all!" Leon yelled.

"Swim across," Billy yelled back. "Make a raft outa wood for your musket. Naw, hell, we got plenty guns over here. Just drop your musket and swim."

"I'm SCARED to swim!" he groaned.

Lenora caught Billy's arm and pulled herself up.

"Leon," she yelled, "go on with Sherman." To see him, she had to look around her mother, who was buttoning the coat. "You're the corporal, Leon. Lead the squad! Get up to South Carolina and free your family!"

It then dawned on Billy that Lenora was not going on with Sherman's army, nor was he. For them, Sherman's march had ended at Ebenezer Creek. Now, at least, he knew where they were *not* going.

"I RATHER go with y'all," Leon mourned, and jumped to shore as the engineers hauled out another pontoon. Hands in his pockets, he walked slope-shouldered up the bank. Billy liked Leon. He did. Still, he wasn't downright sorry to see his only rival for Lenora's fancy going the other way.

With his bayonet he chopped down a forked dogwood trunk to make a crutch for her. Reba padded it with a piece of blanket. Together the three of them moved slowly toward her parents' spring wagon. They passed through the battle wreckage of dead horses and soldiers—men so pitifully ragged the freed people hadn't bothered to strip them. Only their weapons had been worth taking. He looked into the mashed face of a soldier his own age, barely able to grow whiskers. Billy's one good eye ranged down the bloodied corpse. Except in a few places where the waxed thread still held, the man's shoe soles hung free of the uppers. Inside the leather his sockless feet were black with dirt.

"Look at'em," he said, "ain't an officer one amongst'em. It's just a bunch of Peckerwood privates and one corporal."

"No gentlemen," Lenora said, "no cavaliers."

If Billy had stuck with the Georgia Guard, he might have been among this crew. The dirty feet would have been his own.

'They fightin for honor, they fightin for liberty," Billy said. "That's what the woman vedette told me. She never had no slaves, but she was fightin for liberty to own'em."

Lenora June shook her head in wonder.

"Don't they fight hard! Don't they show courage. They always do. In a better cause, nobody could beat'em."

But she was sagging on her crutch now, teeth clenched. Billy came up on one side, Reba on the other. They helped her to the wagon. He dropped the tailboard and eased her up to sit. She ran light fingers over the stained fabric of her breeches.

"Blood won't come out," she said.

"We give it cold water soak," her mother told her. "Patch that hole. It come good again."

Clustered around them were other wagons and several carriages. People drifted toward them. Billy recognized those from the Forge, and at least Ezra and Martha from Hunnicutt's. Munching a hoecake, Lovage walked boldly up to Billy.

"You give me another penny?"

Billy was too weary now to fish into his soaked trouser pockets. His eye was hurting worse.

"Ain't got no more, Lovage," he lied.

Still the boy smiled and held out a grubby hand.

"Give you bite a'my hoecake."

Billy grabbed it, bit into it and growled. The corn meal gritted pleasantly between his teeth, sweetening as he chewed. Giggling, Lovage danced backwards, then came forward to reclaim the rest. John Marion came up leading Billy's and Lenora's horses, which he'd found grazing in a pasture downstream along with a half-dozen of the Confederate mounts. Their precious store of Spencer cartridges was still in their saddle bags.

"But y'all ain't travelin hoss-back for yet awhile," he told Billy and Lenora. "Y'all stop in that wagon bed till you better."

Billy was ready to stop. The pain in his eye was spreading back into his head, making the whole thing ache. His teeth ached. Charley Broomfield showed up, still limping from the shell fragment wound in his backside.

"Best thing I ever seen," Charley told Lenora and Billy, "way y'all rise up shootin out that creek. We took a lickin from them slave drivers. Time when we saw y'all, we figured we had enough. We start fightin back."

"Where's your fiddle, Charley?" Billy asked him.

"In that buggy. If I get a chance, I play tonight."

With others still gathering around the wagon, John Marion said:

"*Where* you gonna play tonight? That bridge is gone. Where we go from here?"

Billy was the lieutenant, but they all looked at Lenora June, a genuine U. S. Army sergeant, even if she was wearing a patchwork quilt. She shrugged.

"We could start toward those north Georgia mountains. We've got weapons for nearly forty people. With the Secesh trying to stop Sherman, they can't worry much about us. We could get on up into the Blue Ridge. Up there they don't like the Confederacy."

"Don't like colored neither," John Marion said.

Billy knew this argument. He'd been through it before, with Lenora June taking the other side.

"Anyhow," she said, "up there they won't try to make slaves of us."

"Good land in that Blue Ridge already took up," Isaac Stoneman said. "No land there for us."

She smiled and nodded at Billy.

"He says we can go to the mountains, and then go to Kansas."

"Yes!" Pleased to be noticed, Billy felt a grin widen toward his ears. Even the grin made his eye hurt. But he said: "They got abolitionists in Kansas. Gonna be free homestead land yonder—not no forty acres and a mule, either. It's a hunnerd sixty acres free land. Lenora saw it in that Baltimore paper."

"Homestead land?" John Marion snorted. "For colored?"

"May be."

"Go to KANSAS!" shouted Charley Broomfield.

"How to HELL we get out yonder?" Isaac demanded.

Long ago Lenora had showed Billy a newspaper map of the United States, which included Kansas as a territory. He knew how far it was. He said:

"First, let's just get on up to them mountains."

Epilogue

The Tragedy

Virtually from the moment of Lincoln's death on the morning of April 15, 1865, all the possibilities bound up in the Emancipation Proclamation began rapidly to unravel, and within a dozen years, the freed slaves of the South had been recaptured by the ex-Confederate ruling class in a weir of economic dependency, political intimidation and racial terror.
—Allen C. Guelzo in his "Lincoln's Emancipation Proclamation."

UNION BOYS DID WIN THE battles, the decisive ones. Civil War combat ended less than five months after Union Gen. Jefferson Davis stranded thousands of freed people at Ebenezer Creek, permitting their return to slavery. Outrage in the North over that incident helped push General Sherman into issuing his Field Order 15. It provided 40-acre farms along the coast and army livestock to 40,000 freed people. After President Abraham Lincoln was murdered, his successor, Andrew Johnson of Tennessee, in 1866 ordered the freed people off the land and returned it to former owners.

Three new amendments to the Constitution abolished slavery, forbade states to abridge the rights of any citizen and guaranteed equal rights to both colored and white citizens, including the right to vote. Even in the South, Negro men and women could legally marry. Even in the South, colored families could no longer be broken up and sold apart. After the war in the great decade of Reconstruction, the Union Freedmen's Bureau did its best to protect freed people even in the South.

Then, having won the battles at great cost, the Union lost the Civil War on the issue that mattered most to the South. The North so yearned for reconciliation with embittered white southerners that, beginning after 1877, the nation handed back to them control over the lives of black people in the South.

This was the tragedy.

With impunity the South violated the new Constitutional amendments and civil rights laws. Confederate General Nathan Bedford Forrest, the former slave trader whose troops murdered surrendered Negro soldiers at Fort Pillow, founded the Ku Klux Klan. While federal lawmen mostly stood aside, the Klan, its allies and successors led a 90-year campaign of terror against black people in the South, lynching, burning homes and churches, attacking anyone who challenged white supremacy. Through violence, poll taxes and literacy tests, most of the South denied black people the right to vote. The U. S. Supreme Court's Plessy vs. Ferguson "separate but equal" decision in 1892 empowered the South to segregate black children in inferior schools and bar black adults from most decent jobs. The South with its Jim Crow laws barred them from service at most restaurants, hotels, hospitals, parks, even public rest rooms and water fountains.

Having lost on the key issue in its first Civil War, the United States of America engaged in a second, mostly non-violent one called the Civil Rights Movement during the 1950s and 60s and 70s. We won, mostly.

Those are the public facts.

A Private Victory

As for the story of Billy and Lenora, they and their friends climbed the north Georgia mountains into the Blue Ridge. From there as winter became spring, some of the friends trekked westward, pausing in towns where they could trade labor for food. John Marion's blacksmithing skills were everywhere useful. Billy and Lenora were legally married by a sour-faced Tennessee justice of the peace, who needed the fee. Only then did Billy get his long-cherished sight of Lenora June's walnut-brown butt, not seen by him since, as children, they had pissed together in the woods at Highland Forge.

They were among the first of the westering freed people later called Exodusters, traveling from St. Louis up the Missouri river and then the Kaw river on a flatboat. They debarked at Lawrence in a Kansas still bleeding from a full decade of warfare over slavery. In 1863 a

Confederate band led by William Quantrill had murdered more than 180 men and burned the town, then known as the free-soil capital of the state. Outside Lawrence, Billy and John Marion staked claims to homesteads. Inside the town, because so few male laborers remained alive, they quickly found work. John Marion forged iron for wagons built by Absolom Dimmery, a colored business owner.

Billy started as a one-eyed apprentice typesetter for the Kansas State Journal. He who could read so well learned a different script, upside-down mirror images of the fancy words he spelled out letter by letter in the galley tray---illumine, ennobling, scholarship, esthetic, beatific, euphonious. He struggled and failed to find a Peckerwood way to pronounce them. When Lenora June heard such words drop pure and sweet from her husband's lips, she would smile and exclaim:

"See, Billy, you *can* speak good English!"

She was prouder still when he later wrote editorials in what, during the 1870s, turned out to be America's losing battle against subjugation of the South's colored people.

Quantrill had burned the Lawrence Contraband School for Negro children. In a new school started at war's end, Lenora volunteered to assist Blanche K. Bruce, a colored teacher. Lenora then was paid as an instructor of the intermediate department in rented quarters at the African Methodist Episcopal church. Her great delight was teaching biology from a recently-published work, *The Origin of Species.* This caused trouble, but down the years she was never quite silenced on the subject. Lenora June educated students whose great grandchildren would soldier for black rights as America finally won its second Civil War—most notably just 40 miles west of Lawrence in the 1954 case titled Brown vs. Topeka Board of Education.

As she had predicted during Sherman's march, Kansas proved far from perfect. They were indeed shunned by most of their white, and even colored, neighbors, though they did find friends. The grapes in their homestead vineyard were tender enough, but—notwithstanding the Song of Solomon—Billy's pomegranates froze out. Then, soon after they settled into their new cabin roofed and sided with shakes split from a huge shingle oak tree, the Douglas County sheriff arrested Billy for "cohabiting in an illegal manner with a colored woman." A neighbor had reported the crime. What saved him was the marriage license certified, no less, by a state of the former Confederate South. Some schools and other facilities in Kansas remained segregated throughout the lifetimes of Billy and Lenora and long after. Still, Kansas offered colored people a better life than its neighbor, Missouri, and infinitely more than the South.

In 1870 August and Essie Leidig came on the Union Pacific to visit their son, their daughter-in-law and three grandchildren the color of creamed coffee. The Leidigs stayed nearly a month. Billy and— yes—Lenora June as well returned several times to visit his parents at Highland Forge. It cannot be said that Essie and Lenora ever really liked each other. Still, they got along as well as most mothers of only sons and the women lucky enough to marry those precious boys.

Acknowledgments

I am in debt to the entire great tribe of Civil War historians. Sexual abuses by a former South Carolina Governor and U. S. Senator—as told by Aaron and Hubert in this novel—were documented in *Secret and Sacred—the Diaries of James Henry Hammond, a Southern Slaveholder,* by Carol Bleser. For the extravagant Southron character of Desdemona Piermont and much of her flowery speech, I'm indebted to Mary Gay, a Georgia woman of the period, whose language was passed on by A. A. Hoehling in his *Last Train from Atlanta.* The Forge Master's prediction of a 2,000-year future for slavery and much of his phrasing derives from the 1856 letter Gen. Robert E. Lee wrote to his wife, as reported in *The Making of Robert E. Lee* by Michael Fellman. William A. Fletcher, a Confederate soldier, was himself scalded by a southern housewife defending her store of parched corn. That tale was suggested by Fletcher's *Rebel Private: Front and Rear,* from which I also borrowed his chicken-stealing technique. My understanding of emancipation as the cause for which the war was fought came in major part from James M. McPherson through such works as *Battle Cry of Freedom* and *For Cause and Comrades.*

Others to whom I am indebted are William Andrews and Louis Gates, jr., for their *Civitas Anthology of African American Slave Narratives*; Ira Berlin, Marc Favreau and Steven F. Miller for their editing of, *Remembering Slavery*; Burke Davis for his *Sherman's March*; Mark Coburn for *Terrible Innocence*; Charles Dew for his marvelous *Bond of Iron—Master and Slave at Buffalo Forge*; Thomas G. Dyer for his *Secret Yankees—the Union Circle in Confederate Atlanta*; David Goldfield for *Still Fighting the Civil War*; Allen C. Guelzo for his *Lincoln's Emancipation Proclamation*; Herman Hattaway and Archer Jones for *How the North Won*; Jeffrey Rogers Hummel for his *Emancipating Slaves, Enslaving Free Men*; Peter Kadzis for his *Blood—Stories of Life and Death from the Civil War*; Richard M. McMurry for *Atlanta, 1864*; Reid Mitchell for his *Civil War Soldiers*; Clarence L. Mohr for his *On the Threshold of Freedom—Masters and Slaves in Civil War Georgia*; George Ward Nichols, who served under Sherman, for his *The Story of the Great March*; Alfred Nofi for *A Civil War Treasury*; Charles Royster for *The Destructive War*; Marie Jenkins Schwartz for her *Born in Bondage—Growing Up Enslaved in the Antebellum South*; Eileen Southern for her *The Music of Black Americans*; Michael J. Varhola for his *Everyday Life During the Civil War*; Charles Edmund Vetter for *Sherman—Merchant of Terror, Advocate of Peace*; Richard Wheeler for his *Sherman's March* ; Bell Irvin Wiley for *The Civil War Soldier*; Stanley Harrold for his *Civil War and Reconstruction*, Earl J. Hess for his *The Union Soldier in Battle*, and Russell S. Bonds for his *War Like the Thunderbolt—The Battle and Burning of Atlanta.*

About the Author

AFTER A U. S. ARMY tour in Germany during the Cold War, Charles Hammer became a reporter for the Kansas City Star. In 1968 as both rewrite man and street reporter he covered the riot that occurred after the Rev. Martin Luther King, jr., was assassinated. He won the 1972 Kansas Bar Association award based in part on his reporting of police brutality cases. He won a Stanford Journalism Fellowship and a Presbyterian Interracial Council award for many reports documenting the Real Estate Board's role in fostering racial turnover and resegregation of neighborhoods. Later he taught journalism for 20 years at the University of Missouri-Kansas City. He co-authored a sports history, *Unsportsmanlike Conduct,* published by University of Michigan Press and wrote two youth novels for Farrar, Straus & Giroux.

LaVergne, TN USA
21 September 2010
197914LV00005B/1/P